M000040130

BE A
people
HELPER

KEYS TO HELP OTHERS
WORK THROUGH PROBLEMS

Dr. Chuck Lynch

Living Foundation Ministries

"People Helping People"

BE A PEOPLE HELPER

By Chuck Lynch

ISBN: 978 1 5136 5005 0

Living Foundation Ministries, Inc.
611 R.D. Mize Road
Blue Springs, Missouri 64014
U.S.A.
☎ 816-229-5000
www.help4living.org

Cover & Layout Design: Adrián Fonseca

DEDICATION

It is my privilege to dedicate
this book to a dear colleague,
Shelia D. Benzon,
who has celebrated more than 20 years
as a biblical people-helper
with
Living Foundation Ministries.

ACKNOWLEDGEMENTS

You only see the author's name on the book, but behind it lies a team of dedicated people who made it possible. I'm deeply indebted to them.

My sincere thanks to Linda Hight who transcribed hundreds of hand-written pages into an intelligible manuscript and skillfully supervised the project to completion.

I cannot say enough in praise of my wife, Linda, who tirelessly edited the early drafts to make sense of her husband's thoughts.

What an invaluable contribution Kathy Schneeberger and Kathy Moran made in applying their professional expertise to increase the quality of the text.

We are deeply grateful to Barbara Moreno who translated the English text into Spanish. A double thanks to Rigo and Luisa Castellanos for editing the Spanish manuscript and designing the interior layout. We admire and greatly appreciate the graphic skill of Adrián Fonseca who did the layout and cover design.

Above all, I give glory to God who impressed these insights on me and enabled us to share them on five continents for over twenty years. May the timeless principles of God's Word motivate and equip you to be a people helper in your world.

CONTENTS

INTRODUCTION

BEFORE YOU START

"This Class Full." Unreal! This large church offered over a dozen adult study groups on Wednesday night. Classes on such crucial topics ranged from *How to Parent a Rebellious Teenager, How to Get Debt Free* to *How to Understand the Doctrine of Election.* But only the last topic on the list, *How to Counsel Biblically,* was followed in small print, "This Class Full." I could understand this class being full if all the other classes were less relevant. What parent doesn't need some fresh parenting tools? Who could not use some financial advice when there is too much month at the end of the paycheck? But why is *this* class full?

WHAT'S THE ATTRACTION?

Interest in lay-counseling programs attracts people for at least three reasons. First, there are those who feel they have a need to learn how to deal with their own personal problems. The growth of church-sponsored support groups is a reflection of the willingness of people today to admit to themselves and to others that they might have unresolved issues. Many have grown weary of stumbling over things they have avoided dealing with for years.

The second reason is to gain people-helping tools in order to be of genuine help to others. True, some may want to help others as an excuse for avoiding their own unprocessed needs and pain (Friel, p. 143), but the vast majority are now beginning to take seriously God's clear command to "bear one another's burdens and thus fulfill, in a practical way, the law of Christ" (Gal. 6:2), but they don't know how to do so.

The third reason is a mixture of both groups. Everyone has personal needs which call for personal growth in Christ. In the midst of the painful awareness of their needs, they also see others struggling with the same or similar issues. They feel a tugging in their spirit to be a part of their growth and healing, but they are not sure what to do or what to say, so they usually do nothing for fear of doing or saying something wrong. There is a practical way to train believers to help other believers work through their problems in living biblically and it will involve a change in perspective.

WHAT CAN I SAY?

This overwhelming response to lay counseling seminars reflects the pain people are facing personally and the desire to help other believers. Many are turning to the church as never before for answers because of political turmoil, social upheaval, economic crisis and the never-ending family conflicts. They feel so helpless because they do not know what to say to a friend who made a panicked late-night call or a son or daughter whose marriage is in crisis. To make it worse, they hear their grandkids screaming out of control in the background on the phone while they try to talk to the parents.

A horrible feeling of helplessness washes over them. Even Solomon knew that a person has a sense of joy when he can give a helpful, timely answer (Prov. 15:23). But fear replaces joy when you don't know what to say.

IDENTIFY YOUR MENTAL ROADBLOCKS

A dear friend once said to me, "Chuck, I would like to be able to counsel people like you do, but I have so many problems of my own to solve before I'm in any position to help others!" What was Marvin's mental road block? Did he think he had to be perfect or problem free before he could offer a *timely word* to a desperate friend?

Close to the feeling that you should be problem-free is the thought that because you may have personal baggage either from what you have done or what was done to you, you are disqualified. Those painful feelings dampen any motivation you might have to help others in their time of need.

HERE'S THE GOOD NEWS

God is looking for at least four qualities in a person whom He would like to use to help others. Yes, prayer, Bible study, church attendance, are all important disciplines. But you may be surprised to learn, if not shocked, that you, with all your problems and historical baggage, may be just the one He is looking for to help others. So, this book will help you accomplish two goals: teach you how to work through your problems in living from Scripture and teach you to train others to work through their problems in living.

GET READY TO GO!

Fasten your safety belt because you are in for a great experience to learn how you can deal with most all problems in living from a biblical perspective both in your life and in the lives of others. Here are just some of the things you will learn:

- How to process your own issues
- How to learn from your past to help in the present
- How to use your life as an illustration to help others
- How to reproduce yourself in others
- How to understand God's purpose for problems
- How to cooperate with God's plan for your life
- How to use the five benefits you have to help others
- How to use anger to identify needs
- How to forgive from the heart
- How to live with forgiven memories

- How to work through relationship conflicts

- How to establish fair fighting rules

- How to end the control of negative emotions (guilt, shame, fear)

- How to actually help others work through problems in living

A STEP AT A TIME

Sounds overwhelming? At first glance it does. But take your time as you go through each chapter. Let God lead, encourage and instruct you one step at a time. Someone's life will be changed for His glory because yours did.

Chuck Lynch

Chapter 1
PROCESS YOUR PAST

If God set up a display table at a job fair to recruit people who could help others work through problems in living, what would be the first question He would ask any prospective candidate? "Are you working through your own personal or relational problems from a biblical perspective?" He will not ask if you just have personal issues. Everyone does. But He wants to hear you say, "Yes, I am working on *whatever* and I am endeavoring to use biblical tools (Scripture) to process them." That will be music to His ears.

WELCOME YOUR PAST

Past or current personal struggles and failures can be the top reasons you may feel would prevent you from helping others with their *stuff.* May I suggest you make a change in your thinking? Ready? View all you have gone through or are going through as working to your advantage, not your detriment. Whether you are struggling with pride, greed, jealousy, fear, shame, guilt, inferiority, anger, rejection, failure, abandonment, or addiction to porn, gambling, drugs or alcohol, it makes no difference. Understand it is not *what* you are going through but *how* you are going through it. Are you choosing to use your biblical tools to work through these issues?

REJECT THE LIES

My friend, Marvin, believed that he had to be near perfect before he was qualified to help others. In fact, he would even feel like a hypocrite if he tried to help someone because he still had issues. Where did that perspective come from? Dr. James Friesen asked the same question. He believed it was unintentionally taught by those who may have hidden their own private struggles while ministering publicly. There was a lack of appropriate transparency and honesty. The huge pressure to be the perfect example pushed them into hiding their own struggles while conveying to believers that successful servants of God have overcome all their struggles and are happy and victorious all the time. If you want to be authentic, you must honestly confront the personal challenges you face. We are all broken! We are all wounded somewhere (Friesen, p.4).

I was listening to a broadcast of one of my favorite preachers, Chuck Swindoll. In the middle of his message he declared that he had been struggling with lust all week long. Can you just feel the shock waves that reverberated throughout that audience? But what integrity!

Gary Smalley invited Linda and me to attend a pastors' conference in Branson, MO, where Swindoll was one of the key-note speakers. There, he addressed the need for us as pastors and Christian workers to be authentic and to face our personal *demons*. In the middle of expressing his own struggles, he revealed that he and his wife, Cynthia, had had some serious marital problems. Then he paused, "I mean separate bedrooms." He divulged they both sought professional counseling. Chuck gave over 500 pastors and leaders permission to acknowledge their private needs and deal with them biblically while serving publicly. God gives you the same permission.

REJECT SATAN'S ACCUSATIONS

Satan will use your past or present failures and struggles to discourage you from being a biblical people-helper. His strategy is to remind you of your stuff, then, insert the lie that you are disqualified to give any counsel because of it. "Who are you to help a couple with marriage problems when you had an affair?" or "Look who's talking. You and your spouse have conflicts."

Sadly, he is only repeating to you his accusation of you to God. He is detailing your faults and failures to God day and night to shame and condemn you (Rev. 12:10b). He does not give up. Yes, he will ultimately be thrown out of heaven and cast into the lake of fire forever (Rev. 20:10), but until then, he is a tireless prosecuting attorney to get God to condemn and give up on you.

Peter strongly urges you to be on the alert at all times and to keep a sharp eye out for your adversary, the devil. Like a starving lion, he is looking for someone to devour and destroy (I Pet. 5:8). He would love to see you rendered ineffective because of your struggles.

Would it surprise you to know that Satan and his demon assistants have the ability to remind you of your failures, struggles and inadequacies using your own voice? It sounds like you, but it is not you. The goal is to get you to think you are so bad that you will not have the faith to believe God can and will use you to help others. Satan tried to do this with Peter.

VIEW YOUR FAILURES AS PREPARATION

It was a long night. Jesus had just instituted what we refer to as the Lord's Supper. The new covenant was being established and the old covenant was being laid aside. In the middle of this very special moment, a big argument broke out among the disciples as to who was the greatest among them. You can just hear them boasting of all their own accomplishments and leadership skills. Then it happened.

The argument abruptly stopped when they heard Jesus say, "Simon, Simon." The disciples may have thought, "Oh no, not loud-mouth Peter." But what followed must have sobered all of them. "Behold, Satan has demanded permission [from Me] to sift you like wheat, but I have prayed for you, that your faith may

17

not fail; and you, when once you have returned again, strengthen your brothers" (Luke 22:31,32). Initially the disciples thought Jesus was declaring Peter as the greatest. Instead, He publicly revealed to Peter how God was going to prepare him to be the leader by first failing as their leader.

Although most of the disciples were fishermen, they were familiar with the winnowing process of separating the wheat from the chaff. But what did God mean by the winnowing process? It's simple. Satan's plan was to get Peter to fail so badly that he would think God would never take him back and his trust in Jesus would break down because he failed so badly. "God would never use me now. You just can't swear you never knew Jesus in the presence of a crowd and believe God would want to take you back, let alone use you." But God did just that (Jn. 21:15-17)!

I don't know what you've done or what was so horrifically done to you. I don't know what you have been through to potentially separate you from your confidence that God would use you. But consider a major change in your perspective right now and declare aloud, "It was to *prepare me* to help others, not to *destroy my potential* for helping others" (2 Cor. 1:3,4).

LOOK WHO GOD USED IN THE PAST

Why in the world do we have 39 books in the Old Testament? What do they have to do with you and me now, let alone with helping others? The apostle Paul gave us a big clue in his first long *email* to the young church in the city of Corinth, Greece. After discussing some of the devastating judgments that Israel experienced for its repeated rebellion and sin (I Cor. 10:7-10), Paul offered this explanation, "Now these things happened [from time-to-time, the use of the imperfect verb tense] to them as examples for us. They were written down [again, from time-to-time] for our instruction upon whom the end of the ages has come" (1 Cor. 10:11).

The word, *instruction* (*tithemi*), is made up of two Greek words: *nous* (mind) and *tithemi* (to put), literally means or *to put into our mind* (Vine, p. 32). We would say, *to drive a point home.* Notice the point God tried to drive home. He recorded the failures and successes of key personalities in the Old Testament to give you and me a balanced picture to document for us that He chooses and uses the weak, flawed, fearful, needy people to accomplish His will in other peoples' lives. You have not done or experienced anything worse than they did, yet God still chose them. David sexually violated one of the wives of his thirty mighty men, Uriah, then, had him murdered (2 Sam. 11).

LEARN FROM PIZZA

Picture a big pizza with your favorite toppings divided into six equal slices. You are ready to devour it. Then, to your shock, you notice a fly landed on one of the slices and is stuck in the melted cheese. Yuck! So, you remove the one contaminated slice and dig in and have yourself a feast. One piece is flawed, contaminated; that's a reality, but then there are five other good ones. That is exactly what God did in most of those great Old Testament stories. He could have only recorded how perfect those Old Testament people were, but in His integrity, He included their flaws, failures and weaknesses and uses them as examples of men and women of faith (Heb. 11). "For whatever things were written before were written for our learning, that we, through the patience and comfort of the [Old Testament] Scriptures, might have hope" (Rom. 15:4). Hope? Yes, hope that God will use you to make a difference in someone's life, even if you are weak like Charles Spurgeon.

Spurgeon was a great preacher in the last century who pastored a large church in England. Preachers today read and study his sermons. What most people don't know is that he struggled so much with depression that his deacons had to help get him out of bed on Sunday mornings to preach. He was weak but powerful, just like Gideon. Take a peek at Gideon's life. You might think you are his clone after you see what God recorded about this man of faith (Heb. 11:32). Notice where God found him and what he was doing.

STUCK IN THE PIT

The Midianites had conquered Israel. They were in total control, even confiscating the Israelites' harvested crops. God wanted to deliver Israel from their slavery so He recruited Gideon. And what was he doing when God approached him? He was in a wine vat dug in the ground for crushed grapes. What was Gideon doing in that pit? He was trying to winnow wheat without being detected by the Midianites, totally dysfunctional. Sound familiar? You may be hiding in your own pit, hoping no one will discover your dysfunctional ways. The last thing you want to do is get close to someone to help them and then have them discover you are in a deep pit yourself.

RECOGNIZE THE PIT

What was Gideon's thinking when God recruited him to deliver Israel? Look at his response to the angel of the Lord after calling him a *valiant warrior* (Judg. 6:12). His response revealed six deep issues Gideon was struggling with in his *pit.*

First, in Jud. 6:13, Gideon responded to the angel of the Lord's greeting, "Oh my Lord … if the Lord is with us…" (implying, "I don't think He is"). Gideon questioned God's presence. He did not believe God was with him in his personal pain. In fact, he later blamed God for it. His logic was, "If God is with me, why am I suffering like this?" Sound familiar?

Second, Gideon questioned God's protection. He said, "Why then has all this happened to us?" He was hurt, bitter and felt totally powerless and vulnerable. He struggled with anger issues. He felt God had failed to protect him. You probably have felt that way and have been ashamed of yourself for it and concluded God would never choose you. But He will if you are working through your problems biblically.

Third, Gideon questioned God's power, "And where are all His miracles which our fathers told us about saying, 'Did not the Lord bring us up from Egypt?' But what happened that you cannot come through for us now?" Gideon could not hide his anger and his disappointment with God. This is a common feeling that explains the popularity of Phillip Yancey's book, *Disappointment with God*. Gideon was stating a strong feeling of disappointment that God and His Word works for everyone else but him. Feeling helpless and powerless, he questioned God's power. Have you ever felt God and His Word seemed to work for everyone else but you? "Why would God want me when I feel that life just does not seem to work for me?"

Next, this had to be hard for Gideon to tell the angel of the Lord, "I feel You do not care and have abandoned us." This is probably the deepest human fear, to feel totally abandoned and alone, especially by God. Being alone was the only negative thing said about God's creation, "It is not good for man to be alone" (Gen. 2:18). Abandonment is frightening! Almost every book describing the characteristics of the grown child raised in a dysfunctional family devotes significant coverage to fear of abandonment.

Have you felt that God's promises are for everyone else, but not for you? You may still be struggling through these deep feelings, but, to your credit, you are still processing them with God. The fact you are still processing them and not quitting qualifies you to help someone who is or has been in a similar pit. You are going through a learning experience.

Furthermore, Gideon felt deeply that God was unfair. "God, look what You have allowed." He said, "…You have given us into the hands of the Midianites. [It's Your fault. This is not fair]." This too, may have a familiar ring in your mind.

Finally, Gideon questioned God's choice of him. "Oh Lord, how shall I deliver Israel? Behold, my family is the least family in the tribe of Manasseh, and [to make matters worse] I am the youngest in my father's house." (Judges 6:15) In his pit, he struggled deeply with inferiority issues. Think about this. Gideon questioned God's presence, protection, power, care, fairness and choice, and still He did not walk away. Friend, I have good news for you.

If you struggle with issues like Gideon did and feel overwhelmed by your own inadequacies, you just might make the best recruit for a people-helper. You qualify! You have the ingredients to be in God's "Who's Who" as listed in Hebrews Chapter 11. You possess the first basic ingredient of an effective people-helper if you are facing your issues head on and are using scriptural tools to deal with them. God would say, "Here, sign on the dotted line. You are just the one I'm looking for" (Matt. 11:28,29). Basket cases seem to make the best recruits for people-helpers.

CONSIDER THIS LIST

In another Old Testament example, Jeremiah begged off from being a prophet because he did not know how to speak. He was not claiming that he was physically unable to talk but felt he was not able to speak well enough for such a public ministry (Jer. 1:6). Plus, he claimed to be only a child, a Hebrew word for infant (Ex. 2:6) or a young man. Jeremiah may have been in his late teens or early 20's, but felt totally ill-prepared to be God's mouthpiece to the nations. God was not looking for an eloquent elder statesman; he was simply looking for someone to be a faithful messenger. Later in ministry, Jeremiah plunged from the height of confidence (Jer. 20:11-13) into the depths of depression. He went so far as to wish that the day he was born had been cursed, that he had never been born (Jer. 20:14-18).

Other Old Testament figures also struggled: Job had similar feelings to Jeremiah (Job 3:1-16). Isaiah thought he was ruined and useless because he felt impure and lived in an environment of impure people (Is. 6:5). Jonah hated the Ninevites and felt they did not deserve to hear of God's mercy, but God sent him anyway via a huge fish (Jonah 1 and 3). Esther was afraid she would be killed if she went to King Ahasuerus to plead for protection for her people, the Jews, who were about to be destroyed by Haman (Esther 4:11-14).

Consider Rahab, the vocational prostitute: immoral, rejected, shamed, worthless and used. What did God do? He led the two spies sent by Joshua to Jericho to her house to protect her and her family (Josh. 2:1). That was just the start. God lists Rahab in His hall of fame of faith (Heb. 11:31). She is even part of our Lord's genealogy (Matt. 1:5), the ancestor of King David through whom Jesus was born. She was *used wrongly* by others but was *used rightfully* by God, just as Kari was.

When Kari came to me to work through the sexual abuse in her past, I told her and her accompanying friend that God would use what she had gone through to help others. But she insisted, "How can I be used by God when I have been so wrongfully used by others as a child?" Kari worked through that question to a point of healing. Later, I received a phone call from her asking if I would meet with her and her pastor. Why? They wanted to set up a ministry, which Kari would lead, for those who had been sexually abused. They just wanted to know how to go about it. The processor became the person God selected to help others in the healing process.

CONSIDER THE NEW TESTAMENT GREATS

Many Christians have the feeling that the Apostle Paul was almost the fourth member of the Trinity. Yes, he did offer himself as a role model to the Thessalonian believers regarding how to live their Christian lives (I Thess. 1:6). Yet Paul made it clear he had not arrived spiritually. Although he wrote thirteen books in the New Testament and established more churches than all the other disciples (Phil. 3:12), he still struggled with sin and hated it (Rom.7:15-25).

In a moment of vulnerability, he revealed to his friends in Corinth, his personal struggle while ministering to them and shared three little-known characteristics of a successful servant of God: "And I was with you in weakness and in fear and in much trembling" (I Cor. 2:3). The repetition of the preposition, *in*, before each descriptive noun, makes them all hold equal weight.

Weakness: an inability to produce results Fear: a fright caused by being scared, feeling dread or terror, having a desire to run away.

Trembling: a physical expression of nervousness due to the personal awareness of potential failure from weakness and fright.

Paul's admission has freed many would-be people-helpers who were held back by unresolved personal needs that still needed work. Needs qualify, not disqualify, you. Clay was one of these kinds of people-helpers.

Clay was well-liked and greatly appreciated as a Christian school chaplain. He also taught Bible classes and coached soccer. The school administrators and parents held him in high esteem. His boldness in witnessing was an example to all. But it was the inner turmoil that finally made him call my office; he could not take any more.

"Chuck," he began, "I am ashamed to admit this to you. You have been my college teacher; you know me; but I can't stand it any longer." Fearing the worst, I asked him if he wanted to tell me about it. "I, I… this is hard… I can't sleep at night…try as I will, until I call my Dad on the phone and have him tell me everything is okay." "Okay?" I asked. "Yeah, I mean, I just want him to reassure me that I am okay and that things in general are all right. Chuck, I am 32 years old, married and have great kids. I am so ashamed....," Clay sobbed. The truth was out. Someone else knew.

Over a period of weeks, Clay came to see that his emotional dependency was as damaging as his parents' alcoholism had been. He had to change his perspective from an emotional dependency on his unpredictable, conditional, performance-oriented parents to an adult dependency on the Lord. He is now much freer to minister and has not had to call his dad for reassurance in years. His counseling ministry now has a greater depth because of his own journey to freedom. People-helpers are processors, just like you.

Even the Apostle Paul's disciple, Timothy, struggled privately while ministering publicly. Paul had to challenge Timothy to deal with intimidation because of his age (I Tim. 4:12) and with shyness that resulted in timidity (II Tim.1:7). Apparently, all this stress created some physical problems that Paul had to address (I Tim. 5:23). Does any of this sound familiar?

Little is mentioned about Elizabeth, the wife of Zacharias, the priest. She lived each day of her life with a personal sense of shame, disgrace and failure. Why? She felt she was defective because she could not bear children. To her and in her culture, childbearing was a validation of worth, value and God's blessing. She and her husband were very old, past the age of childbearing (Luke 1:7).

But Elizabeth miraculously conceived and gave birth to the forerunner of the Messiah, John the Baptist. When she discovered she was pregnant, we learn just how much shame and social rejection she had felt. Dr. Luke tells us she went into seclusion for five months. "How kind the Lord is!" she exclaimed. "He has taken away my disgrace of having no children" (Luke 1:24,25). Matthew explained God's perspective of her pregnancy, that among those born of women there had not risen anyone greater than John the Baptist (Matt. 11:11). God chose to use a woman who felt embarrassed, disgraced and rejected to birth a son who would announce to the world that Jesus the Messiah has come (Luke 1:17; Jn. 1:34).

UNDERSTAND THE PROCESS

When people come to my office for counseling, they often visualize counseling like a banana. You peel it once, eat it and you're done. They think that in one visit they will get *fixed*. Instead, they should picture themselves as an onion. It has many layers. They are going to work through layers of their life to grow into spiritual and emotional maturity, the process of being shaped into the likeness of Christ in their words, actions and attitudes.

It is not complicated. When you became a Christian, you were born again in your spirit (John 3:6), not in your mind (Rom. 12:2). Scripture refers to new-born believers as *babies* (I Pet. 2:2). That clearly indicates you and I must grow up spiritually.

When you became a faith-follower of the Lord Jesus, you were instantly made a saint. Over 60 times in the New Testament, believers are called saints. What does *saint* mean? It is one who is sanctified or set apart for special use by God (I Cor. 6:11). Now the process really begins. You are positionally given a new identity by God, but it takes time to learn how to act, think and speak like who you are. That is called progressive sanctification and it is a life-long process.

But you may rightfully ask, "What does that have to do with me being qualified to help others?" It's easy. You are always going to have trials, afflictions, struggles and temptations. You are never going to be perfect this side of heaven. Maturing, yes; perfect, no. You will be in a growth process until Jesus returns or you go to be with Him (Phil. 1:6).

The Apostle Paul urged the Philippians to get on with the process. He specifically told them to work out their salvation (Phil. 2:12). He meant work into their every-day lives what God has done through their salvation; to incorporate their new identity in Christ into every area of their lives. That is your responsibility, too. Then he stated the process and purpose. "For God is working in you, giving you the desire and power to do what pleases Him" (Phil. 2:13). That is *His* responsibility.

But left to yourself, you probably would not do that. So, James, the half-brother of Jesus, explains God's maturation process. It is very clear, "My brethren, count it all joy when you fall into various trials, knowing that the testing of your faith produces patience" (Jam. 1:2,3). Notice the goal of the process: endurance, maturity, completeness and the ability to handle anything. You don't *fix* a trial, test, affliction or temptation. You *process* it. That takes effort and it takes time (like peeling the onion).

So, who is God looking for to help others? Here is the good news: the first quality God is looking for in a biblical counselor or discipler is someone working on a problem biblically. Jesus is looking for biblical people-helpers like you who are admitting their needs, facing their issues and working through personal problems and meeting those deep-seated needs using biblical tools, just like Bill.

WELCOME THE PAIN AND PREPARATION

Bill was devastated by his wife leaving him with five young children. Shocked, grieving, hurt, disillusioned and angry, he sat in my office wringing his hands. His story was familiar but no less painful. I said to Bill, "What I am going to share with you will accomplish two goals. First, it will give you the tools to work through your own loss. I can't fix it, but I can give you tools so you can process it. Next, I will pray with you that you will be able to share the tools I offer you with someone who is experiencing the same pain. That is at least one of the reasons God has allowed this to happen in your life."

I asked him to read 2 Cor. 1:3,4, "Blessed be the God and Father of our Lord Jesus Christ, the Father of mercies and the God of all comfort…" His eyes glanced up with an "I've-heard-this-before" look. He continued to read, "…who comforts us in all our affliction [hurts] so that we may be able to comfort those who are in any affliction with the comfort with which we ourselves are comforted by God." "So?" he skeptically questioned. "Bill, notice the word, *able*. It means *ability* and *resource*. God is giving you the ability and resource to help others by what you are going through right now."

At the end of our session, I accompanied Bill to the front door. I watched him open his car door, pause, then turn back toward me. With one arm on the car door and the other resting on the top of the car, he cocked his head and said, "Do you tell this to everyone?" Momentarily, my mind flashed back over the past 40 years. "Yes, Bill, I tell it to everyone."

GET READY - SIGN UP

You are one of us. You are dealing with your stuff. It is tough, but you are doing it. Now there is another mental attitude to adopt. If you do this, all that you have experienced in life, the good or bad, will now take on a whole new meaning. You will be amazed just how rich you really are. Do you feel you do not know what to say or are you afraid of saying the wrong thing? Good news, you are ready for the second characteristic of a person God will use to help others. You are a learner.

Chapter 1
PROCESS YOUR PAST

- Process your present or past issues.

- Use your process to prepare you to help others.

- Understand it is not *what* you go through as much as *how* you go through it.

- Reject the lie you must be perfect to help someone.

- Be aware that Satan is out to disqualify you to help others.

- View your failure as preparation to help others.

- Recall who God used in the past.

- Realize maturity is a life-long process.

- Accept pain as part of your preparation.

- Be authentically honest with others.

Chapter 1
SMALL GROUP QUESTIONS

1. Share the issues you have had to work through in your own life.

2. What Scriptures, books, sermons or teachings helped you work through them?

3. What were the obstacles you had to deal with to work through the issues?

4. What lies did you identify about yourself, God or others? What truths replaced them?

5. What major perspectives did you change about God, others or yourself?

6. What failures have you experienced that you can now see how they prepared you to help others?

7. What Old or New Testament person can you identify with most? Why?

8. How did you come to realize that your trials in life were indeed preparation to help others?

Chapter 2
LEARN FROM YOUR PAST

"How many believe in the Great Commission?" I asked of a group of upper-level college students. At 7:30 a.m. their bodies were in class, but their minds were still in the dorm, asleep. So, I quoted it to them, "Go therefore and make disciples of all nations, baptizing them in the name of the Father, Son and the Holy Spirit, teaching them all that I have commanded." "Now, how many really believe in that?" With half-dazed eyes, they dutifully raised their hands in agreement. Then I said, "That's too bad."

Their half-shut eyes instantly widened in disbelief. Did they misunderstand my response? I quoted it again; then, posed the same question, "Do you really believe in it?" The affirmation became more direct. Again, I said, "That's too bad." What is this professor in a Bible college saying? From the back of the class an alert student informed me, "Dr. Lynch, you misquoted Matt. 28:18-20. You left out the words, 'to observe.'" "You just passed the class with flying colors," I affirmed. These well-schooled students had read, memorized and heard this verse taught and preached for almost four years. They got it! But did they?

CLEAN THE FISH

Most of the disciples were fishermen. Jesus called them to become fishers of men (Matt. 4:19). They knew that meant to lead men and women into the kingdom. Today we would call that evangelism. But Jesus did not repeat that same command before He ascended into heaven. Instead, He said, "Go and make disciples" [learners] (Matt. 28:19). What is the difference?

Evangelism is the process of leading men and women into a saving knowledge of the Lord Jesus Christ. The Apostle John referred to it as being *born again* (Jn. 3:7). This time He said, "Make disciples." If evangelism is the process of *catching* fish, then discipleship is the process of *cleaning* fish. Jesus told them to go and make disciples (clean fish). Obviously, you cannot clean what has not been caught. Timothy was told to do the work of an evangelist (2 Tim. 4:5), yet most of the instruction Paul gave him while ministering in Ephesus had to do with discipleship (cleaning fish).

We have 27 books in the New Testament. The first three gospels explain the life of our Lord from three different perspectives: Matthew, Mark and Luke. The gospel of John was written for the expressed purpose of evangelism. John selected seven miracles of Jesus to prove He is God and should be believed (Jn. 20:30,31). But notice something.

Dr. Luke wrote a long letter to Theophilus detailing the spread of the gospel and establishing the church primarily through Peter and Paul in the book of Acts. The next book is Romans which is a systematic treatise on biblical theology revealed to the Apostle Paul directly during his three years alone in the Arabian dessert (Gal. 1:17,18). The following book is 1 Corinthians. What takes place in the first chapter? How to deal with conflict! The next 21 books affirm what God has given us in Christ and how to handle personal issues and conflict facing believers. The final book is Revelation, God's plan for the end of the age!

Only the gospel of John, is dedicated to evangelism. Twenty-one other books deal with problems in living and cleaning fish. What is the logical conclusion? The answer may be in the name believers were called in the first century, followers of the Way (Acts 9:2). That could indicate a way of life, not just a mental ascent to some biblical truths. The disciples were to teach other believers how to live out the new life in Christ. That is cleaning fish. They were not even called Christians until Acts 11:26 in Antioch. The ending, *ian,* means belonging to Jesus.

BE A CLEANER

Jesus clearly stated He wanted His followers to develop disciples. The Greek word for disciple is literally *learner* from the verb *to learn.* It denotes one who follows another's teaching as a disciple. He was not looking only for decisions for salvation, but for disciples.

Jesus further clarified precisely what He meant. He did not merely tell His followers to go and just teach others content. No! His goal for them and for us is to teach us how to *observe* or to *put into practice in our daily lives* all things that He had commanded us. We are now to be fish cleaners. Discipleship counseling is the process of teaching learners how to be like Jesus in the way they think, behave and communicate. Our key identity is LEARNER, not only adherents to a system of thought, but imitators of our Master-teacher, Jesus. God specifically uses our problems in life to stimulate us toward that goal.

BE A LEARNER

The second quality God is looking for is that you are a learner with a teachable heart. In fact, you do not need any prior formal training to sign up with Jesus to be a people-helper. He only desires that you have a strong desire to learn, especially through the trials, tests, temptations, afflictions, pain and losses that you will experience in life. His desire is that you learn wisdom which includes practical answers to difficult situations (2 Tim. 3:16,17). Dr. Gerard Egan, in listing important characteristics for counselors, insists that they first have a commitment to their own growth physically, intellectually, socially, emotionally and spiritually. Counselors are not people who have never had problems in their own lives. (Egan, p. 22-24)

ADOPT GOD'S PRIORITY

The religious scholars realized the disciples were *uneducated* and *unlearned* men and were amazed at the wisdom Peter and John displayed (Acts 4:13). The confident apostles, on one hand, were without any formal training, but, on the other hand, were eager to learn. None of them were formally trained priests, rabbis or scribes. The religious scholars saw the disciples' confidence but could not figure it out. They began to recognize them as having been with Jesus (Acts 4:13). They had not been to the established rabbinical schools of Hillel or Shammai (Robeson, p 52). Jesus Himself was also regarded as uneducated because He did not have degrees from the leading theological schools (Jn. 7:15,16). But the disciples were like you, motivated to learn. They saw how John the Baptist taught his disciples, so they asked Jesus, "Lord, teach us to pray just as John also taught his disciples" (Luke 11:1).

God's priority for you is to adopt the same motivation as His disciples. Specifically, learn how to live the Christian life practically, every day, based on Scripture and not just accumulate a lot of knowledge and platitudes that tend to feed pride (I Cor. 8:1). Get all the formal or informal training you can get but realize some of the most significant learning takes place outside four walls. God does not primarily bless the *knowers* of His Word, only the *doers* (Jam. 1:21-25), so commit to *practice* what you teach.

REALIZE YOUR ADVANTAGE

Years ago, in the Carkhuff and Truax study, lay-helpers were compared with professional, formally trained counselors. The results were amazing! They concluded that "the patients of lay-counselors did as well or better than the patients of professional counselors." (Hughes, p. 14). The Durlak study concluded that "para-professionals or lay-counselors were generally as effective as, and sometimes even more effective, than professional helpers, especially when the counseling involved more specific, targeted problems. Professional mental health education, training and experience did not appear to be necessary prerequisites for an effective people-helper" (Tan, p. 53). You may even have many advantages over professional counselors.

First, you may be closer in relationships to the one being helped. The professional counselor has to build a relationship with his clients before he can effectively help them. You know them as friends and may also know their families. Statistically, people in need turn to a friend first, a pastor second and a mental health professional third.

Next, you know their culture, traditions and language so you are better informed about their family, work situation, beliefs, neighborhood, sources of stress and pressure. This better prepares you to understand problems based on past experiences together (Prov.18:24; 27:6,9,10). Professionals must take the time to learn all these things. As a friend, you are more available than the professional or even their pastor. Professionals rightfully require an appointment. Pastors are busy people. But "a friend loves at all times" (Prov. 17:17). "A man's counsel is sweet to his friend" (Prov. 27:9).

In order for an alcoholic to be involved in an Alcoholics Anonymous program, he must have a sponsor who himself was an alcoholic and is available 24/7 when humanly possible. Also, upon entering the AA program, 90 visits in 90 days is required to break the alcohol cycle with the support of a sponsor. The program works if you work the program.

Furthermore, as a friend, you can communicate in a language which the person can easily understand. You do not have to deal with complicated psychological terms or formulas. When we look at Jesus' ministry, he taught in the common Greek language of His day. And when you analyze His teaching, you can see it dealt with how to be reconciled to God, how to get along with others and how to work out conflicts between His followers.

When the Holy Spirit came at Pentecost, those present heard the gospel in their own language as if spoken by native speakers (Acts 2:8). But all the speakers were Galileans. God could have given the listeners the ability to hear and understand Greek or Aramaic. But He wanted them to hear as if it were spoken by a friend from their home town. And friends tend to be more practical, relaxed and informal. As one psychologist stated, "I'm a practical theologian giving lessons in practical theology." She has a Ph.D. in psychology and knows the advantage of being practical. Good psychology is biblical; it does not contradict Scripture.

Another big advantage you have is not needing to work with complicated psychological personality theories. This alone lets you focus on the person's needs and biblical answers rather than fit them into a systems box. Today we have over 200 personality theories and years ago even the secular news magazines stated that none of them have been proven better than others (Newsweek, January 1998). In 1952 there were 60 recognized mental illnesses. Over fifty years later, there are 410. Today anything can pass for a mental illness. The sad reality is that most, if not all of those theories were designed by atheists. They may have been able to describe human behavior by observation, but with God factored out, their solutions are lacking. "Schools of psychology vary radically from one extreme to another and a variety of theories that contradict one another abound in the behavioral sciences" (Anderson, p. 30). The Apostle Paul explained that in "the wisdom of God, the world through [human] wisdom did not know God, it pleased God through the foolishness of the message preached to save those who believe" (I Cor. 1:21).

DIG DEEP FOR THE GOLD

"The past is the past. I don't need to go there!" Then don't. But learners who want to help people have chosen to go back and dig deeply into their past, process it biblically and utilize the lessons they learned about God, others and themselves. Paul did it. How do you think the Apostle Paul maintained such a high appreciation for grace? How did he develop such a humble attitude that he was the *least valued* of the apostles after all he did for the church? He daily glanced in the rear vision mirror of his life and remembered how he persecuted the church of Christ and tried to destroy it before he was transformed (I Tim. 1:13).

He vividly remembered dragging moms and dads from their houses, possibly as their young children screamed, "Please don't take my mommy and daddy!" (Acts 8:3) Those voices probably rang in his ears until the day he died. Through it all, he met Jesus and instead of Jesus killing him like he deserved, He forgave Paul, bathed him in grace and favor that he did not deserve, and called him to serve the Savior. He would say today, "I am what I am by the grace of God!" (I Cor. 15:9,10). Paul went into the gold mine of his past and dug out the gold. Then he reminded people, "Look at me. If I could be saved from what I have done, He can save you and use you for His glory" (I Tim. 1:12-16). Ask Mike and Shelia.

Shelia's schedule is always full. People come from miles around to see her for counseling. It was not that way 25 years ago. She and Mike sat devastated in my office. Their world had collapsed around them as Mike confessed to a six-month affair with Shelia's best friend. Added to that, Shelia, as a youth, had been sexually, physically, verbally and emotionally abused. Having Mike's full blessing to tell their story publicly, Shelia is now totally free to share what transpired, how both she and Mike were affected and especially how they worked through each tragic issue biblically. She experienced enough pain to last a lifetime and often shares the golden nuggets that God taught her through her experiences. She reads hundreds of books and attends purposeful seminars as an avid learner. Now she is being asked to teach the seminars. She has a wealth of wisdom and practical life experience. But something could have blocked it all. Denial.

Christian denial is denying God access to a hurt that He wants to heal for your benefit and for His glory. Learners are not deniers. They dig deep into their past for the rich gems of life. They view their past as a gold mine of insights and lessons to process rather than as a deep, dark pit to be avoided. A learner's past is a frame around his present life. Often biblical counselors are God-taught through personal experience of walking with Him through any affliction (2 Cor. 1:3,4).

Here is a little-known secret about Shelia. She does not have any college degrees. Her clients are from the least to the most educated you will ever find: pastors, doctors, lawyers, athletes, therapists all ask for her. She does not advertise. Her former clients tell of the changes they made as God used her and the tools she shared. Even the well-educated respect her. She attended a seminar taught by a *learned* psychologist, designed for graduate students only. After the week-long event, people would quietly walk up to her and say, "You should have been teaching this course."

BE FAITHFUL

Although God may not require any prior training in a people-helper, He is looking for the quality of faithfulness in current responsibilities. In other words, He is looking for a good steward (I Cor. 4:1,2), someone who has been entrusted with a lot of life experience and is using it on behalf of others. What is the bottom line for a performance evaluation? Faithfulness in applying God's word to their own lives. This gives hope to many of my friends who have faithfully rebuilt their lives. Just ask Darren.

Darren stopped me as I walked across our church parking lot. He was hurting. He desired to be a church officer but he was divorced. Our particular church policy did not permit divorced persons to be elders or deacons. Whether he should or should not be one was not Darren's need. He felt rejected in life and the church prohibition only exacerbated those feelings. I asked him why he wanted to be a church officer. Did he want the position and perceived status? Did he want the opportunity to serve like an elder or deacon? Did he want the esteem which came with the title? I held my breath. "Well," he began, "I just want to be able to pray with people, counsel, help them with some of their practical needs, be their friend, share the word of God with them, you know."

I would take a hundred *Darrens* in my church. Why? He just wanted to serve others and he was willing to do it without a title. "Darren, God asks each of us to do these things in the church body whether, or not we have an official position or title. The greatest asset you have is your heart to serve and to be a servant. There are no requirements for a servant or steward in Scripture other than to be faithful in current responsibilities. Your marital status of the past has nothing to do with you being a servant in the present. No one can hold you to the requirements of being an elder or deacon if your only title is servant. The big plus-factor is that you do not have to shoulder the luggage of leadership with a cumbersome title and responsibilities. You are free to serve." How often, as a pastor, I wished that those with titles would imitate Darren's attitude.

His eyes lit up. He got it! For years he had operated under the distorted notion that only paid clergy or elected officers of the church could minister to the needs of believers. God gave gifts to the whole church, not just a selected few (I Cor. 12:11).

USE YOUR TEN PERCENT

Do you really have to walk in a person's shoes before you can help them? No! It is not the *quantity* of experiences you have been through that prepares you to help others. It is the *quality* of your experiences and the lessons you learned through them.

You may only experience ten percent of the potential problems of life but that experience can prepare you to handle other problems as well. The Apostle Paul put it this way, "God comforts us [gives hope and strength] in all our affliction so that we will be able [ability and resource] to comfort those who are in ANY affliction with the comfort with which we ourselves have been comforted by God" (2 Cor. 1:4). Notice the words, *all* and *any*; they are the same Greek words. No medical doctor has experienced every illness he treats. Yes, he has experienced some, but he is a master-learner. He utilizes what he has experienced and what he has learned from other sources.

BE WARNED, YOU MAY SPECIALIZE

While speaking at a weekend couples' conference, a lady approached me during a break and asked, "Do you know you have six alcoholics attending?" Glancing over the sixty couples in the auditorium, I saw none. "How do you know?" I asked. "We alcoholics can spot another from miles away." Former alcoholics seem to be the best ones to deal with their addicted friends.

Women tell me they can spot a woman who has been sexually abused either as a child or an adult. Why would God give them that sensitivity if He did not expect them to be a biblical care-giver to those wounded women? Most specialized ministries were birthed by those who had gone through a similar experience. *If Not for Grace*, a post-abortive ministry to men, women and families, was founded by a woman who had an abortion. Many women's lives are being rebuilt and renewed by a processor who chose to learn from it in order to help others.

LEARN FROM OTHER SOURCES

A biblical people-helper can distinguish between capital *T* truth and small *t* truth as he continues to learn. What is capital *T* truth? It is the supernaturally revealed truth contained in Scripture, inspired and preserved by God. The Apostle Peter explained this reality, "But know this first of all, that no prophecy of Scripture is a matter of one's own interpretation, for no prophecy was ever made by an act of human will, but men moved by the Holy Spirit, spoke from God" (2 Pet. 1:20-22).

The Apostle Paul emphasized the Scripture's value to Timothy, "All Scripture is inspired by God and is profitable for teaching, for reproof, for correction, for training [discipling] in righteousness" (2 Tim. 3:16). The Scripture is God's Word and absolute truth.

What is small *t* truth? It is what we learn from observation, research and life experience. But all small *t* truth must always be in submission to God's revealed truth, not equal to it because there are no absolutes in society, psychology or anthropology, only in Scripture.

I have had the privilege to train biblical care-givers on five continents in many countries. When I illustrate small *t* truth, I will ask lay people, pastors and counselors if they have ever heard of or read Dr. Gary Chapman's book, *The Five Love Languages*. Usually there are at least a few raised hands in every group. It is an excellent book and is very helpful in understanding how we can learn to love someone from their perspective and get the greatest benefit. Would you be surprised to learn that there is nothing in the Bible about five love languages? It is small *t* truth that relates in most cultures and is based on research. There are biblical counselors who claim they use only one book, the Bible, but have a library full of books containing small *t* truth. Integrity will admit this reality.

You can learn from many people and resources, but internalize only what matches God's Word in principle or precept. Wise leaders are readers who test what they read by God's Word (I Jn. 4:1; Acts 17:11). Where Scripture is clear, remain firm. Where the Bible is silent, be open to God's Spirit to lead you. Reject every theory or practice that violates God's word. Learn to discern truth and error that even sounds good. As my mother would say, "Eat the chicken and spit out the bones."

Theologians study theology and may not understand people. Those in the mental health field study people but may not understand God. Through scientific observation they are not able to answer the philosophic question, "Why." You can see this when 90 percent of psychologists who develop personality theories are professing atheists.

Their research, however, enables them to observe what the Bible calls, *the flesh* (Jn. 6:63; Rom. 8) and identify the words, actions and attitudes of the fallen nature of humanity, independent of God's wisdom. What distinguishes biblical-discipleship counseling is that God is central in the process. Theologically, it is the process of sanctification, changing step by step into Christ-likeness.

A balanced disciple/counselor will study and seek to understand both Scripture and people. The book of Proverbs provides a wealth of information about God and people.

REMAIN A LEARNER

The person God uses has been through many trials and processes them over time by using God's Word. But it does not stop there. You look at the events of life: the good, the bad and the ugly, and say to yourself, "What a learning experience!" View life as one big learning experience about God, people, and especially yourself. Having learned from your past and present, you have met the second requirement God looks for to help others.

Since you are going to be a biblical care-giver, commit to remain both teachable and faithful in your current responsibilities (I Cor 4:2). Continue to be taught through personal reading as well as through the difficult tests you experience. You are learning. Now, what will you do with it?

Chapter 2
LEARN FROM YOUR PAST

- Remember, disciples are learners.

- Make disciples, not just Christians.

- View yourself as a fish cleaner.

- Focus on being a lifelong learner.

- Adopt God's priority – discipleship.

- Use your advantages as a lay people-helper.

- Dig deep for the gold in your past.

- Realize God may have you specialize.

- Remain faithful in your present responsibilities.

- Test all you believe with His truth.

Chapter 2
SMALL GROUP QUESTIONS

1. What specific lessons have you learned while processing your personal issues about God, others and yourself?

2. What was the hardest lesson you had to learn and accept? Why was it so difficult?

3. What personal benefits have you experienced helping others as a lay people-helper?

4. What responsibilities has God given you that you can honestly say you have been faithful in assuming? Describe how difficult it was to become and remain faithful.

5. What specific events have you experienced and worked through that you feel will be helpful in serving others?

6. What sources beyond Scripture have been a help to you to be better prepared to help others?

Chapter 3

ILLUSTRATE HOW YOU PROCESSED YOUR PAST

As I walked into the dimly lit display room at the Pro Football Hall of Fame museum in Canton, Ohio, I stood amazed. All around the room, rows and rows of brass busts of the greatest football players sat on glass shelves, each individually lit to highlight that player.

As I stood there with my grandson, Dawson, my mind shifted immediately back to God's Hall of Fame, His trophies displayed in Hebrews 11. Yes, they were flawed in areas of their personal lives like Noah, Abraham, Sarah, Moses, Rahab and Sampson. But God encourages us to look at the part of their lives where they did excel, namely their faith. These are examples, patterns to follow. They are trophies of God's grace working in their lives. But there is one thing common with all of them: they are dead, you are alive, and it is your turn.

ILLUSTRATE WITH YOUR LIFE

You have worked hard to process your life. You have even retraced the past and gleaned the gems of life and of faith. Now you are ready for the third step that God says defines a biblical care-giver. You are a classic illustration of how to do it. You are the living breathing example people need to see, hear, feel and touch. You are in God's Hall of Fame even though you might still be flawed in some areas and are still struggling like the rest of us. People are not as inspired with speakers who tell them what to do as much as they are with speakers who can appropriately admit their personal problems and how they dealt with them. Dr. Bernie Zilbergeld maintains that people would solve most problems better by talking to friends, spouses, relatives, or anyone else who appears to be doing well in an area where they believe they are doing poorly! Ask Fred Stoeker.

Fred struggled with sex addiction. He was compulsively turning to pornography and masturbation for sexual release. But he worked through that sexual slavery biblically and achieved the ability to restore the power of choice to his life. He learned how to control strong sexual passions and live a pure life, yet not without a life-long battle. What did Fred do with all that life experience? He founded Living True Ministries to help guys work through their sex addictions and regain control of their lives. He co-authored a gold medallion award-winning book, *Every Man's Battle*. Guys from all walks of life have been helped. He is a trophy, an example of a man who has processed his past, learned from it and now humbly stands before others as an illustration of how to regain sexual sobriety. Jesus is gone. The Old and New Testament greats are gone. Who is left? You!

BE HIS EXAMPLE

As a biblical care-giver, be open to appropriately explain to others how God's Word works both in truth and practice in your life. It is your own personal practical application of God's Word that lays your foundation for people-helping. Yes, academic training can be helpful, but it must not be a substitute for applying God's Word to your own issues, which is a life-long process (Phil. 1:6; 3:12). The Apostle Paul was an example of that pattern.

Remember his *email* to Timothy. He knew it would be tough for Timothy to convince people with a pagan past that the one true God would save them or that they were even worth saving. But Timothy could refer to Paul as being the worst of the worst, the chief of sinners, and yet Paul's life was positive proof that if God could save him, He could save them. Paul demonstrated that greater grace could not be shown than what was shown to him. God could not find a greater sinner that required all of His patience (Nicoll Vol 4 pp. 96-99).

Paul is God's greatest human illustration of His grace, not because he was an apostle, but because of the horrific pain he caused Christians as he planned almost single handedly, to destroy the church of God. People were shocked when they heard of his change. They could not believe he was now preaching the very gospel he had tried to destroy (Acts 9:21; Gal. 1;13).

Paul's past served as a backdrop to display the *grace of God*, as it does in your life. His past was a frame around his life. A frame calls attention to the picture; it highlights it. Your past is not a shame, it is a frame. Your present life may not make sense or be appreciated by others if they do not know your appropriately shared story.

When I stand up to speak for the first time in another country, the people look at me as this white, educated, *rich* American who has all the answers, attempting to help these *poor*, struggling people. Then I drop the bomb. I tell them my father was an alcoholic who abandoned our family when I was about 15 years old. He never came back and we heard nothing from him again. I know the heartache of living in a divorced home, struggling to survive financially.

Shock runs through the audience as they realize, "He's one of us." The atmosphere abruptly changes. They are ready to listen. Why? They are listening to an *illustrator* who has processed a lot of pain, learned a wealth of hard-earned lessons and is an exhibit of God's grace. Now I make sense to them. My transparency and honesty adds authenticity and credibility to our training.

LET PASTORS SET THE EXAMPLE

Remember the Great Commission? It was not only to teach all that Christ had taught them. It was primarily to teach others how to *put into practice* all that He taught. Now we have a problem. All those people are gone, so, God, in His creativity, designed a very simple long-term solution.

Yes, God put pastors [elders] over the church to preach, teach, exhort and rebuke with great patience (2 Tim. 4:2). Then God gave them a huge responsibility and He will hold them accountable at the believers' judgment (I Cor. 3:10-15; 2 Cor. 5:10). Elders of the early church were not to control their churches by verbally lording their position over the people and bossing them around but to lead by example. They were to practice what they preached so the people could see and know how God's Word works. They were to be examples of how the Word of God works in everyday life and in all circumstances and not just on Sundays. God wants people like you in the church who He can point to and tell the others, "Follow their example" (1Peter 5:3).

BE AN IMITATOR

Today we have many great Bible preachers but very few who can say with integrity, "Imitate me, just as I also imitate Christ" (I Cor. 4:16; 2 Thess. 3:7)). But Paul did not leave this responsibility with pastors alone. He told the Ephesian church, "Therefore be imitators of God as dear children" (Eph. 5:1). What did God want them to imitate? The life of Christ in the way they communicate, the way they act and the way they think.

People have been hurt in so many ways in life and do not know what to do with their *stuff*. What God is looking for are believers like you who also have experienced *stuff*, but you are working through it biblically. You've learned a lot from the process and now you stand in God's trophy case as an illustration of what to do. Yes, you! You are the most important person in someone's life. Not just because you are a Christian who can answer some of life's most difficult questions, but because you were teachable and you are now illustrating the process and its fruit.

Trained professionals confirm your value as an illustrator who is applying the Word of God to your own life. Christian psychiatrist, Dr. Frank Minrith, states, "One who knows the Word of God and is living it can probably help 95 percent of the people who come to him." What's more, he adds that such counselors need to know that their success rate may be proportionally higher than other professionals (Bobgan, p. 81). I agree with Dr. Neil Anderson that lay people, well-trained in biblical tools, can be used by God to process 95 percent of the problems people face (Anderson, p. 396).

Think about that! As a processor, learner and illustrator with no degrees you can potentially help 95 percent of the people that a professional can help. We have proved it at Living Foundation Ministries. Guess who comes to us for help? Counselors, therapists, psychologists, doctors, lawyers, professional athletes, school teachers, administrators and pastors. How is that possible? We are talking about problems in living and not the psychiatric disorders like schizophrenia, borderline personalities, etc. Research psychiatrist, E. Fuller Terry states that 75 percent of people who go to a psychiatrist go with problems in living. Only five percent have organic brain disease. Twenty percent need further examination (Bobgan, p. 4).

For example, clinical depression can result from the depletion of serotonin in the brain. This depletion is often a result of unprocessed anger. Scripture explains what to do with anger (Eph. 4:25,26). You do not need a clinical background to deal with anger. Acknowledge the presence of anger, identify the object of anger (person), then, by God's power, forgive them. (We will explore forgiveness further in Chapter 9.) Anger is basically a notifier of the hurt that God wants to heal through forgiveness for your benefit and for His glory (Matt. 5:16).

FOLLOW THE PATTERN

Look what we learn from an Old Testament scribe, Ezra. He returned to Israel from Babylon to instruct the Jewish returnees to Jerusalem how to worship and to serve God. But notice how he did it! "The good hand of his God was upon him. For Ezra had set his heart" to do three things. First, study the Law of the Lord. But what did he do with that information first? He put it into practice personally (processor, learner, illustrator). Then, he began to teach His statues and ordinances in Israel (Ezra 6:10). Sound familiar? This pattern is one of the important ways of God for us to follow. The Word of God went through Ezra's life experience first, not just his head.

How did James, the half-brother of Jesus, emphasize this concept? "Be doers [practitioners] of the Word and not hearers only, deceiving yourselves [thinking you are doing] … he who looks in the perfect law of liberty and continues in it … this one will be blessed in what he does" (Jam. 1:22-25). Do not exchange *listening* for *doing*. That does not work! Psychologist, Dr. Larry Crabb, warns us, "Without an increasing understanding of how the biblical message works in our lives, no amount of training in counseling theory or technique will ever produce a biblical counselor" (Crabb, *Understanding*. p. 72).

BELIEVE WHAT WORKS

To be effective, you must be personally convinced in your heart that Scripture answers every problem in living, specifically or in principle. Your confidence is not misplaced. God Himself affirms this reality apart from your personal experience. Peter, who spent three years living and ministering with Jesus, declared later in life, "God has given us everything we need for living a godly life" (2 Pet. 1:3). No exceptions!

The Apostle Paul reaffirmed this to his disciple, Timothy, that "All Scripture is inspired by God and profitable for teaching, for reproof, for correction, for training in righteousness; so that the man of God may be adequate, equipped for every good work" (2 Tim. 3:16,17). But it will take time to study and will not happen overnight (I Tim. 4:15,16; 2 Tim. 2:15).

If you are going to help anyone, especially with all that you have been through, you will have to agree with the grandfather of biblical counseling, Dr. Jay Adams. "Every change that God promises is possible. Every quality that God requires in His redeemed children can be attained. Every resource that is needed, God has supplied." Yes, we recognize that there are organic, physical, hormonal and legitimate brain disorders, but we are focusing here on problems in living, not organic issues.

Unfortunately, some wrong living patterns are classified as a disease. One might say that a passive-aggressive behavioral pattern is a disease. No, it is an inappropriate way of dealing with anger and you have the biblical tools to deal with it. Co-dependency is not a disease; it is an inappropriate way to deal with the fear of abandonment. It is a form of relational addiction with God removed from the relationship. The co-dependent person relies on another human being to act in the place of God on their behalf. The other person should always be available, automatically know his every need, and able to *fix* every problem. "Lacking any biblical perspective on mental health, secular doctors and psychologists explain the battle for control of the mind as a neurological disorder or chemical imbalance" (Anderson, p. 44).

AVOID THE SHORTCUTS

There are no short-cuts at this point. You are now in a position to illustrate how you used God's tools (principles from Scripture) in your life to form your core curriculum to help others. As you are processing your issues and learning from them, stand tall as an illustrator. This is the only pattern God blesses (Jam. 1:22-25).

It is time to explore a practical list of *problems* in living. Do not be discouraged if you do not have an answer now to each question. Determine to study God, His Word, people, and the lessons from your own personal life. Then be ready to give an answer to everyone who asks you for a reason for your hope and quality of life (I Pet. 3:15). God never wastes life experiences on anyone. If you don't have an answer, tell the questioner you will get back to him and then, research it and ask fellow disciples. In time, you will research fewer issues because God, His Word, godly friends and counselors will help you as you remain a learner for life.

PRAYERFULLY THINK THROUGH THE LIST

• How do I process (control, redirect) anger?

• What should I do when I am lonely instead of using drugs, sex, Internet, pornography, alcohol, unhealthy relationships?

• How do I control lust, fantasy, temptation and avoid pornography or other addictions?

• What do I do when fearful or anxious?

• How do I respond to others' anger?

• What do I do when I fail, make mistakes or offend someone?

• What do I do with guilt, shame and depression?

• How do I pray, study the Bible, witness, give, serve?

• How do I forgive?

• How do I deal with memories of past hurts, failures, forgiven sin?

• How do I deal with problems, trials, afflictions?

• How do I deal with rejection (past or present)?

• How do I rebuild from failure?

• How does one recover from an affair?

• How do I rebuild a broken relationship?

• How do I work through a difficult family or marital conflict?

• How do I work through grief?

Don't get depressed over this list. This book will give you answers to many of these questions. Our website **(www.help4living.org)** is rich with practical information that you can use yourself. There is no charge for these resources, which can be found under the *Training /Tools* tab.

WHY DID ALL THIS HAPPEN?

"Why me, God? Why is this happening to me?" Good questions. Common questions. Painful ones. But by now, you should have a clue why God allowed you to go through all you have experienced in life. You were given the opportunity to use God's tools to give you a better quality of life. You have also learned a great deal about God, others and yourself. Each lesson is worth more than gold (I Pet. 1:6-9). You worked hard for it. Now you can begin to see the value of it all. You can be in God's hall of fame as a living example of how to respond to the trials, tests, afflictions and losses of life.

Now you are ready for the most exciting part. You have earned the right to reproduce. You are going to be an instrument of change in someone else's life because you processed, learned and illustrated. You were born to reproduce.

Chapter 3
ILLUSTRATE HOW YOU PROCESSED YOUR PAST

• View yourself in God's Hall of Fame.

• Be a living example of how God's Word works.

• Remember that your past is God's backdrop for His present work in you.

• Illustrate the process seven days a week.

• Be a person of integrity.

• Understand that you may be as successful as any professional person in helping others.

• Adopt Ezra's strategy: study, apply, then teach.

• Be convinced that Scripture answers every problem in living.

• Avoid shortcuts to maturity.

• Realize your life is someone else's key to freedom.

• Appropriately share your story.

Chapter 3
SMALL GROUP QUESTIONS

1. Who is in your mental hall of fame and how did they get there?

2. What short-cuts have you tried to take to avoid processing and what did it take to get you to do the hard work?

3. What areas of your life are illustrations of what you have processed? Describe what you went through to get there.

4. What pastors/teachers/mentors stand out as examples to you and why?

5. What is your personal pattern of Bible study and how has that better prepared you to help someone else?

6. How did you arrive at the understanding that God's Word is practical for all life situations?

7. Share an experience of someone who may have responded to your illustration of obedience to God.

Chapter 4
REPRODUCE THE PROCESS IN OTHERS

"Dr, Lynch does not have any counselees," announced the host of a Christian counseling training seminar as he introduced me as the presenter. My eyes widened. I, who come to see him," he continued, "am not viewed as a counselee, but a trainee." He got it! I did not realize our philosophy of counseling training was so well known. Why did he say that?

CLEAN FISH HERE

Jesus' instructions were clear, "Make disciples" (Matt. 28:19). But if we had a sign in front of our office advertising the fact that we train disciples to be spiritual care-givers, it would be a long time before anyone would walk through our doors. Perhaps a few curiosity seekers would venture in. But if we announced we offer Christian counseling, that would change things, and it did.

WE DON'T FIX PROBLEMS

Every person who comes for counseling is given a brief form to fill out. Near the end of the form are two very unusual statements. It reads: *Our goal is twofold:*

1. Goal 1 - *to give you tools to work through your issues and*

2. Goal 2 - *to prepare you to assist someone else in working through their problems.*

What is that all about?

Recall Jesus' words, "Make disciples" or *learners* – clean the fish. Each counselee is viewed as a learner (disciple) and we are going to use their *problems* to train them in the practical application of God's Word to life. The tools we will share are either a clear Scripture or a principle from Scripture or an insight that does not violate Scripture.

TOOLS ARE IMPORTANT

Why do we use the concept of *tools*? It's very simple. Tools imply that it is the counselees' responsibility to process their own issues with the tools we provide and coach them to use. Most people expect you to *fix them*. That is not discipleship. Their issues provide opportunities for them to learn more of the Word of God (discipleship) and apply it to real-life situations. God benefits only the *doers* or appliers of His Word, not just the hearers (Jam. 1:25).

The concept of tools has another benefit. The tools you use to build a shed could also be used to build a deck. You don't have to go back to the hardware store to purchase another hammer, saw, or screwdriver for every new project. You use the ones you have. When you have another issue in your life, you can use the tools you learned earlier. Some would call that maturity.

Some Christians never learn the basic tools and are always having to start all over again. This is precisely what the author of Hebrews is talking about when he reminds some of his readers, "You have been Christians a long time and you should be in a position to disciple others [biblical tools], but instead, you need someone to sit down with you and go over again the same basic principles [tools] of God's Word" (Heb. 5:12, paraphrased).

YOUR COUNSELING ISN'T WORKING

From time to time, I will hear a *disciple* report that they feel the counseling is not working. When I hear that, I say, "Good! Please tell me which tool you agreed to use that is not working." Silence. The obvious is evident; they did not use the tool. It is at this time that I remind them that 60 percent of physician's prescribed medications are not taken. Sometimes there are legitimate reasons. But there are very few reasons, if any, not to use a practical tool from God's Word. I have graciously shared, "If you don't take the medicine, you may need to change doctors." Remember, a disciple is a learner who is willing to learn to *apply all* that Jesus taught (Matt. 28:19,20), not just to accumulate information, which could become a real source of pride (I Cor. 8:1).

PASS IT ON

The first thing counselees in our office are told is, "We don't fix problems." Secondly, we tell them that it's our prayer they would be open to share whatever they learn with someone else. Do people always buy into this? No, not up front, however, we have received letters, phone calls and emails, sometimes years later, sharing how people have helped others using the tools they learned here.

Case in point: A former client dropped by our office recently and gifted us with a framed copy of a skillfully crafted handout on communication that she developed from her counseling here more than a decade ago. She also brought in an elaborate Native American talking stick with beads and feathers that she had made to use with the handout. When Native Americans would meet to discuss tribal issues, they would allow only one person to talk at a time. The one holding the stick was the only one who could talk. Then the stick was passed on to the next speaker. This is a practical illustration of Jam. 1:19, "...be quick to hear, slow to speak." Our client explained that she has been offering the printed handout with the talking stick as a wedding gift to engaged couples to help them learn to communicate better.

This brings us full circle. Teach the tools to disciples who then pass them on to others. This is precisely what the Apostle

Paul did with Timothy. In Paul's last letter to his son in the faith, he reminded Timothy, "The things [tools] you have heard from me in the presence of many witnesses, entrust these to faithful men who will be able to teach others also" (2 Tim. 2:2).

BE A REPRODUCER

Heidi's emotional pain was real and deep. She was sexually abused by her older brother and beaten often by a mother who was impossible to please. Dad was a workaholic, always gone, and never witnessed the abuse in the home. When she told her story, I ached for her. I validated her emotions. I could see we had our work cut out for us. Later, I explained to her that perhaps someday she would be able to help other women who are going through similar painful issues. Her response was very common from those who have experienced so much trauma in their developmental years, "I've always wanted to help people." Does everyone respond so positively? No. When you are in pain, usually helping others is not at the top of your *to do* list. Yet, I have found that as soon as I can appropriately interject that thought, the faster they can gain hope that they will make it and, just maybe, there is a purpose for their pain.

Biblical people-helpers have a desire to reproduce other caregivers who will in turn be able to help others work through their problems in living from God's Word. There is a reason for that. Biblical counselors have viewed their own personal trials, hurts, losses, failures and tests as their personal preparation to help others. Dr. Friesen expresses it this way, "People who conquer a problem often end up helping others conquer the same problem. Many professionals are people who have been through traumas themselves and are helping others with theirs. One former alcoholic founded Alcoholics Anonymous" (Friesen, p. 36).

Remember, you are a processor. You have learned and are learning a lot through the process. You are a living illustration of how God's tools work and now you are ready to reproduce them in others. As Dawson Trotman, the founder of the Navigators, often stated, "We were born to reproduce."

Biblical counselors should not use counseling as a means to fill a hole in their own soul or ignore a hole that exists. Much training is given to people who have ignored their own past issues and want to be trained to help others. This is not necessarily wrong but it is not how God works. Everyone has fallen short of God's holy standards (Rom. 3:23) and have grown up in a home with less than perfect parents. Everyone ends up in adulthood with wounds from life. But you have acknowledged that and are dealing with them while using your biblical tools.

ADJUST YOUR VISION

Picture anyone with whom you share an insight, Scripture or principle as a learner (disciple) even if it is one sentence. "Like apples of gold in settings of silver is a word spoken in right circumstances" (Prov. 25:11). King Solomon echoed the same thought, "A man has joy in an apt answer, and how delightful is a timely word" (Prov. 15:23).

The apostle Paul clearly states God's perspective on the whole process of counseling. 2 Cor. 1:3,4, "Praise be to the God of all comfort ...who comforts us in all our affliction so that [purpose] we will be able to comfort those who are in any affliction with the comfort with which we ourselves are comforted by God." This is Betty's story in a nutshell.

"Chuck, would you talk to Betty on the phone? It sounds urgent." Betty's husband wanted out of the marriage and had filed for divorce. I urged her to see me as soon as possible.

I slowly worked with her through all the agonizing issues of being rejected, abandoned, unemployed and a single parent. We shared many tools and applied them then and there, working through denial, acknowledging the legitimate anger and speaking truth to the lies she believed about herself. She was given permission to feel the full range of emotions and finally over time came to accept and live with the loss. There were many issues to grieve that we worked through, one at a time.

A month later I received a call from another *Betty*. Notice what we did. I met with this woman once; then I asked her if she would be willing to meet with Betty, who had gone through a similar painful experience and to allow Betty to walk with her through this. I assured her that if there were any questions Betty could not answer, she could call me directly and get all the help she needed. She graciously agreed. Fast forward ten years.

I was asked to speak at my former church. Following the service, Linda and I stood in the church lobby greeting old friends. Suddenly, I heard my name called out across the room, "Chuck!" A woman rushed up to me and asked, "Do you remember me? You helped me when my husband divorced me." Before I could respond, she said, "You can't believe the ministry God has given me over these past ten years. He has allowed me to minister to scores of hurting women and even those who have been abused." She gave Linda and me warm hugs and abruptly left telling us to "Please stay in touch."

Where did God find this care-giver? She was hurt but she allowed it to be the doorway to healing. She learned much more on her own and went way beyond me in this particular area. Betty is a living example of how the Word of God transforms the painful wounds of life. She is a reproducer. This is the way of God.

CONNECT PAIN TO PREPARATION

Most hurting people experience a deep desire to help others, especially those going through personal pain. But few people help them connect how processing their pain is personal preparation for ministry, even if their pain is self-inflicted. It is like a mental wall is erected between life's pain and God's preparation to help others. When the fish are caught (evangelized) and cleaned (discipled) they are ready to reproduce, especially if the mental wall has been removed so they can connect their past to preparation to help others.

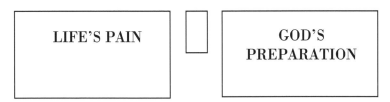

Joseph is a classic Old Testament example of one who connected the events of being kidnapped by his brothers at age 16 and sold as a slave to the Ishmaelites as preparation to save his family from starvation. When Joseph, later in life, revealed himself to his brothers who felt guilt and anger for what they had done to him, he told them to stop it. He shifted their focus from themselves to God who, "sent me before you to preserve life" (Gen. 45:5). Did Joseph always see God at work? No! Before he revealed his identity to his brothers, they admitted guilt for not responding to Joseph's begging and pleading to take him from the pit where they had thrown him before they planned to kill him (Gen. 42:21). Joseph was not praising the Lord in the pit at that moment.

While in prison, Joseph correctly interpreted Pharaoh's cup-bearer's dream. When the cup-bearer was to be restored to his position, Joseph pleaded with him to tell Pharaoh how he was kidnapped and enslaved and had done nothing to deserve the dungeon (Gen. 40:14,15). "I'm innocent! This is totally unfair!" Joseph was not quoting as it were, "All things work together for good for those who love God..." (Rom 8:28). However, Joseph later connected the dots between the abuse he suffered and God's plan for his life.

Did Joseph simply overlook what his brothers did to him? No. He held them responsible for their actions, but he did something else. He was able to factor God into the abuse and clearly stated their responsibility and God's purpose, "....you meant [intended] evil against me but God meant it for good in order to bring about this present result [deliverance from starvation] to preserve many people alive" (Gen. 50:20).

The hardest word in verse 20 is the word, *good*. We all have painful experiences. My father walked out the door and never came back while I was a young teen. Alcoholism, abandonment, rejection and living on the edge of poverty with unmentionable shame. *Not good!* Yet, today I have the undeserved opportunity to explain firsthand how to forgive from the heart and have watched thousands of lives change on five continents. That is GOOD! My first book, *I Should Forgive, But...*, was dedicated to my praying mom and forgiven dad.

One of the privileges you have as a biblical people-helper is to help others to work through their pain and visualize how they will be able to help someone else. Even if they initially fail to see what personal or spiritual benefit their experience can offer them or others, you can help them make the connection, as the Apostle Paul did. He encouraged those in Corinth who were experiencing suffering, to connect the dots of their pain as preparation to help others (2 Cor. 1:6).

IT IS NOT A NEW IDEA

"You'll never last," was Moses' father-in-law Jethro's honest comment to him. He watched Moses being overwhelmed attempting to judge all the people's cases. He was headed for total exhaustion (Ex. 18:17,18). Jethro counseled Moses to select able men and teach them God's statutes and laws in dealing with life's problems. We would call that discipleship. By doing so, Moses would only have to handle the most difficult issues and the people would get the justice they needed and would go home in peace (Ex. 18:21-23).

IT IS NOT COMPLICATED

Moses chose able men and made them heads (judges) over the people, rulers over thousands, hundreds, fifties and tens. Problems in living had to go through four layers before they reached him. But notice, Moses did not only delegate responsibility to leaders, he also had to teach, train (disciple) these men so that they could practically apply God's Word to specific problems in life. The lower level judges and counselors may not have had all the insights the higher-level leaders had, but it was a starting point. We witnessed this first hand in Venezuela.

"Where did they all come from?" was my first reaction to the large packed room of lay people who wanted to be trained to counsel others. We took them through the basic course of ten topics in a week. But that was just a start. Francisco and Yrma, our disciples in Venezuela, returned to that city every week for ten weeks. They expanded my one-and-a-half-hour session to eight hours with many personal application examples. A year later we returned and participated in a graduating class of 20 trainees. Then it was announced that 40 had already signed up for the next training to be conducted by Francisco and Yrma. The pastor of this church of 500 stood up at the end and shared that the church had adopted the goal to have the entire church go through the training. For the record, you could not graduate if you missed a class.

Later, all those who had taken the training met with me for hours asking questions about specific situations. What was amazing was that as we would address each real situation and teach them how to apply the biblical tools, fewer and fewer questions were asked. They got it! I was impressed to learn that the pastor had made it perfectly clear that all the trainees, for good reason, had to also be working on their own issues. Biblical people-helpers must have integrity in order to be believed by others. We are all wounded warriors helping others with their wounds.

WHO IS TOP PRIORITY?

"What one practical action could you do that would fulfill the entire law of Christ?" When I ask this question to groups all over the world, the answer is the same, "Love the Lord with all your heart, soul and mind and your neighbor as yourself" (Matt. 22:37-39). They did not hear the question. I asked what specific action, deed, could one do that would fulfill the law.

Love is an attitude of the heart. The Apostle Paul describes attitudes in I Cor. 13 that reflect love. But no one action was identified that would fulfill the law of Christ. However, he did reveal the answer to the Galatian believers. "Bear one another's burdens, and so fulfill the law of Christ [which is love]" (Gal. 6:2).

God puts a high priority on helping fellow believers work through problems in life. Why? The Great Commission was to make disciples, not just Christians. God is not only interested in our catching fish but also cleaning fish, the process of discipleship. "So then, while we have opportunity let us do good to all people and especially to those who are of the household of faith" (Gal. 6:10). Christians helping one another is a command, not advice. Why?

GOD LIMITS HIMSELF

Would it surprise you to hear that an all-powerful God would limit Himself? When I ask an audience, "Can you and God alone handle every burden you carry?" the answer is often, "Yes!" However, God has chosen to limit His power to work through people and that includes you!

He *commanded* us to help carry one another's burdens. It was not just advice. God refers to the church as the body of Christ where the members need one another to function (I Cor.

66

12:12-27). A fellow believer may have a need that you could meet. God could do it without you, but He purposely limits Himself to work through you.

HELP!

Every believer, sometime in life, will need another's help. The Apostle Paul urges, "Brethren, even if anyone is caught in any trespass, you, who are spiritual, restore such a one in the spirit of gentleness; each one looking to yourself, so that you will not be tempted" (Gal. 6:1). When he said, "you who are spiritual", he was not referring to an official position, but to anyone who knows God and how to apply His Word, regardless of their qualifications.

God does not need you! For His own reasons, He has chosen to limit His power and use you to restore to effectiveness a brother or sister who has been overwhelmed, who feels hopeless and powerless. A single parent recently wrote after a visit, "Although I needed lodging, I was coming for more than that. You have always been so accepting of me even when there has been lots of garbage inside of me. I want you to know that your love for me has paid off. I came so you could understand how the Lord has been working and, yes, I must admit, I came for some more of that love because my spirit was tired. You did not disappoint me."

James, historically the first book written in the New Testament, summons believers to help fellow believers. "My brethren, if any among you strays from the truth and someone turns him back, let him know that he who turns a sinner from the error of his way will save his soul from death and cover a multitude of sins" (Jam. 5:19,20). The one who has strayed may feel like he is standing in the middle of his house while it is burning and all he has is a glass of water to fight the flames.

James is encouraging you to engage the wanderer who has fallen away from the faith to return to a faith walk with Christ.

The "lost ones" or "sick ones" in the church family need to be restored to the church fellowship. The issue is not evangelism; it is restoration - not catching the fish but cleaning the fish.

The sins of the restored one are covered as if a holy veil was thrown over them. Now he can move on again and grow in spiritual maturity. God could have done that Himself. He is able! But He chose to limit Himself to work through you and me to bring greater spiritual maturity to the body of Christ. The helped believer can now carry his own lighter load (Gal. 6:5).

HOW DOES IT REALLY WORK?

Shelia (in chapter two) had been a preschool teacher for years. She also had a passion to help other women work through their past and present hurts that continued to control their lives. She did this through personal discipleship. When she would get stuck, she would bring the woman into my office and the three of us would work together.

Over the course of years, Shelia brought fewer and fewer women in to see me. I asked her to consider working with us as a biblical counselor and continued to ask her over a five-year period. Finally, one day she said she felt free to leave her teaching position and serve at Living Foundation Ministries. She worked as a receptionist and would often sit in with me as I counseled. In time, I asked her if she would be open to see some women alone. Cautiously, she agreed. She has been with us 18 plus years and there is usually a waiting list to see her.

THIS WAS GOD'S IDEA

Dr. Luke sent a long letter to Theophilus mentioning his first letter, which we know as the gospel of Luke. He reminded Theophilus why he wrote the gospel, which was to explain all that Jesus began to do and to teach (show and tell). Dr. Luke, in one short sentence, summarized the whole process of discipleship. Jesus was the pattern. It had at least six simple aspects.

Observation and Instruction: Jesus had His disciples follow Him around, listen to Him teach and observe His ministry. At this point the disciples just listened and watched (Luke 6:17).

When I am asked by pastors to sit in on their counseling sessions and give them an honest evaluation, often they are doing a great job. I usually ask, "Who is watching you do this?" These sessions would be a great learning experience for many. This is exactly how the disciples learned from Jesus. They watched and observed.

Participation Under Supervision: It did not take long before Jesus included the disciples in ministry under his close supervision. We see this in the feeding of the five thousand (Matt. 14:13-21). This is exactly how we trained Steve. He sat in on scores of hours of counseling with me. Periodically, I would ask Steve what he thought about an issue we were dealing with in someone's life. As I listened to his answers, I knew he, like Shelia, was ready to be launched. He had studied through all our training materials, had hours of observation and now participation. He was ready.

Participation Without Supervision: Jesus felt his disciples had seen and heard enough. It was time to be sent out on their own. He sent them out two by two like a team (Luke 9:1-6). They, too, felt they were ready. They knew His teaching and were given power and authority to perform the miracles.

Participation Report: When the disciples returned, they were ecstatic and full of joy. What an incredible experience they had had! They felt so empowered they reported to Jesus that even the demons were subject to them when they addressed them in the name of Jesus (Luke 10:17). This was true because the authority Jesus had given them broke Satan's power. Jesus must have been thrilled as the disciples told their stories just as I was filled with joy listening to Shelia and Steve share victory after victory in the difficult situations they dealt with.

Correct and Clarify: After listening to His disciples and observing their joy, He also noted some things that needed to be adjusted. In their excitement, they felt elated about the power they had over demons. Men love power and their response was normal. But Jesus challenged their source of joy, "Do not rejoice in this, that the spirits are subject to you, but rejoice that your names are recorded in heaven" (Luke 10:20). He made it clear our joy should come from our relationship *with* Him and not our accomplishments *for* Him.

Commission and Release: Three years had passed. Every minute was packed as Jesus taught His disciples and showed them what to do. Now it was time. Following His death and resurrection, Jesus appeared over the next 50 days. In His final farewell, He passed His authority on to His disciples "And Jesus came and spoke to them, saying, 'All authority has been given to Me in heaven and on earth. [19] Go therefore and make disciples of all the nations, baptizing them in the name of the Father and of the Son and of the Holy Spirit, [20] teaching them to observe all things that I have commanded you; and lo, I am with you always, even to the end of the age.'" Amen (Matthew 28:18-20).

The on-site training was over. The teacher had gone to be with the Father. The first eye witnesses of His life and teachings were to go and tell and show others how to disciple. They were not to build their own kingdom, but God's kingdom. They were not to collect people, but to reproduce and send them out. Twenty-one of the 27 books of the New Testament were written to explain how to clean the fish and how to prepare His people for His coming (Eph. 5:25-27).

TRAINERS CHANGE ROLES

I often questioned why our Venezuelan team wanted me to return to Venezuela and teach when I knew they were now better equipped than I to do the job of training people-helpers. They

70

know the language and the culture. However, there was one piece of the discipleship procedure I did not realize. They finally told me, "You are coming for us, you are our mentor."

Francisco and Yrma have trained over five thousand people in small groups in the last ten years. They are good! But they taught me that a reproducer's role should ultimately change from a direct trainer to a mentor who is available, who will release and let go and fervently pray for them. It is not *catch and release*. It is *train and release*.

TOUR OUR HALL OF FAME

Along the back wall of our reception area is a row of pictures of our staff. There is one characteristic of each one. They all came in initially for counseling.

Shelia and Mike dealt with an affair. Della told me she was about to commit suicide. Now she is our number one prayer warrior. Fran had been in an abusive marriage, her youngest daughter died at age eleven, then, her oldest at age 18. She became an alcoholic. Now she specializes in grief and addiction counseling. Steve had some blended family issues and had experienced some major set-backs in his life. He is now one of our counselors and specializes in marriage/family issues. Linda and her husband, Jim, worked through some marriage challenges and now she has managed the office for over ten years. Karee tried to take her life, but she was helped to work through the sources of her pain. She serves as our bookkeeper.

Where did God find these people-helpers? They had some serious issues but worked through them biblically. Sharing insights with the rest of us, each one is a learner through what they have experienced and what they glean from reading. They are in our hall of fame as illustrations of what God has done in their lives.

Finally, they are all reproducers. Karee is in training to help others as she serves as our bookkeeper. Our office manager trains new volunteers who are former counselees. She shares godly insight with people in the reception area waiting for their appointments.

BUT WHY ME?

Some big questions will stare you in the face as you seek to help someone in crisis. They will ask, "Why did this happen to me?" "Why didn't God stop it?" "What possible good could come out of this?" "Why did He let them die?"

These are real questions that have been asked thousands of times. You have probably asked them yourself and are still wondering. So, let's ask God, "Why does He allow problems?"

Chapter 4
REPRODUCE THE PROCESS IN OTHERS

• Make reproducing Christ in others a life-long process.

• Offer tools; don't fix problems.

• View each counselee as a future people-helper.

• Teach others to be fish cleaners.

• Continue to learn more counseling tools as you counsel. Evaluate your counseling by the tools you actually used.

• Challenge others to pass on the tools.

• God has chosen to limit Himself to work through you.

• Help people connect their pain with preparation.

• Your priority is helping other believers.

• Recall the strategy: observe, participate, report, clarify, send.

Chapter 4
SMALL GROUP QUESTIONS

1. What was your personal experience of being discipled? What were the benefits? If you were never discipled, in what areas do you wish you had been?

2. Describe an incident when someone expected you to fix them while they were failing to be responsible.

3. What are some of your favorite biblical or relational tools? How did you use them? What was the response?

4. How different would a person counsel if he viewed the counselee as a trainer?

5. What painful experiences have you had that you can now connect as being preparation to help others?

6. What does this statement mean to you? *God has chosen to limit Himself to work through you?*

7. Who have you observed helping someone else and what did you learn personally from that experience?

8. How would your life be different if you truly believed that you are the most important person in someone's life?

Chapter 5
UNDERSTAND GOD'S PURPOSE
FOR PROBLEMS

WELCOME PAIN AND LOSS

Pain and loss are no fun. When you experience a severe tragedy, heartache, catastrophic loss, it feels undeserved. Something down deep screams, "WHY? What did I do to deserve this?" Understand, first of all, it is not wrong to ask the question. This response to loss and pain is normal. God chose to address this very topic in Job, one of the earliest books written in the Old Testament. It is probably one of the best-known examples of undeserved suffering and loss recorded in Scripture (Walvoord, OT, p. 715).

Job lost his material possessions, all his children and his health. He even lost the emotional support of his wife, who, out of her own bitterness, told him to curse God [revenge] and die [escape] (Job 2:9). Statistically, fifty percent of couples who lose a child in death, divorce. Anger, in the grief process, can cause couples to turn on each other.

But to add insult to injury, Job's friends condemned and shamed him because they believed he had been a fraud and hypocrite who harbored secret sins. Watching this unfold, you cannot help but wonder, "How much more could Job take and not turn on God?"

Turning to the New Testament, in the book of James, guess what issue he first addressed? Pain and loss. It is a letter that was written to the twelve tribes of Israel who had lost everything and were now scattered in Babylon and Mesopotamia. They lost their homes, possessions, many friends, family connections and anything familiar as they relocated to a strange, dangerous environment; total loss of security! Acknowledging the reality of pain and loss is a high priority to God as reflected in those two books.

Jesus' disciples reflect the same belief Job's friends expressed, that all physical and emotional pain is the result of and punishment for sin. They, so much as said so when they saw a blind man from birth and asked Jesus, "Rabbi, who sinned, this man or his parents, that he was born blind?" (Jn. 9:2).

The disciples faced a troubling theological problem. They believed the only purpose for pain and suffering was punishment so that the handicap a person was born with was a result of sin. Their only possible explanations were that he sinned in his mother's womb or his parents had sinned (Ex. 20:5). But logically, how does a baby sin in his mothers' womb? They were reflecting the Old Testament perspective of pain and loss. If you obeyed God, you were blessed. If you sinned, you were punished (CF Deut. 11:26-28). You will hear this same thinking today. "Is God punishing me through my son's death?" "Cancer! Why is this happening to me?" Elaine asked me the same question. Her husband was a pastor and they were both involved in ministry until he developed cancer and died. She was left with three kids and no job.

If you stood before the cross as Jesus was crucified, the most painful death possible, you would hear the Son of God ask the same question, "My God, My God, why have You forsaken Me?" (Mark 15:34). That was Jesus speaking while wracked with pain. His Father abandoned Him in a judicial, not a relational sense. Why? Because Jesus was bearing the curse of sin and God's judgment on sin (2 Cor. 5:21; Gal. 3:13). Jesus experienced the unfathomable horror of separation from God while dying on behalf of our sin.

WHAT'S THE PROBLEM?

Ironically, the word, *problem*, does not appear in the English King James Version of the Bible. The word appears two times in the New American Standard (Dan. 5:12,16) and three times in the New International Bible (Deut. 1:12; Dan. 5:12,16)

When I tell classes the word, *problem*, technically is not in the Bible, I get a lot of bewildered looks. Apparently, God does not view tragedies, hurts and losses as problems. He calls them trials, tests, temptations, afflictions, tribulations or sufferings, but not problems. God uses these words to describe a process that people go through FOR A PURPOSE. He views these painful things as opportunities for you to experience positive benefits. Many writers have contributed to a possible list of reasons for these events in our lives.

WHAT ARE THE BENEFITS OF PROBLEMS?

Growth in Character: One practical question you can ask yourself is, "What character quality is this building in me?" "But I don't need character; I need relief!" you may think. Take a step back for a moment. Remember what James wrote to the Jews who were suffering because of their losses.

He had the nerve to tell those believers to put an entirely new meaning on their losses. Instead of grief from loss, he challenged them to consider their loss as a source of joy (Jam. 1:2). And he understood that they were surrounded by trials everywhere they turned. But he does not stop there. Verse three is the key: "...knowing that the testing of your faith [trust in God] is the process He uses to build in them the quality of endurance."

The word, *knowing,* is a present participle which means the *knowing* is taking place at the same time as the trial. If you know (believe) that this is a test for the purpose of strengthening your faith, you *CAN* rejoice. You win even in the midst of loss. As a result, you will be able to handle anything that comes along later in life (Jam. 1:4b). Rewards in eternity are just an added blessing.

But if you fail to put that meaning on your loss or hurt now, you will stay immature and every future test will be met with grief, anger or bitterness and a major loss of the quality of life that God has planned for you. Why are there so many immature believers? One reason is their failure to put a good meaning on *bad* experiences and grow through them. The choice is simple: be bitter or be blessed.

What will separate you from most *advice-givers* in well-meaning circles? You, by applying the truth of God's purpose in trials, will be able to gently share with others that God is more concerned that they develop Christ-like character than just having Him fix problems or relieve pain. Some issues like cancer, may not get fixed, but they can offer other opportunities to grow in spirit when suffering physically and emotionally.

Gain Insights in His Word: As Amy poured out her pain because of her husband's affair, she paused in the middle of her tears, anger and grief and acknowledged, "I have found myself reading my Bible more than I ever have in all my life. For some reason, it has come alive to me and it is not just words, especially the Psalms." Thankfully, Amy was learning the second benefit of processing problems with God: He will reveal insights that you may never have learned without the trial.

I would have never chosen what I lived through as a kid because of my dad's unfaithfulness. God did not choose this; my dad did and so did Amy's husband. But God will meet us in the midst of our suffering with comfort which gives hope when it looks hopeless and strength when we are weak from crying our eyes out.

What insights are you learning from His word as you go through your own painful experiences? The Psalmist expressed a hard-to-live-out truth in the midst of pain, "It is good for me to be afflicted, that I may learn [more about] Your statutes" (Ps.

119:71). Do not let trials keep you from going to God's word for help and comfort. Then record them in a journal so that you can share them with others later.

Deepen Your Understanding of His Ways: How many times have you acted out of your own understanding and had it blow up in your face? God expects you to use your mind. But it may take a minor or even a major trial, which I call a learning experience, to follow His ways of dealing with life. Psychologist, Larry Crabb, said it has been his experience that many of the obstacles and ensuing spiritual/psychological disorders are, in reality, the result of the sinful pursuit of life apart from God. People desire to remain independent of God and still make life work (Crabb, Understanding, p. 21, 106).

A proverb that I cite often simply states, "There is a way [of thinking and acting] that seems right [logical, level and straight] to a man, but the end [result] is the way of death" (Prov. 14:12). There is physical death which is the separation of body and spirit. There is spiritual death which is the separation of us from God as non-believers. There is relational death, as in divorce. Solomon was referring here to physical death because of sin.

Many of our responses to difficult people or circumstances are more human than godly. It is our way of dealing with them, not His way. One good reason to experience these *inconvenient* challenges is to learn *how* to respond in a Christ-like fashion, differently than we have done in the past. We call that growth.

Much of my *coaching* is training people how to act, think and speak in a Christ-like way when they are dealing with a relational crisis. If you were a fly on the wall in my office, you would hear me say repeatedly, "What a learning experience!" Now, what did you discover that did not work and what can you learn that would work and reflect His ways? God describes just how badly we need this, "For My thoughts are not your thoughts, nor are your ways My ways, says the Lord. For as the heavens are higher than the earth, so are My ways higher than your ways and My thoughts than your thoughts" (Is. 55:8-9). Jesus, too, challenged the way people thought and acted right from the beginning of His ministry, "You have heard it said…but I say to you." Six times Jesus attempted to change their perspective of life to reflect His way of life (Matt. 5:21, 27, 31, 33, 38, 43). Each change had to do with thinking and/or action.

Deepen Your Relationship with Him: What is God's number one priority for you? Relationships! First, with Him and second, with others. Jesus clarified this priority to the Pharisees who asked which was the greatest commandment (Matt. 22:37-40). His answer was simple: "Love God, love others." But the first one is to love God with all your heart, soul and mind. Why? He wants a relationship with you that is deeper than a casual association on Sunday.

Ellen once confessed to me after experiencing a major tragedy in her life that she had never prayed so hard or felt God so near as she had during all the turmoil. She learned what Job came to realize after all his losses. "I have heard of You by the hearing of the ear but now my eye sees You" (Job 42:5). Or, we would say Job heard a lot about God and that was good. But after all the physical, material and emotional loss, he could see God with new understanding.

This new view of God was a spiritual insight, not necessarily a physical vision. It deepened his perspective and appreciation of God. It not only changed his life but the lives of millions who have read of his struggles and identified with his pain and agony and personal loss. They have learned you can go through such loss and pain, be angry and even question God and feel abandoned and still come out with your faith and relationship intact.

Illustrate How to Respond: I overheard a dad sharing his frustration regarding the financial challenges he was facing, none of which were his own making. After a pause, his friend asked if it was possible that God was using these stressful trials to give him an opportunity to illustrate to his three daughters how to respond in difficult situations. A good question to ask yourself is, "Who will benefit from my godly response to a challenging situation?" Wives are encouraged when they see their husbands struggle in a crisis and throw themselves completely on the grace and mercy of God. Struggles without faith are discouraging, but conflicts with faith are encouraging.

The Apostle Paul was always facing one conflict after another. But out of the corner of his eye, he observed who was watching him and wondered what his influence would be on them. He expressed the reason he experienced so many conflicts. "God comforts us [Paul and his team] in all our troubles so that we are able to comfort those who are in any trouble with the comfort with which we are comforted by God...For when we, ourselves, are comforted, we will certainly comfort you. Then you can patiently endure the same things we suffer" (2 Cor 1:4,6). When He said *able to comfort*, he meant ability and resource. Also, the words *all* and *any* are the same Greek word.

People were encouraged to be more vocal about their faith in Christ because they observed Paul's response to his trials. People are looking for a pattern to follow. Your godly response to your struggles and trials might just provide what they are looking for.

Glorify Him: When you are in excruciating pain, or you just lost the dearest thing on earth to you, the last thing that enters your mind, if you are normal, is how can I glorify God through this? You are in shock! You cannot believe it is happening! It does not make sense. Anger even seeps in; then you start playing the *if only* game.

81

Welcome to grief. Though deeply saddened, in time, you will come to acceptance. And what does acceptance mean? You can accept the loss and be ready to move on. Acceptance does not mean you like it; it just means you can adjust your life to the new reality and take the next step. However, failure to come to this understanding of acceptance will keep you stuck emotionally, losing the opportunity to illustrate how a godly person should deal with loss and glorify God through it. Your Christ-like response automatically gives glory to God.

Remember the man born blind in John 9 and how the disciples questioned if his blindness was punishment for the man's or his parents' sins. What a loss! But Jesus added a third option; "It was so that the works of God might be displayed and illustrated in him" (Jn. 9:3 Amp). When Mary and Martha's brother, Lazarus, was seriously ill, Jesus explained the purpose, "This sickness is not to end in death, but for the glory of God so that the Son of God may be glorified by it" (Jn.11:4).

You may question during the darkest hours of your devastating pain, "God, how am I to glorify You through this?" or, "Lord, how do You want my light [life] to shine in such a way that people will see my godly response and glorify You?" (Matt 5:16). This takes submission. This takes maturity. This takes trust that He will glorify Himself through it all.

Correct Wrong Behaviors: It was not a great Thanksgiving holiday for Kent. He had been in jail. His family did not hear from him for a few days. Earlier in his teen years he bragged how he loved to drive fast which resulted in many speeding tickets. He grew out of his need for speed. At least he thought so until he got another ticket years later and failed to pay it. Not good. There was a warrant out for his arrest and the judge said he could choose which two days to spend in jail. He chose Thanksgiving so he would not miss work. When he told his granddad, he ended his confession with a statement his granddad had used with him on other difficult occasions, "What a learning experience!"

God loved Kent so much He allowed him to experience the result of his decisions. God, in His love, gives us the power of choice, the responsibility for our choices and the opportunity to experience the consequences of our choices. Why? To correct words, actions or attitudes that do not reflect the presence of Christ in our lives.

When we sin, we can count on God to discipline us (Heb. 12:6a). Discipline is not punishment. Christ has taken all the punishment for our sin (Rom. 8:1). But He will discipline us as one means of discipling us so that we can learn to share His holiness (Heb. 12: 10b). We win!

Kent's behavior has taken a more wholesome turn because of his *learning experience*. The purpose for God's discipline is not to punish but to correct a pattern that can ruin your quality of life. God focuses on correction, not punishment. In a *learning experience*, you will learn a lot about God (His love, grace, mercy), others and, especially, yourself. But if you keep doing the same thing over-and-over again and expect different results, it is not just a definition of insanity, it is a description of immaturity.

Reduce Pride, Increase Humility: How do you think Kent felt when he had to explain to his parents why he didn't come for Thanksgiving dinner? With eyes lowered, he shared the details of his *learning experience,* not just once, but multiple times, to each relative who innocently inquired.

There are many Scriptures on the negative use of pride. You probably know them. We may excuse or ignore pride but God does not. He hates it (Prov. 6:16,17; Ps. 101:5). He will allow you to experience a trial, affliction or loss [because of your proud, independent choices], in order to break that shell of pride and develop greater humility that attracts us to Him (I Pet. 5:5).

Strengthen Your Faith: **I heard an interesting insight in** graduate school, "You may or may not live out what you believe from day to day, but you will always live out what you believe in a crisis." Job is a classic illustration of that. Recall he had lost his sons, daughters, sheep, camels, oxen, donkeys, servants, both by enemies and supernatural events (Job 1:13-19). It is easy to trust God in luxury but what about devastating loss? Job had a faith that trusted God regardless (Job 1:20,21).

Remember James' purpose for trials? It was to test [mature] your faith or trust in God (Jam. 1:3). Peter expressed it this way, "In this you greatly rejoice, even though now for a little while, if necessary, you are distressed by various trials [why] so that the proof [or genuineness] of your faith being more precious [to you] than gold, which is perishable, even though tested by fire, may be found to result in praise and glory and honor at the revelation of Jesus Christ" [at His second coming] (I Pet.1:6,7).

All genuine relationships are based on trust or faith that a person is who he says he is or will do what he says he will do. That relationship of faith and trust grows as you go through the experiences of life. You learn to trust in a deeper way when tested by difficult challenges. So it is with God. What you have gone through may be one of the greatest opportunities you have had or will have to trust Him and to draw close to Him, instead of abandoning your faith and your relationship with Him. Your struggles, rightly faced, will reduce your dependence on people, places or things and grow your faith in the heavenly Father.

Prepares You to Help Others: We have come full circle exploring why God allows problems: to develop character, better understand His ways, deepen your insights into His Word, and your relationship with Him and others, be an example to onlookers, glorify Him, correct behavior, learn obedience and strengthen your faith. Those are only some of the benefits of your struggles. But whatever you have gone through was, in reality, preparation to help others. How do you do it? That is what others want to know.

Testimonies are great. Often they bless, but sadly, they do not instruct. You will hear someone tell what happened to them. Then we hear, "God dealt with me in a powerful way." This is then followed by the great transformation in the person's life. But something is missing.

As you listen you become a little resentful. Why? Why didn't God do that in my life? What is wrong with me? The testimony left out an important component: *HOW* did God work in their life? What did *they* have to do? Did someone help them through it? How did they struggle? What were their doubts, frustrations, periods of anger? What Scriptures did God use?

What people want to know are the *how's*, not just the *what's*. How did you actually process it? Be honest and explain the process. It was not a quick fix. God does not fix trials. He takes you through them so that you might glorify Him and be a blessing to someone else. Your pain is preparation! God gives you comfort [hope and strength] in all your troubles with the comfort you received from God (2 Cor. 1:4).

DON'T WASTE ANYTHING

God does not waste any of the events of your life, whether things you did or things done to you or around you. There is a divine purpose for everything. Nothing is an accident with God. Nothing happens in a vacuum even if Satan is behind it (2 Cor. 12:7).

While thinking about what I would speak on one night at a Christian family camp, I was approached by a woman camper. Knowing I was the speaker, she said, "I hate Romans 8:28," then, walked away. I stood there stunned for a moment. Later I learned her husband had recently been killed in a car accident and she had been badly injured. Some well-meaning person may have come up to her at the funeral and said, "Remember Jan, 'All things work together for good for those who love God and are called according to His purpose.'"

At that stage of grief, it was the last thing she wanted to hear. It is rarely a good idea to add truth to pain. The Scripture does not say to lecture those who weep, but to "weep with those who weep" (Rom. 12;15). She had been in shock. She was angry. She had replayed that wreck over in her mind a thousand times, dealing with her *if only*. Sadness had become her constant companion. Acceptance was still miles away. Usually the purpose for our pain, tragedy, trial or crisis does not come to us immediately. It may take time, but it will come. And yes, one of those purposes will be to prepare you to help someone else. It is a process, not a waste.

GROW THROUGH THEM

God's purpose is not to fix your problems but to lead you through them for your maturity and for His glory. Personal growth takes time. It takes six months to grow a squash and fifty years to grow an oak tree. None of us would build a house with squash. That spiritual growth takes time is a shock to some. Many believers feel that if you just pull the *God lever*, everything will change instantly. And when relief is not forth-coming, disillusionment turns to anger and to distancing oneself from God. The Apostle Paul learned this the hard way.

Paul had a *problem*, a thorn in the flesh, something physically painful. To make matters worse, it was inflicted by Satan (2 Cor. 12:7). Remember, Paul was in full-time Christian service. He healed others, no problem. He would just ask God and "poof!" this thorn would be gone. He prayed once for himself and it did not work. The second time he made it clear to God he wanted it removed. Still no answer. Why wasn't this working? This had to be a surprise to Paul because he was even able to raise the dead (Acts 20:7-12). What was wrong? He was desperate now! This *quick pray, quick fix* pattern was not working for him. The request probably turned into a plea the third time. Then God *tweeted* Paul a short two-sentence answer, first, "My gracious favor is all you need" [there will be no change]. Not good! Second, "My power works best in your weakness" (2 Cor. 12:9). Oh! That is good.

What a learning experience! God believed Paul needed two things and neither of them was healing. Paul needed *grace* for the pain and *purpose* for the pain. He finally learned God's purpose for his pain, to reduce his pride and to make him strong. Now God could have simply sent Paul an *email* without this hassle of the thorn experience and shared those two insights. But the issue was not just information. Surprise! It was a process he had to go through personally to further prepare him to help others in a very powerful way.

Only one thing did change: Paul's attitude, not the thorn. "Therefore, most gladly I will rather boast in my infirmities [and not hide them in order] that the power of Christ may rest upon me. Therefore, I take pleasure in infirmities, in reproaches, in needs, in persecutions, in distresses for Christ's sake. [Why?] For when I am weak then I am strong" (2 Cor. 12:9, 10).

Now he could say to others with conviction, "Rejoice always; pray without ceasing; in everything give thanks; for this is God's will for you in Christ Jesus" (I Thess. 5:16-18). God never intended for you to merely cope with your trials but to welcome them, learn from them, grow through them by using your biblical tools and then tell others how to do it themselves.

The late Andraé Crouch put this whole process to song and it has been one of my favorites for many years.

THROUGH IT ALL

I've had many tears and sorrows,
I've had questions for tomorrow,
there's been times I didn't know right from wrong.
But in every situation,
God gave me blessed consolation,
that my trials come to only make me strong.
Through it all,
through it all,
I've learned to trust in Jesus,
I've learned to trust in God.

Through it all,
through it all,
I've learned to depend upon His Word.
I've been to lots of places,
I've seen a lot of faces,
there's been times I felt so all alone.
But in my lonely hours,
yes, those precious lonely hours,
Jesus lets me know that I was His own.
I thank God for the mountains,
and I thank Him for the valleys,
I thank Him for the storms He brought me through.
For if I'd never had a problem,
I wouldn't know God could solve them,
I'd never know what faith in God could do.

There is an even more beneficial reason God allows *problems*. They hold the key to unlock the greatest benefit you could ever experience in life. Interestingly, I learned it in a dentist's chair.

Chapter 5
UNDERSTAND GOD'S PURPOSE
FOR PROBLEMS

• Welcome pain and loss as part of preparation to help others.

• Realize God does not call difficult situations, problems.

• Survey the possible benefits to life's challenges.

• Use trials as opportunities to grow.

• Record the insights you learned in pain.

• Remember, people are watching your responses.

• Be willing to change wrong behavior.

• Be patient with yourself; growth takes time.

• Understand God does not waste events of life.

• Use your problems as building blocks of maturity.

Chapter 5
SMALL GROUP QUESTIONS

1. When have you seriously questioned God about why something happened and how did you come to accept it?

2. Describe the hardest trial you have experienced and what benefits you have come to realize after going through it.

3. What have others learned by watching you go through a challenging difficulty?

4. Describe a difficult time in your life and what Scripture became meaningful to you during that time.

5. What have you changed in your thinking about how God works in your or someone else's life?

6. Have you ever lost someone special to you and how did you personally experience the various aspects of grief?

7. Being discipled by God is usually not fun. Describe a time and event where you experienced His discipline and what did you learn from it?

8. Growth in faith is gradual, but sometimes we get hit with a big faith challenge. Describe your biggest faith challenge and how you came through it?

Chapter 6
CO-OPERATE WITH GOD'S PLAN
FOR YOUR LIFE

I moved my family to a Midwest Christian college where I was to assume a new faculty administrative position. With relocation comes the added task of finding a new family physician and dentist.

My first visit with Dr. Schopper provided a clear illustration of why God allows problems. As this experienced dentist skillfully prepared to refill a cracked filling, he carefully explained each procedure in detail. I was unaccustomed to this special treatment. I felt a part of it. In fact, it felt as if he was trying to recruit me as a prospective dental assistant. Then it happened. Out of exasperation this patient dentist firmly requested that I make a special effort to keep my mouth open. I was disillusioned. What I thought was a recruitment strategy was instead an effort to explain what he was doing to get me to co-operate by opening my mouth wider. He thought if he described each procedure, I would be a more co-operative patient.

GOD EXPLAINS THE DETAILS

Why doesn't God simply do to you what He wants? He is God: He *can* do it! But He has the same motivation Dr. Schopper had with me. God explains His growth procedure so you will co-operate with Him as He shapes you into Christ-likeness. All through the New Testament God explains what He wants you to say, think and act. Also, He explains how He is going to accomplish His goal in you so that you will not react against the process, but co-operate with it.

James could have told all his Jewish friends just to rejoice when they experienced their whole world falling apart around them (Jam. 1:2). Grit your teeth and bear it! But that is not how God works. James explained that there is a process going on inside you when you go through tough times. God knows that if you understand the process, you will be more motivated to co-operate with it without resistance, thinking it strange having to go through it (I Peter 4:12). The only way any reasonable person would joyfully call a trial a good thing is if he can see how it benefits him personally. And what is the personal benefit? Maturity. Mature people who have co-operated with God's process usually have a better quality of life than those who do not co-operate and fight God at every turn. Problems are only one means God uses to help you see where you are in your Christian growth and where He wants you to be for your benefit and His glory.

WHAT IS GOD'S GOAL?

While I was conducting a training for Christian counselors in St. Lucia in the Caribbean, I asked a gentleman from the audience to leave the room and remain outside for five minutes. I asked him to do one thing while he was outside. The request was simple. "While you are out there I want you to conform yourself into the image of Christ." I ushered him to the door and told him I would call for him in five minutes. Bewildered, he complied, and I closed the door and went on with the training. A few minutes later I asked him to return to the classroom and asked him what he did to be like Jesus. Glancing back and forth, he finally just shrugged his shoulders appearing confused. That assignment seemed to him as practical as the proverbial screen door on a submarine.

You are often told that you should focus on being conformed to the image of God. It is God's will (Rom. 12:2). You are in Christ

(Eph. 2:13), and Christ is in you (Col. 1:27). To fashion your life like Jesus is the utmost desire of His heart. But there is one small problem: it is the same one my friend in St. Lucia had. How do you do it? Do you grow a beard and long hair, wear a robe and sandals? You may have been told to double down on your Christian disciplines: pray, read your Bible and fast.

Yes, intense study of His Word is important. Prayer is a must. Obedience is a command, never an option. Yet, one of the most practical ways God matures you is through, you guessed it, trials, afflictions, loss, pain and suffering.

BIG SURPRISE

God never intended you to cope with your trials. He expects you to work through them with the goal of maturing spiritually and reflecting the life of Christ in all that you say, do and think. The goal of biblical counseling or focused discipleship may not be the elimination of all mental, emotional or physical symptoms related to suffering. That may be the goal of psychology. God's ultimate goal is holiness, not happiness, and spiritual health, not the absence of mental, spiritual or emotional conflict. (Tan, p. 37). It is your goal to help each person to mature in Christ.

Who would not want to get rid of, avoid or escape from various kinds of pain? The brain hates pain. That is why psychologists tell us that the brain has at least 40 ways to avoid mental and emotional pain. Denial is number one. It is the most common defense of an addict. They lie to themselves and to others.

God has designed a *breaker switch* in the brain that if you experience intense physical or mental pain, you either go into shock or faint. If you didn't, you could go crazy. Insanity is one of nature's ways of helping troubled individuals find a less painful world in which they can exist and cope (Hughes, p. 65). Moses warned Israel of this possibility if they rebelled against God. "The Lord will strike you with madness and blindness and confusion of heart. So, you shall be driven mad [insane] because of the sights which your eyes see" (Deut. 28:28,34). Even the human body has to defend itself against further injury and hurt when damaged. A cut finger develops a scab to ward off disease-carrying germs until the wound has healed.

WHAT'S THE PLAN?

First, fasten your mental safety belt. This Christ-like lifestyle is God's life-long plan for you. The Apostle Paul described it this way to the Philippian believers. "I am confident of this very thing, that He who began a good work in you will perfect [mature] it until the day of Christ Jesus" [His return] (Phil. 1:6). Paul had come to a settled conviction earlier that God would continue to complete the good work of maturing them in Christ that He had begun.

Next, His strategy has a dual responsibility. We work. God works. It is like a two-sided coin with different impressions on each side but it remains one coin. Paul expressed this dual function this way, "…continue to work out your salvation [in everyday life] with fear and trembling for it is God [the Holy Spirit] who is at work in you both to will and to do [work, energize] for His good pleasure" [purpose] (Phil. 2:12b-13).

Don't get confused. He is not telling you to work *for* your salvation. They were already called *saints in Christ Jesus* (Phil. 1:1). You are not saved by *how* you believe; you are saved by *what* you believe. The phrase, *work out*, literally means *to work down*, like kneading (mixing) dry flour into a lump of dough that contains too much moisture. Simply put, it means to work the benefits of your salvation into your everyday life. Your trials, tests or afflictions are designed to accomplish that kneading process. There is no such thing as instant maturity.

God hates compartmental lifestyles where there may be one lifestyle at church and a completely different one at home or work. Therefore, one of the reasons God allows *problems* is to motivate you to incorporate the benefits of your salvation into every aspect of your life for your benefit and His glory. James warned of the loss of potential blessing if you only *listened* to God's Word but failed to incorporate it into your life (Jam. 1:22-25). That is selective amnesia. Remember, believers were first called *followers of the Way* (way of life) (Acts 9:2) before they were called Christians (Acts 11:26). Jesus Himself was called *The Way* (Jn. 14:6) and left you an example to follow in His steps (I Pet. 2:21).

Finally, this plan was a predestined goal even before creation. It is not a new idea. Paul explained how long ago God designed His plan to develop Christ-like character in you. "For whom He foreknew, He also predestined [not to become Christians, but] to become conformed [engraved] to the image of His Son" (Rom. 8:29). *Foreknew* does not mean God's simple awareness of you. It means a meaningful awareness of you based on God's choice in eternity before creation. "He chose us in Him before the creation of the world" (Eph. 1:4). But it was more than just establishing a relationship. You were predestined to fashion yourself into the image (character) of Jesus Christ. Discipleship counseling is the process of building the life of Christ into one another.

The word, *image*, means to stamp and engrave through pressure. What are you going through or have gone through that involved a lot of pressure and stress? That is how diamonds are formed. They are mere pieces of coal put under pressure for years. Picture yourself as a chunk of coal under pressure developing into a beautiful and valuable diamond.

The word, *conform*, is equally interesting. It means having the same form as another. For us, it is not an external or physical form. In those respects, we are all different. It is referring to internal character. Notice, however, Satan has a plan for you also. He would desire that you be pressed into the mold of his secular society and not conformed to Christ and His character (Rom. 12:2).

WHAT DOES IT LOOK LIKE?

It is not complicated. Just picture a triangle. Then imagine a circle in the middle of it. Each point represents one of the three most important aspects of your life: Communication (words, tone of voice, body language), conduct (physical actions, habits) and core beliefs of the heart (attitudes, values). When you

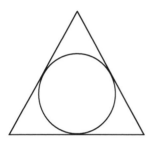 became a faith follower of Jesus, it was as if you were born again as a triangle with Christ in your heart represented by a circle. It is God's plan for you to round off the sharp areas of your life (old, selfish flesh patterns) in all three areas to become more like the *circle,* Jesus.

One of the main purposes of biblical counseling or focused discipleship is to mentor, disciple or coach a person to mature in these three areas where he may fall short in reflecting God's character. God does not focus on fixing people but reshaping them to conform to a practical picture of one who talks, thinks and acts like Jesus. But getting fixed may be your friends' expectation of you if you endeavor to help them. Remember, you are sharing tools and mentoring them to use the tools for the next challenge they will face.

Why did Paul write thirteen letters under the direction (inspiration) of the Holy Spirit? In Gal. 4:19 he explains, "My children with whom I am again in labor until Christ is formed in you." The word, *labor,* means to be in the *throes of birth pain.* The word, *again,* refers to the first birth experience leading to salvation and the travail that Paul is now involved in to bring them to maturity. In their case, it delivered them from the lies of the false teachers that were testing them.

Then he changes metaphors with the expression, "...until Christ is formed in you." He is now attempting to transform us to take on another form, Christ. "This expression *describes the* Christian life as a kind of reincarnation of Christ in a believer's life. This is, in fact, God's ideal and purpose – for Christ to live His life in and through each believer" (Walvoord NT p. 602). Paul expressed the same idea in his personal testimony, "I have been crucified with Christ; it is no longer I who live, but Christ lives in me; and the life which I now live in the flesh I live by the faith in the Son of God, who loved me and gave Himself for me" (Gal. 2:20).

Knowing there is an ultimate predestined goal is crucial to disciplers and Christian counselors. We know what God's ultimate goal is for our lives. Aristotle said, "Like archers, we stand a better chance of hitting the target if we can see it" (Hughes, *Helping*, p.18). If we know what we are aiming for and can see it, we are more apt to achieve it. This concept separates us from the rest of people-helpers because we are not fixing problems or seeking pain relief. However, we would hope that would be accomplished by applying God's tools to the most difficult challenges. Dr. Hughes warns us, "When we lose sight of the goal, we tend to focus on the parts or details of the crisis, like the airplane pilot who announced to his passengers, 'I'm afraid we are lost, but cheer up, wherever we are going, we are making good time'" (Hughes, p 18).

Failure to know and understand God's ultimate goal explains why some spiritual leaders and other people-helpers do not know what to do in a crisis situation. They do not know or have forgotten the goal that this crisis is designed to accomplish.

WHERE DO YOU START?

No one ever walked into my office and asked if I would help them to be conformed into Christ-likeness. Some have expressed a desire to be like Him but rarely has anyone connected their present conflict with that process. This was certainly true with Mark and Sherry when they came to see me for marriage counseling, I asked how I could serve them. They began to explain the conflicts they were experiencing in their marriage. They did not realize they were explaining to me where they were *AT* in their relationship. "We can't communicate." "He always loses his temper." "She keeps talking over me." "He doesn't support me with the kids." I wrote down every issue they mentioned. When they paused, I would ask them to tell me more. I wanted to know everything.

Then I took a piece of paper and put a big *AT* on the left side of the page and listed in summary, every issue they mentioned. Then I wrote a large *BE* on the right side of the page and asked them to tell me where they would like to be in each of these categories.

AT	BE
We can't talk	Able to communicate
Bad temper	Calm spirits
Mutual hurts	Mutual forgiveness
Yelling	Peaceful communication
Criticism	Affirmation
Disrespect	Respect

The list was lengthy. Then I asked if they would like to be mentored to go from where they were *at* to where they wanted to *be*. Their mutual glance said it all, "Yes!" That took an hour. I agree with Dr. Neil Anderson, "Discipleship counseling is an attempt to meet people where they are and help them resolve their personal and spiritual conflicts so that they can be established alive and free in Christ" (Anderson, p. 14). I gave them some homework to complete before they returned. After our closing prayer, Mark said, "We have been to many counselors before, but we accomplished more in this one hour than we have in all of the other counseling." They were so grateful that they later began to invest financially in Living Foundation Ministries.

Did you notice that all the issues sprang from words, attitudes and actions and that where they wanted to be basically reflected the character of Christ? I usually ask couples to choose their most problematic issue and start there. Not surprisingly, it is usually communication. We have designated a complete chapter on what Dr. Norman Wright would call, *Fair Fighting Rules* (chapter 13) that are very practical.

You will soon notice you will not need to address every issue on your list. Often, as you learn enough tools to address the top two or three, the rest fall into place. But I must issue a caution here. Even when a couple or individual can identify where they are *at* and agree where they ought to *be*, do not be surprised if they start for the *be* direction, stop, and turn right back to where they were *at.* Not everyone wants to be where they and God agree they should be, even if it creates a better quality of life. There are at least three reasons.

They have lost sight of the personal benefit to themselves.

They believe they cannot do what it takes to effect change. They want the benefits without the work.

They are addicted to misery. The absence of the adrenaline rush from conflict may result in boredom as far as they are concerned.

CHRIST-LIKE COMMUNICATION

The first point of this equilateral triangle is communication. Words represent only seven percent of communication. Body language and tone of voice represents 93 percent. Yet words are very important. When destructive words are being used in any communication, they should be identified and replaced with constructive words. The apostle Paul described it this way, "Do not let any unwholesome [foul, profane, shaming, devaluing, vulgar] words ever come out of your mouth, but only such speech as is good for building up others, according to the need and the occasion so that it will be a blessing to those who hear you speak" (Eph. 4:29 Amp).

The phrase, *good for building up*, is actually *edification*. It is a construction term. The primary building material in Christ's day was mud, brick or stone. They were specifically and purposefully placed to construct a building or wall. Our choice is either to randomly *throw* our words to hurt and distance a person from us or to strategically *place* our words to build a person up and connect with us. You are who you are today because of the words someone said to you, whether they were helpful or hurtful. Also some of you are in pain because of the words that were never said to you, like Fred.

When his dad had taken a turn for the worse, Fred's family was asked to come to the hospital. Standing by his father's side, he pleaded with his dad to say just once that he loved him. His dad replied, "I don't have time for that," rolled over in bed and died.

My files are full of cases of those who had been damaged severely because of *foul, profane, devaluing* and *vulgar* words and equally painful was the absence of *nurturing* words while a son or daughter was growing up. One damaging result of the latter is that a person then concludes they are unlovable, worthless, inadequate or rejected.

Former First Lady and presidential candidate, Hillary Rodham Clinton, has shared about her father's never affirming her as a child. When she was in high school, she brought home a straight A report card. She showed it to her dad hoping for a word of commendation. Instead, he commented, "Well, you must have been attending an easy school." Thirty-five years later the remark still burned in Mrs. Clinton's mind. His thoughtless remark may have represented nothing more than a casual comment, but it created a point of pain that has endured to this day. (Washington Post, 3 April 1993). It is Satan's goal to use words, or the absence of words, to destroy the work of God in your life.

Yelling or screaming (verbal terrorism) needs to stop. These are not evidence of the fruit of the Holy Spirit in one's life. They are selfish attempts to control, to change or to manipulate someone's behavior. Instead, they should be replaced with calm, cool communication. Words must always be filled with grace, favor, respect, value and seasoned, as it were, with salt so that you may know how you should respond to each other (Col. 4:6; CF Prov. 15:1; Jam. 1:19-29).

Criticism needs to be acknowledged and replaced with praise, affirmation and encouragement. The Apostle Paul used an ugly word picture to describe words that were especially negative, painfully demeaning and critical. "But if you bite and devour one another, take care lest you be consumed by one another" (Gal. 5:15). He is talking about relational cannibalism. A cannibal ate his enemy for he believed by doing so, he could steal his enemy's power. This brings us back to the need for power, control and manipulation.

Constant complaining needs to stop and to be replaced with gratefulness. "Do all things without grumbling or disputing" (Phil. 2:14). The order of the Greek words focuses on everything a believer does, *in everything*. The verb, *do,* is in the present continuous tense which means that this is to be done continually without stopping.

Instead of *complaining* (CF I Cor. 10:10), "In everything give thanks; [why?] for this is the will of God in Christ Jesus for you" (I Thess. 5:18). How can we give thanks to God in every circumstance of life? It is a choice, not a feeling. We will come to see now or in eternity that God does work everything together for good, even when others meant to hurt you. God defines whom He is referring to; it is for those who love Him (Rom. 8:28).

CHRIST-LIKE ACTIONS

Often, I am asked, "What is the most difficult obstacle you face when teaching in various countries?" Because I am training people to help other people work through problems in living, the number one issue is culture. All our attendees are Christians. Most of the root issues are the same but may manifest in different ways in each culture. What you grew up with, you think is normal. As a result, you deal with conflicts in relationships from a cultural perspective which may not be a Christ-like way. One of the primary reasons God allows conflicts is to reveal the behavioral patterns that are not reflecting Christ so you can identify them and correct them for your benefit. If a man's father was domineering and controlling, his son may follow the same pattern in his marriage. If a woman had a critical mother, she may find herself doing the same thing and think nothing about it until someone reacts negatively.

Culture shapes our behavioral patterns. Therefore, God says, "Do not be conformed [any longer] to this world [its superficial values, customs, behaviors, lifestyle] but be transformed [how?] by the renewing of your mind" [or change the way you think] (Rom. 12:2a). The phrase, *be transformed*, is a command, which means we are to keep allowing ourselves to be changed from the inside out. This is the process of *renewing our minds* as our thinking is being changed by the Word of God.

God has a good reason for you to avoid looking around and establishing your life based on what you see in the culture. This lifestyle is based on this *evil age* (Gal. 1:4). Satan is the god of this world and has blinded the minds of unbelievers (2 Cor. 4:4).

Why does God allow conflict, pain, loss or failure? One reason might be that you are behaving in a manner that is totally permissible to you and your native culture but is totally unacceptable to Him. Left to ourselves, most of us are not highly motivated to make major changes in our lives because what we grew up with is our *normal*.

For example, selfishness comes naturally to all of us. Identifying it is just the start. Ask God, day by day, to help you replace selfish motives with generosity and sacrifice. It is more beneficial to you and others to give without focusing on getting (Acts 20:35). That is like Jesus, "though He was rich, yet for your sakes He became poor, that you through His poverty might become rich" (2 Cor. 8:9). From the splendor of heaven Christ came to the squalor of earth. The incarnation was an incomprehensible renunciation of spiritual and material glory. The one who was rich, who had everything, became poor, making Himself nothing (Phil. 2:7). He assumed your debt of sin and paid the entire price demanded for it by sacrificing His life (Phil. 2:8). He became what you are (poor) so that you could become what He was and now is... rich (Walvoord, NT p. 574). This is the new standard.

All abusive behavior must be recognized for what it is and renounced and replaced with loving actions. It is never to be tolerated. An abusive husband who manipulates with *God words* such as *submission*, is under a higher law. Christ is above him and he is accountable directly to Him. The Apostle John firmly declares, "He who does not love, does not know God for God is love" (1 Jn. 4:8). Jesus is another name for love. Behavior that does not reflect God's definition of love (I Cor. 13) needs to be identified, repented of and replaced with Christ's own character.

Immorality in all its forms must be honestly faced, repented of and replaced with a holy lifestyle like that of Jesus. Immorality results in a legion of conflicts, hurts, losses, tragedies, guilt and shame – just for starters. One survey indicated that 62 percent of Christian men are engaging in pornography to the destruction of their very souls. God's will is not complicated, "this is the will of God [you don't even have to pray about this to determine His will], namely, your sanctification" [personal holiness]. If that is not clear enough God says, "Abstain from sexual immorality" (I

Thess. 4:3). You were chosen to be holy before the foundation of the world (Eph. 1:4).

Sexual purity is one of the hardest struggles on planet earth. The godliest man in the Old Testament, King David, was destroyed by sexual sin. The wisest man, Solomon, was also destroyed because of sexual obsession. The strongest man, Sampson, was destroyed because of out of control sex. If any of you think you are standing strong and can withstand any sexual temptation, be careful lest you give in to your own lust (I Cor. 10:12). God counterbalanced that fear with a promise that nothing will overtake you from behind that you can't deal with. God is faithful and He will provide a way of escape, but you must choose to take it (I Cor. 10:13). It is up to you to use your power of choice (Rom. 6:11-14).

Rejecting others, whether subtly or overtly, must be replaced with accepting them as valued by God. "Wherefore accept one another, just as Christ also accepted us to the glory of God" (Rom. 15:7). Acceptance is not approval of wrong behavior; it is granting respect, worth and value for who they are in Christ. Newborns in Christ need a lot of acceptance, affirmation and patience while they mature and correct many wrong patterns of conduct, communication and faulty thinking.

Revenge must be replaced by forgiveness. Revenge, in and of itself, is not wrong. The desire for revenge can be the back door to forgiveness. Justice must be satisfied. Without the shedding of blood there is no forgiveness (Heb. 9:22). But revenge is God's responsibility. He makes it perfectly clear, "Never take your own revenge, beloved, but [instead] leave room [get out of the way] for the wrath of God, for it is written, 'Vengeance is Mine [God owns it], I will [definitely] repay', says the Lord" (Rom. 12:19). We will answer a lot of the *what if* questions in chapter ten.

CHRIST-LIKE CORE BELIEFS

Attitude correction is the hardest challenge you or others will face. Words can be deceptive. Actions can present a false impression that all is well within. Attitudes can be hidden. Problems can reveal these submerged icebergs that are ready to rip the heart out of any relationship. Scripture calls your core belief system, *the heart* (Prov. 4:23; Matt. 12:34). It contains all your thoughts (reasonings) and memories of things you did or were done to you or around you (history), whether consciously or subconsciously. Even emotions, whether negative or positive, are recorded and stored. Your total belief system is on file whether it is based on truths or lies. Perceived entitlements or rights are ready to be accessed when something negative enters your life. Logically you think things just happen and you respond. It may seem like it because the response is so fast. But the truth is, it instantly filters through your belief system, and then you respond.

Peter found himself in prison for preaching the gospel (Acts 5:17-42). He and his disciples were whipped on their bare backs and then threatened again and warned not to preach about Christ. Those events went through Peter's belief system. He believed that being beaten for preaching Christ was an honor. Wow! That was the meaning he put on it. We read, "So they went on then from the presence of the Sanhedrin council, rejoicing." Why? They believed that God considered them worthy to suffer shame for His name (vs 41). Then, they went right on teaching in the temple and preaching Christ from house to house (vs 42). What kind of negative meaning have you put on something in your life that you need to identify, acknowledge and correct in order have a better quality of life?

Lords versus Servants: When Dennis and Susan came for marriage counseling, the situation was very apparent. Dennis controlled everything that took place in the home and in the relationship. He controlled all the money with no accountability while she had to account for every dime. She was not allowed to have an opinion if it was different from his. You get the picture. Why did he do that? What were his core beliefs that were reflected in his outward actions? It is not complicated.

Dennis had a belief system that said he was the boss, only his opinions mattered and hers were not even a factor. He was the lord of the ring. She was his servant and his sexual ATM machine. It was either his way or the highway. I could have coached him to behave differently. But because of his selfish sense of entitlement in his core belief system it would only be a matter of time before the past behavior would be repeated in the future.

That explains why general repentance does not last. Usually we focus on a person changing his behavior. Rarely do we have the person declare specifically and openly that his thinking is wrong and needs to be changed. Dennis had to come to the place where he was willing to change from being the self-centered lord of his ring to being the servant. Christ-likeness means "having this attitude [belief] in yourself which was also in Christ Jesus. He emptied Himself taking on the form of a bond servant and He humbled Himself by becoming obedient to the point of death" (Phil. 2:5-8). Matthew describes what this would look like. "Just as the son of man did not come to be served, but to serve and to give His life a ransom for many" (Mark 10:45). Jesus was still King of kings and Lord of lords when He took off His outer robe, wrapped a towel around His waist, knelt down and washed His disciples' feet. Yes, He wore the crown, but He also wore the towel. Men want to be the head (wear the crown) but often refuse to wear the towel. Paul explained what *wearing the towel* looks like: "Husbands, love your wives, just as [in like manner] Christ also loved the church [how?] and gave Himself up [sacrificed] for her" (Eph. 5:25). By changing his core belief from lord to servant (Christ-likeness), Dennis could dynamically change his marriage almost overnight.

Pride versus Humility: God has killed more people for pride than for prostitution (Acts 12:21-23). He hates it (Prov. 6:16,17), resists it (Jam. 4:6) and will allow many trials, tests and conflicts to reduce the presence of pride. Everyone who is proud in heart is an abomination to the Lord (Prov. 16:5). It may take some deep pain before one is willing to see the failure of his pride and choose to humble himself before others. If God resists the proud, other people are likely to do so as well (Jam. 4:6). But God gives incredible grace (value, power) to the humble; so do people. If you can say the three hardest words in the English language, "I was wrong," that humility will open up many closed relationships. Humility also ends the argument. What more can you say to a person who just said, "I was wrong?"

Jealousy versus Security: What is jealousy? It is rooted in the fear of being replaced. Why did the Jews kill Jesus? Was it because He claimed to be God, predicted He could destroy the Temple, broke some of the Jewish laws? No. The Scripture is very clear. Pilate knew that the Jews handed Jesus over to him to kill him not out of loyalty to Rome, but out of envy. The Jews were angry at Jesus because He had what they wanted. After the gospel began to spread throughout the then-known world, Jews in many regions saw the power and impact Peter had through the gospel and "they were filled with jealousy" (Acts 5:17). They had a fear of being replaced.

Earlier we discussed our counselee, Dennis. He would often accuse Susan of having an affair. She was shocked at these accusations. He would accuse her of looking at other men, wanting to be with other men, and he interpreted her every action as wanting to leave him. With a stunned expression on her face, she would desperately and tearfully try to convince him that there was not one piece of evidence to support all these accusations. It was just the opposite. She bent over backward to tell him where she went, what she did and whom she talked to.

He would call her multiple times a day asking her to explain all the above. Why?

Deep in Dennis' core belief system, he did not believe he could keep a wife because he believed all women were unfaithful (like his mother). He lived in constant turmoil of the fear of abandonment and of being replaced. When your ultimate security is anchored in your personal relationship with Christ, you do not have to fear being replaced in a human relationship. Nothing can separate you from the love of Christ (Rom. 8:38-39). That reality is adult-thinking, but the fear of abandonment is a childlike, immature perspective. It took a lot of effort to change Dennis' core belief from a fear of abandonment to a bedrock security in Christ. We will explain in Chapters 14 and 15 just how it can be done.

Covetousness must be replaced with contentment (Phil 4:11,12; I Tim. 6:8). A cold, distant heart needs to be replaced with a warm loving heart (I Cor. 13:1-13). Harshness needs to be identified for what it is and replaced with gentleness (Eph. 4:31-32).

REPLACE PERFECTIONISM WITH BALANCE

When Dr. Williams came home for the evening, everyone scattered. The chief inspector was about to enter the house and nothing escaped his critical eye. No greeting, warm embraces, inquiry about their day, just inspection. The stairs, railing, walls and rooms all received a white glove inspection. It was during this time that he and his physician wife entered my office.

What was behind his actions? As a perfectionist, he was motivated by three core emotions: guilt, shame and fear. The biggest one was fear. It has three parts: the fear of discovery, the fear of rejection and the ultimate fear, the fear of abandonment. Things and the order of things are more important than relationships. The primary emotion expressed by Dr. Williams was anger that was designed to change, to control and to manipulate. The Apostle Paul dealt with the perfectionistic Pharisees who were making the same mistake in Gal. 3:1-3.

I could have told Dr. Williams to *stop it* and sent him home. He could modify his behavior for a while, but if the fears were not identified and dealt with, he would only be able to *gut it through* so long and the behavior would return.

It did not take long to discover that his physician father constantly criticized him and told him he would never be a doctor. That core belief turned him into an obsessive person that kept him intellectually avoiding negative emotions at all cost. We will explain how to undo that in the same way we deal with jealousy in Chapters 14 and 15.

WHY THE CRISIS?

A crisis is any event that threatens your well-being and interferes with your ability to properly handle it (Hughes, pp. 112-113). Dr. Norman Wright would say it results in a "time of turmoil with a high level of distress" (Wright, p. 54). He would further ask, "What causes a major crisis to become a restrictive, crippling, eternal tragedy rather than a growth producing experience in spite of pain? Our attitudes." Or we would say, our core belief system.

Ask Dr. Mason. As a Bible College president and professor, he taught all of the senior theology classes with an emphasis on the sovereignty of God. He strongly believed God was going to prompt the US government to give to the college all the near-by decommissioned air force base buildings including the chapel. Instead, the government awarded the chapel to a new local church so that both the college and the church could utilize it. Upon learning this, Dr. Mason responded with a total mental and emotional breakdown and could not get out of bed for days. A board member spent a lot of time just reading Scripture to him. The crisis revealed his true belief of sovereignty in his heart. He could not trust God with the decision of allowing joint use of the chapel for the church and college. The crisis did not create the trust failure, it *revealed* it. Why did God allow the crisis to happen? It's obvious. God wanted to take him to a greater depth of maturity by testing his faith, even in this huge disappointment. As teachers, we face a stricter judgment with a higher standard than others (James 3:1). Instead of embracing the loss with grace, Dr. Mason became angry and embittered. He flunked the faith test and greatly diminished his testimony.

James' answer for the reason for quarrels and conflicts is very informative (Jam. 4:1-3). Quarrels and conflicts could possibly reveal:

· Selfishness (inner sexual desires, pride)
· Lack of self-control (hedonism, the pleasure goal of life)
· Unsatisfied lust for things (covetousness, discontentment)
· Murderous actions (anger, bitterness, hatred)
· Envy (angry at what others have)
· Unsatisfied desires (expectations)
· Fighting to get what you want (at others' expense)
· Selfish prayer patterns (to squander on yourself)

Did you notice the obvious source of all those things? Core beliefs of the heart. The outward quarreling and fights were a response to deeply held beliefs that were selfish and un-Christ-like.

IT DOESN'T WORK FOR GOD

It's no surprise to you that God desires you to grow up in His grace and His Word to be confident to deal with life and to reflect spiritual maturity. Children in adult bodies look grotesque. God wants you to be a mature man or woman (Eph. 4:13). By maturity, James means *having reached its end, finished, mature, complete.* When he says complete, he means in *all* spiritual aspects. Immature behavior reflects lack of growth, not who you really are in Christ. Remaining immature does not please the Lord and it robs you of a better quality of life.

While teaching in a Christian college, one of my responsibilities was to lead the Pastoral Studies Department. As a faculty advisor, I had to approve the selection of classes each student wanted to take. Often I would inquire about other areas of their lives and listen to some normal frustrations: jealousy, selfishness and immaturity. I sought to help them through these issues. Some students would remind me that they were there to get an education, not a character development course. They signed up for a full schedule of classes but God signed them up in courses, such as difficult roommate 101, cold water in the showers 201, bad cafeteria food 309, insensitive professors 410. God fully intended to prepare these pastoral students not only academically, but spiritually. Theologically, some passed academically but failed relationally and later, in ministry. They were not complete (mature) in all their parts of life.

How does one become mature? Gary Thomas has one practical suggestion. "If you want to become more like Jesus, I can't imagine any better thing to do than get married. Being married forces you to face some character issues you'd never have to face otherwise" (*Sacred Marriage*, p. 21). Maturity takes work. Psychologist Dr. Friesen clarifies that reality. "Maturity is not a spiritual gift nor is it a product of salvation. It is something we must work at our whole life." He further states, "Raising one's maturity level greatly increases the possibility of having a satisfactory marriage, great parenting and family leadership skills" (Friesen, p. 27).

HEAVEN'S SAD HEART

There are probably not too many things that sadden the heart of God more than to observe believers' long-term immaturity, both spiritually and emotionally. "For though by this time you ought to be teachers [or disciplers], you have need again for someone to [re]teach you the elementary principles of the oracles of God, and you have come to need milk [like babies] not solid food" (Heb. 5:12). Or as Peter would say, "You have become blind and short-sighted, stumbling through life" (2 Pet. 1:9). Solid food gives strength for adult challenges that liquid diets do not provide.

The Apostle Paul joined in the chorus to express his frustration with spiritual immaturity in those who should have been more mature (I Cor. 3:1-3). They lacked the tools and maturity to deal with problems in living. So what did God do? He allowed conflicts to arise to show the need and urged them to grow up by first alerting them to where they were *AT*, selfish, and where they should *BE*, mature.

Adult infants will always be needy and unable to meet the needs of others. They are unable to care for themselves emotionally or spiritually. They can't appropriately receive important information from others that would be helpful to them. They fail to ask for what they need because they dysfunctionally believe if you really cared for them, you would figure out what they need. They do not grow; therefore, they remain emotionally and spiritually handicapped (Friesen, pp. 20,21). The church suffers from immature members and spiritual babies, especially *newborns* in the faith who should not be allowed to have major leadership roles (I Tim. 3:6).

GOD IS NOT WAITING

God will design challenging times or opportunities to stimulate your faith and to correct misbeliefs of your heart and adjust your behavior to look like Jesus. He is not going to wait until you are ready or until it is convenient for you. I have never had a convenient trial. They seem so untimely. How many times have I said to myself, "Why did this have to happen at this time?" From God's perspective, "Here it comes, ready or not" (2 Chron. 32:31; Jn. 6:5b-6; Deut. 8:16). It is a faith test. He expects your cooperation for your benefit.

God desires you to reflect Christ to others while you are going through the trial, test, affliction, loss or pain in life. "Maturity will be most clearly visible in the way people relate to each other. The task of biblical counseling or focused discipleship is identical to the task of the church in promoting maturity" (Crabb, p. 195).

IT'S YOUR TURN NOW

Why does God allow *problems*? For you to reflect His glory and to prepare you to train others how to grow through their issues in order that they, too, may reflect His glory. You can do it! Take baby steps. Co-operate with God. Process your issues, learn from them and live as an illustration of how to do it. Then ask God to bring people into your life so you can share with and reproduce yourself in them. That is God's ultimate reason for allowing problems in your life. Remember, biblical counseling does not require that you have a particular spiritual gift. It does require Christ-like character, the ability to apply biblical tools and a strong dependence on God.

But, you say, I have no professional training; I feel at a disadvantage. I have some good news for you. You have at least five benefits to work through problems in living and help others with theirs. You are going to be pleasantly surprised and encouraged as you read them.

Chapter 6
CO-OPERATE WITH GOD'S PLAN
FOR YOUR LIFE

• Identify and co-operate with God's plan.

• Focus on God's goal for you to become like Him.

• Use problems to measure your spiritual growth.

• Do not use coping as a substitute for processing.

• Focus on God's life-long plan for you.

• Work your benefits of salvation into everyday life.

• Acknowledge what words, actions and attitudes need to change.

• Welcome a crisis as an opportunity to grow.

• Realize immaturity does not please God.

• Remember, trials are your preparation for ministry.

Chapter 6
SMALL GROUP QUESTIONS

1. In what area(s) is it a struggle for you to co-operate with God?

2. When you hear the phrase, *Christ-likeness,* what comes to mind and what does it mean to you?

3. What kind of defense mechanisms have you found yourself using? How have you reduced their influence in your life?

4. What spiritual truths have you made a special effort to incorporate in your life?

5. Explain the difference between *fixing* and *growing.* How have they been reflected in your life?

6. What are some areas in your life that you find yourself *AT* and where do you want to *BE*?

7. What aspects of communication are you working on? What kind of conflict motivated you to change?

8. Selfish attitudes and actions are hard to change. What are some you have identified in yourself? What practical steps are you taking to change them?

9. Negative attitudes are also hard to change. What are some you struggle with? What have you found is helpful in changing them? What benefits have you noticed with the changes?

10. What was the biggest crisis you ever faced? What positive changes did it bring into your life and/or the lives of those around you?

Chapter 7
UTILIZE YOUR BENEFITS TO HELP OTHERS

One of the biggest surprises that face new and even older believers is the reality that they will still experience many of the same problems that non-believers face. Couples who divorce or don't divorce, argue over the same things.

Why the shock? Because believers may have been given the impression that everything in life would be better upon committing their lives to Christ at salvation. Doesn't the Apostle Paul say, "If anyone is in Christ, he is a new creation; old things have passed away, behold, all things have become new" (2 Cor. 5:17). Paul is referring to the old life of slavery to selfishness and sin. The new life means we now have the power of choice to change our attitudes and behavioral patterns from the past; however, it does not erase history.

Remember, only your spirit was born again, not your mind. "That which is born of the flesh is flesh and that which is born of the Spirit is spirit" (Jn. 3:6). Your spirit is spirit. Your mind is flesh and has to go through a transformation process similar to a butterfly which starts as a caterpillar, turns into a cocoon, and finally emerges as a butterfly. This process is called metamorphosis. This is the same Greek word Paul uses in Rom. 12:2 when he says, "be transformed by the renewing of your mind." It is a process that will take place from the inside out over time with life experience and spiritual growth.

The Scripture explains just how common problems are, whether you are a Christian or not. "No temptation [trial] has overtaken you but such as is common to man." Then Paul goes on to say "and God is faithful, who will not allow you to be tempted [tested] beyond what you are able [to endure] but with the temptation will provide a way of escape so that you will be able to endure it" (I Cor. 10:13). The word, *temptation,* is used in a broad sense which includes tests, trials, temptations, and afflictions. Peter uses the same Greek word but it is translated *trials* (I Pet. 1:6).

The phrase, *overtaken you,* describes a situation which has seized (grabbed) you from behind and continues to hold you in its grasp to the present (perfect active verb). It is something that is *common to man* or common to people everywhere. There is no difference regardless of nationality or culture. Fear is fear. Worry is worry. Rejection is rejection. Though trials may have some unique features in each culture, they are similar in nature.

THE BIG QUESTION

Steve and Linda were not religious. They were invited by their friends to visit their church and were very impressed with the friendliness, music, sermon, and expressions of happiness. They wanted whatever those people had. They acknowledged they were sinners like the rest of us and that Christ died on the cross, paid for their sin and was raised from the dead to give them a full pardon for sin. That felt great!

Then they went home, and, in a few minutes, they were having an argument. What a shock! "We just got saved less than three hours ago and here we are doing the same thing we have always done." Discouragement settled in along with a little guilt and shame. However, they decided to go back to church the next Sunday and were blessed again. But back home they found themselves treating each other the same old way. What conclusion did they come to? Christianity may work for others, but it does not work for us. Gradually they stopped attending church. "Apparently, Christianity is for some people, but not for everybody."

So, do believers have any advantage over non-believers in dealing with troubles in life? The good news is you do have at least five benefits for working through problems in living from a biblical perspective and for helping others to work through their problems. What are these five benefits?

1. God gives you biblical TOOLS to deal with problems.

2. God gives you POWER to use the tools.

3. God gives you the TRAINING to use the tools.

4. God gives you SUPPORT as you use the tools.

5. God gives you REWARDS for using the tools.

WHAT ARE THE TOOLS?

Steve and Linda were freshly caught *fish*, newborn babes in Christ. They had been spiritually transferred out of the kingdom of darkness into the kingdom of light (Col. 1:13), but they were babes. They needed to grow. It will take time. Spiritual growth takes discipleship.

If they go back to church, they can learn how to pray, read their Bible, witness, share their financial resources and serve in several areas of the church that begs for *new recruits*. But nothing has changed at home. The fish has been caught but not cleaned. They do not know the tools to deal with conflict. They may have been told that they just need to pray and study their Bibles more and even start fasting. These are good disciplines. But when you read the 21 letters in the New Testament from I Corinthians to Jude, there are more tools than just those three in the toolbox of Scripture. Someone needs to tell them what the tools are and *how to use them*. Tools are either specific, applicable Scriptures or principles from Scripture or lessons we have learned by experience and research that does not violate Scripture. All lessons and empirical insights must be subject to Scripture. Tools can be techniques or practical strategies in applying those Scriptures. If the tools are biblical, they must be transferrable from one person to another. That is the whole point of biblical counseling.

If Steve and Linda came to you and asked for help, what would you do? First, you would ask them to clearly explain what words, actions or attitudes have resulted in turmoil in the family. Have them describe where are they *At?* You may quickly discover there is yelling, name-calling, criticizing, blame-shifting and a host of other dynamics.

We have explained the importance of identifying where they are *At* and gaining an individual commitment as to where they want to *Be.* Most marriage counselors would agree that just identifying the *At-Be* positions is at least 60 percent of the battle. But now we have a practical question. We know where they are *At* and have an agreement of where they want to *Be,* but how do you guide them to go from *At* to *Be?* In Chapter 16 we will provide a basic plan. Now, let's focus on the concept of tools.

Steve and Linda need a basic course on fair fighting rules that we will expand in Chapter 13. The first one is to stop interrupting or talking over each other and start listening for understanding (Jam. 1:19). In discipling them, you will get their commitment to use the *honor* tool and train them to be devoted to one another in brotherly love, giving preference to one another in honor (Rom. 12:10). *Giving preference to one another* means to try to outdo one another in showing honor.

With that said, you now refer to Jam. 1:19b, "But everyone must be quick to hear [and understand], slow to speak and slow to anger." So, the communication tool of not interrupting or talking over each other is a practical application of Jam. 1:19. If you sat down with Steve and Linda, explained those two verses and described their practical application, they would begin to see that the Word of God is very practical when it is understood and applied.

I have watched scores of couples' relationships change with the application of just this one tool. However, you need to coach them by having them practice it *in your presence*. Do not just tell them to go home and do it. That may not work. What does our national football team, the Chiefs, do here in Kansas City? They practice five days a week as if they are in a real game. They practice plays, drills and strategies under the supervision of the coaches. Hard practice five days a week gives them the ability to play an opponent with skill and to do it almost automatically. Likewise, by practicing this communication tool with you, people are more apt to use it effectively at home. This will accomplish two goals: they will see the personal benefit of it and will be assured that they *can* do it.

Most new believers want a better quality of life, but they don't know how to get it. That is where you come in. You will teach them more tools than they may need right now, but they will have them in their toolbox when the need arises. The good news is that "By His divine power, God has given us everything we need for living a godly life" (2 Peter 1:3). Tools are only as good as the understanding of how to apply them. "All Scripture is inspired by God and is PROFITABLE for teaching, for reproof [rebuke], for correction, for training [discipline] in righteousness" [right kind of living] (2 Tim, 3:16). Remember, it must start with you learning to apply His Word yourself and then illustrating with your life how it works.

POWER TO USE THE TOOLS

If you were discipling Steve and Linda, it would not take long before you might hear, "I can't do this. It's too hard. It sounds good, but I don't think it will work for us." That is not bad. Admitting they can't do it themselves is a good thing. Why?

God is the one who gives His power to use the tools. One of the major distinctions of Christianity from all other religions is that they can tell you what to do, but they cannot give you the power to do it. It is all based on human effort. They can only guilt-trip you, shame you, scare you or manipulate you. God never expected you to *power-up* yourself. He said to His disciples who were about to travel into all the then-known world and make disciples, "But you shall receive power [that you don't have now] when the Holy Spirit has come upon you, and you shall be witnesses to Me…to the end of the earth" (Acts1:8), strongly implying "Men, you could never do it yourselves."

In contrast, the Apostle Paul reminded the believers in Philippi how he was able to do all that he was able to do. "I can do all things through Him [Christ] who strengthens me" (Phil. 4:13). I like the way Dr. Jay Adams paraphrased this verse. "I can do anything that God expects me to do through Christ who gives me the strength to do it." Never accept the excuse, "I can't do it." It may be because they do not *want* to do it or they are shielding their pride. In addictions people may have given the control of their lives over to a substance or habit. They may need another person or team to intervene to stop the addictive cycle. God expects believers to come alongside and help restore a brother or sister (Gal. 6:1, 2).

But we are back to why people may not change. They see no personal benefit and think they can't do it. God comes along and simply asks them to take baby steps of faith, but He will not take the steps for us. Remember, God has restored our power of choice at salvation. However, some believers have given their power of choice over to addictions, like pornography. It is sad to learn from one survey that 62 percent of Christian men are actively involved in *photo prostitution* (pornography) by choice.

Paul reminded Timothy that God had not given him a spirit [attitude] of fear [timidity, cowardice], but of POWER and a sound mind (2 Tim. 1:7). He gave Timothy a practical tool: to run from sexual lust (2 Tim. 2:22). Though God would give him the power to run, Timothy had to get his own feet moving.

STAY CONNECTED

The best electronic device in the world is totally ineffective if it is *not* plugged in. Likewise, you get power to use God's tools when you connect by faith at salvation and then stay in fellowship with Him through obedience. "If we say we have fellowship with Him [plugged in] and yet walk in darkness [disobedience], we lie and do not practice the truth. But [in contrast] if we walk [live] in the light [by obedience] as He Himself is in the light [truth, reality], we have fellowship with one another [you and Him], and the blood of Jesus His Son cleanses us from all sin" (I Jn. 1:6,7). There is no godly power available to you if you *unplug* and walk back to darkness where Satan rules (Heb. 6:1-6). God will not give you power to disobey. That comes naturally from the flesh and therefore makes it hard to live obediently.

But it is an enigma that God's power is made more evident when you are in touch with the reality of your own personal weakness. Paul is a trophy of one who had been given physical pain with no relief in sight, totally weak on one hand but amazingly powerful on the other hand (2 Cor. 12:9). He traveled farther than any of the other disciples, wrote more books and established more churches than any of the original disciples.

When you return to a purposeful reading of God's Word and endeavor to apply each truth personally, you will gain power that is beyond your own understanding. Have lengthy conversations with God in prayer, continue to focus on personal holiness, not happiness. Attend a church that faithfully teaches the Word of God and involve yourself in a small group of like-minded believers (Heb. 10:25) for personal encouragement and support. But there is another advantage you may not have even considered.

TRAINING TO USE THE TOOLS

Why does God allow problems? Simple. To teach you and me how to use Scripture and its principles to deal with the stuff

123

of life. Other ways of describing God's training program are trials, troubles, afflictions, temptations or testing. These are experiences to increase your quality of life and to benefit someone in your life. Just ask Peter.

Peter is a classic illustration of this training preparation through a trial. Jesus wanted to train Peter to help someone who has failed. "And Jesus said to Peter, 'Simon, Simon, indeed Satan has asked for you, that he may sift [test] you as wheat [separate the grain from the chaff]. But I have prayed for you, that your faith [in Me] should not fail, and when you have returned to Me [you're trained now] STRENGTHEN your brethren'" (Luke 22:31,32). Satan wanted Peter to fail so badly and experience a loss so great that he would lose (or be separated from) his faith and turn away from God and doubt that Jesus would ever accept him back after he cursed and denied that he even knew Him.

Jesus knew Peter was going to fail, but He prayed that Peter would still trust Him to take him back after the failure. God had a plan for Peter's experience of failure (the trial). He was going to use his failure to prepare Peter to help people who failed a faith test in their own lives. Peter learned to use the *trust* tool through failure.

Peter was later able to describe the training process he went through to those who had just undergone persecution. "Blessed be the God and Father of the Lord Jesus Christ who according to His great mercy has caused us to be born again to a living hope... in this you greatly rejoice, even though now for a little while [but it feels like an eternity], if necessary, you have been distressed by various trials [why?] so that the proof of your [own] faith, being more precious than gold [to you] which is perishable, even though tested by fire may result in praise, honor and glory when Jesus Christ is revealed" (I Pet. 1:3-7).

How do you learn the tool of faith? By going through a trial. How do you learn to forgive from the heart? By being deeply hurt. How do you develop the tool of prayer? By experiencing a deep loss, tragedy, illness or personal conflict. How can you learn the tools of love and respect? By dealing with a troubled marriage. How do you learn to resist the devil? By being attacked by him, especially at your weakest point. How do you learn the tools of confession and forgiveness? You guessed it! After you have fallen into the cesspool of sin.

What tool do you really know how to use without any experience of using it? If the tools in your toolbox look nice and shiny, you probably know about them academically but not experientially. If you have put on the whole armor of God and used it, the helmet of salvation should be dented, the sword of the Spirit should have nicks in it, the breastplate of righteousness should look like someone hammered on it. That's why Paul finally acknowledged at the end of his life, "I have fought a good fight" (2 Tim, 4:7a), not as a spectator but as a battle-worn warrior. God has a whole hardware store of biblical tools that are free and at your disposal. All you need to do is discover the right tool or tools to deal with your past or present and go to work. It will be a great learning experience.

GOD GIVES US SUPPORT TO USE THE TOOLS

God may choose to give you support physically, spiritually or emotionally through other believers providing you are willing to humble yourself and share your needs with them. He has limited Himself in many of your trials so that fellow believers can help carry your crushing overloads. "Bear one another's burdens [crushing overloads] and thereby fulfill the law of Christ (Gal. 6:2) which is to love one another" (Jn. 13:35). The verb, bear, is a command in the Greek, not a suggestion. And its construction means to keep on caring without stopping.

Patti wrote me while going through a deep trial and shared this, "My Wednesday night class circled around me and had a prayer time. I finally opened up to them a little bit and asked for prayer support. They cancelled the lesson and they prayed the whole time. I felt encircled by the love of God. They cried with me and prayed prayers from their heart. It was a special healing time for me. Much needed." God could have done that Himself but He limited Himself to work through Patti's friends to give some badly needed support from people just like you.

In Venezuela, at the end of the presentation on forgiveness, a medical doctor stood up and shared in tears the abuse he received as a child and that now he forgave his dad. I watched people all over the room get up and walk over to him and hold him and cry with him. He was not alone! Support came from everywhere. That is a huge advantage you have as a Christian.

When you are going through a tough time and share it appropriately, other believers will give you personal support through encouragement. "But encourage one another day after day, as long as it is still called today so that none of you will be hardened by the deceitfulness of sin" (Heb. 3:13). Volumes have been written about lives that were dramatically changed by someone's personal encouragement. Believers can share out of personal finances, material resources, or even their time. My wife, Linda, goes over periodically to help a friend who has a debilitating disease with tasks she no longer can do.

One day prophets came from Jerusalem to Antioch and Agabus told the believers a great famine was coming. So, the disciples in Antioch took a collection to send relief to the brothers in Judah (Acts 11:27-30). The roles had reversed. The church in Jerusalem always helped others. They felt good about that. There was a tendency to look down on those who were not from Jerusalem. So, to bring those two groups together, God used the need of one and the financial support from another to bind the two churches together (Rom. 15:27). Needs bring people together.

God may also choose to support you directly. "Blessed be the God and Father of our Lord Jesus Christ, the Father of mercies and God of all comfort who comforts us in all our tribulations [why?] that we may be able to comfort those who are in any [all] trouble [tribulation or affliction] with the comfort with which we ourselves are comforted by God" (2 Cor. 1:3-4).

Honestly, sometimes people will let you down and fail to support you for whatever reason. Paul knew it firsthand. "At my first defense [in Rome] no one stood with me [supported me], but all forsook me, but the Lord stood with me and strengthened me, so that the message might be preached fully through me" (2 Tim. 4:16-17).

Finally, the Holy Spirit is our best prayer supporter. "In the same way the Spirit also helps [supports us] in our physical, emotional and spiritual weaknesses for we do not [always] know how to pray as we should, but the Spirit Himself intercedes [pleads our case] for us with groanings too deep for words" (Rom. 8:26). In fact, the Holy Spirit is called the comforter (Jn. 14:16, 26) and that Greek word means "to call alongside of." Often, He will use His Word as a major source of support and comfort (Rom. 15:4).

GOD GIVES US REWARDS FOR USING THE TOOLS

God's time clock does not have hands on it because He is an eternal Being. As such, He encourages us to take the hands off our clocks and choose to live from an eternal perspective now, instead of a temporal one (2 Cor. 4:18).

The early apostles were about to suffer some severe physical and emotional pain through persecution. They did not know it was coming, so Jesus had to prepare them for it in the very beginning of His public ministry. Notice how He did it. "Blessed are you when they revile and persecute you and say all kinds of evil against you falsely for my sake. Rejoice and be exceedingly glad, for great is your reward in heaven [not earth], for so they persecuted the prophets who were before you" (Matt. 5:11-12).

Jesus tells them to get ecstatically glad for the pain and loss. That advice had to be a shock to them. They believed if they obeyed God they would be greatly blessed on earth; only sinners received bad things on earth. But Jesus challenged them to take the hands off their temporal clocks and switch the focus to eternity without time and the great rewards they would receive in heaven.

This is the first time the word, *reward,* is used in the New Testament. A future reward was not consciously in their thinking but a literal kingdom on earth now with Jesus as King and they, as rulers with Him. You can expect some losses eventually, whether physically, materially or relationally. However, your godly responses by using biblical tools is investing in spiritual riches to enjoy in heaven forever.

Sharon's husband left her and their three kids for another woman. What a devastating loss! One of the fastest ways to poverty is to become a single mom. Her husband was having the time of his life now - plenty of sex, no responsibility, just fun and games. Her losses were great: betrayal, emotional damage to herself and the children, a struggle to make ends meet. Her car and things in the house will need repair. Loneliness is inevitable. Humanly speaking, it is totally unfair. But as she uses her biblical tools of trust, forgiveness and prayer and remains a faithful, godly mother, she is storing up spiritual riches to enjoy forever.

What about her husband? He even professed to be a Christian. I shared the same verse with him as I shared with her. "For we must all appear before the judgment seat of Christ, so that each one may be recompensed [rewarded] for his deeds in the body according to what he has done, whether good or bad" (2 Cor. 5:10). This is not the great white throne judgment where non-believers will be judged and delivered into hell forever (Rev. 20:11-13; Rom. 14:10). This is the bema seat or reward seat where our works are tried by fire in order to be rewarded so we can enjoy the reward forever.

Disobedient believers will experience a loss of rewards (I Cor. 3:15). That is what is awaiting Sharon's husband. It is not a loss of salvation because that was a gift based on grace (Eph. 2:8, 9). Sadly, I think my dad will face a loss of rewards. He abandoned my mom and us three boys and left us to support ourselves. It was as if we had vanished off the planet. We did not receive a dime, which led each of us to seek work so we could keep the family together.

My mom literally laid down her life for us. My oldest brother went to the University of Southern California and graduated debt free. I was privileged to earn four degrees, debt free. My younger brother attended the police academy and retired after a great law enforcement career. Mom received little on earth but when she stands before Jesus, He will say, "Great is your reward" (Matt. 5:12; 16:27). Mom lost big time on earth but is one wealthy lady in heaven now.

Yes, you will probably lose something of value in time. It will hurt. If you choose to live godly in Christ Jesus, you could well expect to suffer (2 Tim. 3:12). In fact, we are selected out of the world both to be with Him and to suffer for Him (1 Pet. 2:20, 21). The unfairness of this life will not even be worthy to compare to the rich reward you will receive and enjoy forever (Rom. 8:18).

This all sounds good but how do you determine what tool to use to help a friend? You practice the same procedure a mother uses to determine the need of her baby. She learns to read his cries.

Chapter 7
UTILIZE YOUR BENEFITS TO HELP OTHERS

• Understand salvation did not change everything.

• Identify your five benefits for processing.

• Discover and use your biblical tools.

• Learn how to apply biblical tools to specific issues.

• Take baby steps in the use of your tools.

• Celebrate the fact God has given you all you need to live a godly life.

• Stay plugged into God's power to use your tools.

• Use trials to learn to use the tools.

• Identify friends who can support you as you use the tools.

• Anticipate God's generous rewards for using the tools.

Chapter 7
SMALL GROUP QUESTIONS

1. What experience have you had of people telling you that only trained professionals should be counseling people?

2. What surprises did you experience after you became a believer as it relates to your new life in Christ?

3. What practical value do you see in viewing specific Scripture or principles from Scripture as tools and not just verses?

4. What are some of your favorite tools that you use regularly?

5. Share some personal illustrations of times God empowered you to do something that you knew was beyond your physical or spiritual strength.

6. What are some personal disciplines that have kept you connected in fellowship with the Lord?

7. Share a personal experience when you felt so very weak and God provided special energy when you knew it was beyond your control.

8. Share a trial you experienced where you learned to use a new tool.

9. Share a time you experienced extra support from other believers when you really needed it.

10. What is the most practical benefit you have experienced as a faithful follower of the Lord Jesus?

Chapter 8
LEARN TO READ THEIR CRIES

More than once I was bewildered by how my wife, Linda, seemed to discern the various baby cries. She would tell me that our daughter was hungry. I would say, "How do you know? Maybe she needs her diaper changed." Various other options would race through my mind, but Linda would say, "Well, it could be, but it sounds like a hungry cry." And she was usually right. God gave her the ability to read the baby's cry and discern the need.

If there is a frustration that even professional people-helpers experience, it is that of *reading the cries* – or discerning the basic needs of clients. Dr. Larry Crabb has asserted that "All behavior is motivated by some need and makes sense when understood" (Crabb). Even bizarre behavioral actions can be traced to unmet needs.

Charles Rothenberg drove to a motel with his six-year-old son after a fun-filled day at Disneyland. At the motel that evening, he gave his son a sleeping pill. Taking a five-gallon jug of kerosene, he poured it over his sleeping son's body and bed, lit it and left the room. A block away he heard the explosion. Miraculously, the son lived because a patron in the next room heard his painful screams and rescued him from the inferno. A week later, Charles was arrested and confessed to the police that he tried to kill his son because he decided that, "If I can't have him, nobody can."

Two nights before, Charles had argued over the phone with his ex-wife. She angrily told him he had no right to keep their son, and he would never see his son again once he was returned to New York. What possible need did Charles have that would motivate him to attempt this senseless murder? It would have to start with his prostitute mother who deposited him at an orphanage door and visited him only periodically. Feeling deeply rejected, he embarked on a life of crime.

Psychologists who specialize in child murder and abuse say it is difficult to identify common denominators among parents who inflict such violent physical harm or even death on their children. There are, however, common threads that are woven in such a parent's thought process and background, such as, low self-esteem, social isolation, neglect or abuse as a child and feelings of being out of control in their own lives. But what is baffling to mental health professionals is why other parents, who have been terrorized as children by their own families, never hurt anyone.

All behavior is moving toward a conscious or unconscious goal to get either real or imagined needs met. Dr. Hughes states that, "Most psychological problems are the result of a person trying to cope with unmet needs" (Hughes, *Helping*. p. 36). The motivation to get these needs met is tremendously powerful and strong. If you can identify what need a person is trying to fulfill by his behavior, you may have discovered a beginning point in understanding his problem.

One of my favorite "social scientists," Ann Landers, received a letter that further aids us in *reading the cry* (which at first glance may defy logic). At fourteen, Mary in Michigan wrote that when she told her mother that the mother's live-in boyfriend had sexually abused her since she was six, her mother accused Mary of lying. Even after he admitted it, her mother stayed with him and turned cold toward the daughter, as if she was the one who caused the problem. At 20, the daughter felt her mother had abandoned her to save the relationship. That boyfriend, now the mother's husband, would not let the daughter's name even be spoken in the house. He treated the mother like dirt, but she refused to leave him.

Ann perceptibly responded and precisely identified the mother's unmet needs, "Your mother probably has a pathological fear of being alone. She is willing to tolerate anything rather than be on her own. It's the tragedy of a woman who is an emotional cripple" (KC Star, 01-21-91).

HISTORICAL DEVELOPMENT OF NEEDS

As a biblical counselor, several questions have helped me to read the cries: has the person's observable behavior always been this way, have the needs always been the same or has a drastic change occurred? As a biblical people-helper, you may need a basic understanding of people's past behaviors before you can learn to *read the present cries* and meet those needs.

Jesus said that the whole law and prophets depend on two commandments, to love the Lord with all your heart, soul and mind and to love your neighbor as yourself (Matt. 22:37-40). Similarly, the understanding of three major events of history will give you the pegs on which to hang His tools for serving one another in love. These historical people-helping pegs are first, creation, then separation, and finally, restoration. We will not discuss them chronologically as they appeared in history, but instead we will look at them as they are observed in people today. The chart below summarizes these three events.

BIBLICAL PERSPECTIVE OF NEEDS

Creation: Before the fall of man	Restoration: After the fall of man	In Christ
Valuable	Loss of worth and value	Valuable through love
Belonging	Socially isolated	Belonging
Competent	Inadequate	Adequate
Secure	Insecure	Secure
Intimate with God	Estranged from God	Fellowship with God
Intimate with others	Superficial relationships	Fellowship with Others
Purposeful	Purposeless	Purposeful

135

SEPARATION

The lush tropical paradise called Eden only had two residents, Adam and Eve. These perfect people, living in a perfect environment void of any social ills, made a bad decision. Through the verbal manipulation and deception of Satan, in the form of a snake, Eve fell for the subtle trap to disobey God. She believed the lie that she was deficient and that she could be like God (Gen. 3:5b). Adam, who was with her, also ate the forbidden fruit and instantly something happened. Their core belief system (heart) became damaged and fear, shame and insecurity instantly entered the human experience. It is not surprising that anxiety disorders are the number one mental health problem in the world today followed by depression.

The first tangible evidence of a damaged heart was the shame they felt from their nakedness, which they hastily covered with fig-leaf garments. The human race has been in hiding ever since.

The second hint that something dreadful had happened was that instead of anticipating their time with God, they hid themselves in fear (Gen. 3:10). They foolishly tried to hide from an omniscient God, fearful of His rejection.

LOW SELF-ESTEEM

What is the evidence in people's lives that this separation has happened? The psychologist who editorialized Charles' attempted murder of his six-year-old son suggested that one factor was his *low self-esteem*, feeling of little worth and value.

King David struggled with similar feelings, "What is man [or the value of man] that you take thought of him?" (Ps. 8:4). "But I am a worm, and not a man" (Ps. 22:6). "For He Himself knows our frame, He is mindful that we are but dust" (Ps. 103:14).

Charles' mother had her own reasons for leaving him on the steps of the orphanage. But whatever her motive may have been, her action communicated the lie that he was of no worth or value to her. Adopted children tend to struggle with this issue although the adoption may have been the best alternative for them at the time.

SOCIAL ISOLATION

The second evidence of separation which springs from the feeling of personal rejection is social isolation. The reasoning is basic, "If I feel of no worth or value, others must feel the same about me, so before they have a chance to reject me, I will reject them and withdraw myself from any potential painful loss of rejection." And so we create the proverbial *comfort zone* of self-protection, usually fenced in by fear.

The pain of rejection is traced throughout the scriptures. Ahithophel, counselor to King David, was once highly regarded as one who inquired of the Lord. He made a poor choice in aligning himself with Absalom, David's rebellious son, (2 Sam. 15:31). When Absalom later rejected his counsel, Ahithophel felt his personal value was gone because it had been wrapped up in his position. So, "He saddled his donkey and arose and went home to his city, and set his house in order and hanged himself and he died" (2 Sam. 17:23).

INADEQUACY

It was said of the attempted murder that Charles was out of control and felt deeply inadequate, which is the third indication of separation that a people-helper will come to readily identify.

Even Moses had feelings of inadequacy and reminded God, as if He did not understand. "Please Lord, I have never been eloquent, neither recently nor in time past, nor since You have spoken to your servant; for I am slow of speech and slow of tongue" (Ex. 4:10). He felt he was not a prime candidate to represent God to a hostile national figure like Pharaoh. Many great men and women of Scripture perceived themselves as not being adequate to do God's will. This common feeling was spawned in Eden and transmitted genetically to every generation since.

INSECURITY

The orphanage steps became the symbol of Charles' deepest pain – the ever-present fear of abandonment resulting in insecurity. The need for security was evident in the Jews who had Jesus killed. "Therefore, the chief priests and Pharisees convened a council, and were saying, 'What are we doing? For this man is performing many signs. If we let Him go on like this, all men will believe in Him and the Romans will come and take away both our place and our nation.' So, from that day on they planned together to kill Him" (Jn. 11:47- 48, 53). Why? They were insecure and feared losing their religious and political positions. As a way to cover their insecurity, they publicly accused Jesus of blasphemy (Matt. 26:65).

ESTRANGEMENT FROM GOD

Perhaps it goes without saying that Charles had a heightened sense of estrangement from God, the fifth characteristic of separation. Isaiah recorded the same feelings Adam and Eve must have felt when they hid themselves from the presence of God. "Your iniquities have made a separation between you and your God, and your sins have hidden His face from you, so that He does not hear" (Is. 59:1, 2).

It is difficult to have experienced abandonment in your birth family and feel acceptance by God. Abandonment by a child's first authority, the parents, makes it hard to trust God, the ultimate authority in adulthood. Much wife abuse occurs when a man is emotionally dependent on women for his security but fears being abandoned by his wife. He will go into an angry rage, hurt her, realize what he has done, drop to his knees and beg for forgiveness.

SUPERFICIAL RELATIONSHIPS

Feeling rejected and wanting to prevent future painful loss can result in superficial relationships. You see this played out in extreme loneliness and withdrawal, even when one could have many associations with others.

Commitment-phobic men (playboys) and emotionally estranged men feel that they could not sustain a healthy relationship with a woman. Their fear of rejection keeps the relationship superficial and primarily physical. A man can have sex with repeated partners and not have an emotional attachment in the relationship. His fear of intimacy results in sex addiction and perversion and only leads to more superficial relationships. As a people-helper, you may even discover that some couples never had a deep relationship to begin with.

Paul knew first-hand about shallow relationships in contrast to his relationship with Timothy, his son in the faith. "For I have no one else of kindred spirit [like Timothy] who will genuinely be concerned for your welfare for they all seek after their own interests, not those of Christ Jesus" (Phil. 2:20, 21). King David confessed in a vulnerable moment, that he was *lonely and afflicted* (Ps. 25:16) and that at one time, he had become estranged from his own brothers (Ps. 69:8).

Part of the punishment for the first murder drove Cain from intimate contact with others. Cain cried out that "You have driven me from Your face and I shall be a vagrant and a wanderer on the earth ..." (Gen. 4:14). The result of separation played itself out in Cain's life thereafter, in superficiality with others and a deep sense of loneliness.

PURPOSELESSNESS

"What do I have to lose? Why go on? Why shouldn't I just end it all now?" These statements reflect one of the most painful parts of separation... purposelessness. Who needs me? What use am I now? This logic explains the early death of men who didn't prepare for a purposeful retirement because their whole purpose for living was wrapped up in their jobs.

Separation from the purpose-Giver leaves you to your own resources and brings you to the same conclusion as Solomon, "I considered all my activities which my hands had done, and the labor which I exerted and behold, all was vanity and striving after wind and there was no profit [purpose] under the sun" (Ecc. 2:11). This man who had everything but a purpose cried out in despair, "Vanity of vanities! All is vanity" [futile and worthless] (Ecc. 1:2).

Most stories you will hear could be reduced to these unmet needs. But was it always like this? Has man always struggled with these unmet needs?

CREATION

What did God have in mind for man in creation? Did God create such a needy person so that he would struggle in vain all the days of his life? Creation helps us understand what we need to do for restoration because we have a glimpse of what the original looked like.

VALUE VERSUS LOW SELF-ESTEEM

God went on record to affirm what He thought of His original creation. In the Genesis account of creation, "God saw all that He made, and it was very good" (Gen. 1:31). When God pronounces something good it also carries with it intrinsic value. It was created good for His honor and praise. Man was created good without flaw or sin. He was of greater value than the animal kingdom. There were no struggles with self-worth or self-condemnation. There was no separation yet because of sin.

BELONGING VERSUS REJECTION

Whose image is stamped on you? The Creator Himself stamped His own image on you. "Then God said, 'Let us make man in our own image, according to our likeness'; and God created man in His own image in the image of God He created him; male and female He created them" (Gen. 1:26a-27). How are we like Him? We can reason and communicate spirit-to-spirit. We have a living soul. Man never felt more like he belonged than he did in Eden. Acceptance was not even an issue because they were created in God's image.

COMPETENT (ADEQUATE) VERSUS INADEQUATE

How do we know man was adequate at creation? Because God made man fully capable of fulfilling all his delegated responsibilities. This adequacy was part of God's blessing to man. "And God blessed them, and God said to them, 'be fruitful and multiply, and fill the earth, and subdue it, and rule over the fish of the sea and the birds of the sky; and every living thing that moves on the earth'" (Gen. 1:28).

What a job description! This assignment was a blessing that man would enjoy. God gave him the power of choice and he chose the names of all living creatures. Feelings of inadequacy or failure never entered the picture. There was no hint of being overwhelmed. Man was in control and fully accountable to God.

SECURITY VERSUS INSECURITY

Before the separation which began with Adam and Eve's willful disobedience to God's clear instruction, there was only one criteria for security: food. God said, "Behold I will give you every plant yielding seed that is on the surface of the earth, and every tree which has fruit yielding seeds; it shall be food for you" (Gen. 1:29).

After the separation, clothing was added as a second requirement. Paul clarified this to Timothy, "And if we have food and covering, with these we will be content" (I Tim. 6:8). If you can't eat it or wear it, you basically don't need it.

Every known civilization has struggled to provide these two basic necessities. Before the separation, Adam and Eve lived in a perfect climate and environment. Because sin had not entered the picture, there was no sense of shame. After the separation, clothes were needed and God provided their apparel. He knew Adam and Eve's fig-leaf wardrobe was not very durable so He made them clothes from animal skins (Gen. 3:7, 21).

Loss had not been any part of the human experience prior to the separation, so there was no fear of it. Security had been rooted firmly in God's provisions.

INTIMACY WITH GOD VERSUS ESTRANGEMENT FROM GOD

Before the separation, God met with Adam and Eve regularly for fellowship. In fact, He initiated this creator-creature communication. It was before one of these regular visits that the first family attempted to hide from God, "and they heard the sound of the Lord God walking in the garden in the cool of the day and Adam and his wife hid themselves from the presence of the Lord God among the trees of the garden. Then the Lord God called to Adam and said to him, 'Where are you?'" (Gen. 3:8, 9).

God created man to have fellowship with Him. He initiated it. God ultimately desires fellowship with you. Heart-to-heart and spirit-to-spirit communication is the essence of intimacy, which is often confused with sex. Sharing heart-to-heart is not a physical issue; it is a spirit issue. Jesus said, "God is spirit, and those who worship Him must worship Him in spirit and in truth" (Jn. 4:24). Adam and Eve enjoyed unbroken fellowship and unbroken communication with God and one another which made intimacy possible.

INTIMACY VERSUS SUPERFICIALITY

A perfect environment did not meet Adam's needs for companionship. Loneliness is not sin, and apparently Adam was lonely. God agreed that it was not good for man to be alone. "I will make him a helper suitable for him" (Gen. 2:18). The word, "suitable" means responding to him spiritually, mentally, volitionally, emotionally and physically. Although animals provided a measure of companionship, Adam was not able to find one creature in the animal kingdom that met all of the criteria of a suitable responder. It was not until Adam named all the animals of the world that God created Eve and brought her to him (Gen. 2:20-22). What was Adam's first response? "This is bone of my bone and flesh of my flesh; she shall be called woman, because she was taken out of man" (Gen. 2:23). How special was she to be to him? "For this reason a man shall leave his father and his mother, and shall be joined to his wife, and they shall become one flesh" (Gen. 2: 24). They had a deep sense of belonging, not only with God, but with each other.

Emotional and spiritual intimacy was not hindered by marital selfishness. There were not any marital hurts to fracture their relationship. They were open to one another all the time because there was no need to be closed, aloof or protective.

PURPOSE VERSUS VANITY (PURPOSELESSNESS)

The Garden of Eden was not an early retirement center. Although it was a perfect environment, there was pleasant work to do. This was one job of which it could be said, "no sweat." It was not until after the separation that God said it would be, "by the sweat of your brow you will have food to eat because cursed is the ground because of you" (Gen. 3:19, 17). God had purposeful work designed into the creation. "The Lord God took the man and put him into the Garden of Eden to cultivate it and keep it" (Gen. 2:15). The assignment was basic and fulfilling.

Work, however, was never designed to take the place of fellowship with one's wife or with his God. That all began after the separation.

Although this has not been an in-depth study of life before sin, a people-helper can begin to see what God intended man to be before the separation, what has happened as a result and what needs to be restored by spiritual care-givers in Christ.

The late Conrad Graham served as Vice-President of Living Foundation Ministries from its inception. One of his favorite hobbies was restoring antique cars. For months he showed me pictures of various stages in the restoration of a 1939 Cadillac. The first pictures were barely distinguishable shells of two rusted cars sunken in mud. Conrad had seen pictures of the original condition of other '39 Cadillacs and he could visualize the restoration. He combined the best parts of those two cars and accomplished it.

Today the finished product is white-glove perfect in every detail. The rusted hunks of steel may have hinted of their past beauty, but they needed countless hours of skilled restoration to return them to mint condition. How was he able to do that? He knew what the original looked like. Our job is to help restore the lives of those who have been wrecked by sin and neglect because we know who they should look like – Christ.

TRANSITION

One event in history took an incalculable toll on humanity. The idyllic state was destroyed. "Therefore, just as through one man, sin entered into the world, and death through sin, and so death spread to all men, because all sinned" (Rom. 5:12). Disobedience to God's clear instructions brought forth sin and resulted in separation. However, God did not abandon us in the junkyard of life to deteriorate into rusted hunks of uselessness. How did it happen?

"And you were dead in your trespasses and sins, in which you formerly walked according to the course of this world, according to the prince of power of the air, of the spirit that is now working in the sons of disobedience. Among them we too all formerly lived in the lusts of our flesh, indulging the desires of the flesh and of the mind, and were by nature children of wrath, even as the rest. 4) But God, being rich in mercy, because of His great love with which He loved us, 5) even when we were dead in our transgressions, made us alive together with Christ..." (Eph. 2:1-5).

Receiving Christ as your Lord and Savior is the first step in beginning to reverse the negative effects of sin in your life. "But as many as receive Him [power of choice] to them He gave the right [authority] to become the children of God, even [specifically] to those who believe in His name" (Jn. 1:12).

How is this reversal process begun? "That if you confess with your mouth, Jesus is Lord and believe in your heart that God raised Him from the dead, you shall be saved; for with the heart man believes, resulting in righteousness, and with the mouth he confesses, resulting in salvation" (Rom. 10:9, 10).

A basic prayer could be, "Dear Father, I acknowledge that I have sinned and sin has separated me from You. I receive Jesus as my Savior and will follow Him as my Lord. Thank You for saving me and for the promise of eternal life."

Now the restoration process begins but changes are made over a lifetime, not just at a decision point. "So then, my beloved, just as you have always obeyed, not as in my presence only, but now much more in my absence, work out your salvation [into life], with fear and trembling, for it is God who is at work in you both to will and to work for His good pleasure" (Phil. 2:12, 13).

RESTORATION

Christian people-helpers have a great advantage for at least three reasons. First, they know that it is God's responsibility to work on a stubborn will to make a person willing to be obedient. Secondly, it is also God's responsibility to give us the ability or power to change. The basic unmet needs that prompt much of our negative behavior can be met in a personal relationship with Christ. Thirdly, God has given us every possible spiritual resource necessary to live a godly life (2 Pet. 1:3). This is more than any other people-helper system has to offer. In a growing relationship with Christ, we can be assured that basic needs will be met. It is all part of the restoration process.

As I gazed on Conrad's restored 1939 Cadillac, it looked as good, if not better, than when it came off the showroom floor. True, there was still some evidence of age. Even so when God restores your life through Christ, there will be residual side effects of the past decay because of sin, but some day you will be like Him. "Beloved, now we are children of God, and it has not appeared as yet what we shall be. We know that when He appears, we shall be like Him because we shall see Him just as He is" (I Jn. 3:2). That's great! But meanwhile back on planet Earth, daily reality is a different story. How does God restore you now? How are your needs met now?

VALUED THROUGH LOVE

When you feel loved, you feel valued and accepted. When you feel unloved, you feel worthless and rejected. Biblical people-helpers know that a person's ultimate acceptance is found in Christ's love for him and not in the person's love for Christ. The Apostle John explained it this way; "In this is love, not that we loved God, but that He loved us and sent His Son to be the propitiation [sacrifice] for our sins;" and in response, "if God so loved us, we also ought to love one another" (I Jn. 4:10,11).

The often-quoted verse in Eph. 1:6, which in the King James translation says, "He has made us accepted in the beloved" is rendered in the NAS. "...His grace which He freely bestowed

146

on us in the beloved [Christ]." The word, *karitow* from *karis,* translated is *freely bestowed* or *accepted,* to endow with grace, to find favor. It implies more than favor because favor can be earned or deserved. Grace, however, is not earned; it is a gift. God highly favors you. Think about that! This grace, which is not earned, is a gift delivered through His love to you.

Biblical people-helpers approach worthlessness not on a person's self-acceptance level but on the love level as God does. "See how great love the Father has bestowed upon us, that we should be called the children of God, and such we are. For this reason, the world does not know us because it did not know Him" (I Jn. 3:1).

Man stresses personal performance to gain acceptability by God and others. He strives with good intentions to be worthy (valuable) apart from God, but God equates your good works with filthy rags in Is. 64:6. It is a graphic word picture. The word, *filthy,* comes from a Hebrew word which means, *menstruation.*

Self-esteem can be the human effort of a deceived heart to cast a positive vote for self instead of seeing himself loved in Christ and accepted by grace. One's value comes from a personal relationship with Christ and not from human performance to earn acceptance. God established your value through your identity in Christ.

Self-image is appropriate if you mean the image of yourself in Christ and not the image of yourself looking at yourself. The latter is a dead end if your self-acceptance depends on you accepting yourself. What will you do on the days you do not like yourself? Depravity never did like depravity.

God grants you value (grace) as a gift which is an antidote for anxiety. "Are not two sparrows sold for a cent? And yet not one of them will fall to the ground apart from your Father. You are of more value that many sparrows" (Matt. 10:29, 31). In

Christ, the worthless, rusted hulk is restored and granted favor and value that cannot be earned or lost. It is based on a gift, not a reward (Eph. 2:8,9). Loved people are valued people.

BELONGING

Charles felt painfully isolated and rejected. The memories of the orphanage underscored that rejection. But how does God restore a sense of belonging in the midst of so much pain and abandonment? Loneliness is one of the most painful emotions one can feel, whether a Christian or not.

John MacArthur used to say that if a man walked down the beaches of Southern California in a bathrobe he could gain a following. People are desperate to belong to someone or something to have a sense of belonging. This is the basic draw of gang membership, terrorist recruitment and cults. Look at the high cost of hazing by fraternities or street gangs. These are synthetic substitutes, but what is the real thing? The church. God created this new family structure to meet our basic need to belong and to reduce the isolation. The church is God's primary plan for a tangible place to feel like you belong. In fact, it is to be so integrated that it is compared to the human body. "So we, who are many, are one body in Christ, and individually members one of another" (Rom. 12:5).

How does the body function to build up each member? God did not expect us to do it on our own. He gave spiritual gifts to the church. "And He gave some as apostles, and some as prophets, and some as evangelists, and some as pastors and teachers, for the equipping of the saints for the work of service, to the building up of the body of Christ" (Eph. 4:11-12).

God designed the church as a channel through which He could significantly touch the lives of those who are stressed and under the weight of heavy problems. He has called the body of Christ to help people who are struggling with thoughts, emotions and behaviors that are causing havoc in their lives. It is estimated that "95 percent of the problems and potential problems of living can be alleviated by the large or small group ministries in the local church."

Ironically, in the one place where people should be met with acceptance and love, they may be confronted by rejection, hostility and even favoritism. God attempted to stop prejudicial acceptance in the first book written in the New Testament. It was addressed to new Christians who had just come out of a high performance-oriented religion, Judaism. James sought to put an end to partiality and favoritism. "My brethren, do not hold your faith in our glorious Lord Jesus Christ with an attitude of personal favoritism. But if you show partiality, you are committing sin and are convicted by the law as transgressors" (Jam. 2:1,9).

The church is meant to be a center of love and care, however, as Selwyn Hughes observed, "It's a problem, the greatest scandal of the universe, that a church modeled on a God who cared enough for us to give His own Son to die on a cross, should be so bereft of tender, loving care" (Hughes, p. 5). The Harvard psychologist, Gordon Allport, called the church "incomparably the greatest psychotherapeutic agent in the universe and that the Christian church knows more about this than anyone in today's secular society," but he regretted the "age long failures of religion to turn doctrine into practice" (Hughes, p. 61). The church that is loving and accepting without tolerating sin is actively playing a restorative part in God's plan to communicate a sense of belonging in an alienating world.

ADEQUATE

We have no record that Adam and Eve felt overwhelmed by their God-assigned tasks. Since the separation, failure seems to loom just around the corner, either actually or perceptually. The fear of failure is man's greatest fear. In Christ, we now can meet all of God's expectations of us. Paul affirmed, "I can do all things God expects of me through Christ who gives the strength to do it" (Phil. 4:13 paraphrase).

Christians may never fully lose their feelings of inadequacy, but now they realize from where adequacy comes, "And such is the confidence we have through Christ toward God. Not that we are adequate in ourselves to consider anything as coming from ourselves, but our adequacy is from God, who also makes us adequate as servants of the new covenant ..." (2 Cor. 3:4-6a).

Usually, the fear of an impending failure comes from our effort but without picturing God's power to accomplish it. Christians gain a quiet confidence in God's ability to accomplish whatever He calls us to do. "For I am confident of this very thing, that He who began a good work in you will perfect it until the day of Christ Jesus" (Phil. 1:6).

SECURITY

If acceptance is rooted in the bedrock of God's love, so is its bedfellow, security. The fear of separation produces insecurity. Paul asks a rhetorical question that covers all separation options. "What will separate us from the love of God? Tribulation, famine, nakedness, peril, sword, death, life, angels, principalities, things present or future, powers, height, depth, or any created thing? He is convinced that nothing shall separate us from the love of God which is in Christ Jesus our Lord" (Rom. 8:35-39).

What can daily remind us of our security? God's leading in our daily lives as His sons/daughters. "For all who have been led by the Spirit of God, these are the sons of God" (Rom. 8:14). Our security is further established because it is in a person, Christ, not in our performance. "For you have died and your life is hidden with Christ in God" (Col. 3:3).

Christians still struggle for control of their lives to prevent further painful loss. They are learning the balance between human responsibility and God's responsibility. King David tried to strike the balance by stating, "Unless the Lord guards the city, the watchman keeps awake in vain" (Ps. 127:1b). He does not say the watchman is to take an extended coffee break and leave the *total* care to God. But the watchman is to do his part and fulfill his own responsibilities with full awareness that he is ultimately trusting God to protect the city.

As a parent, I kept watchful care over our children. But I am fallible. I did my best to protect while trusting God for that ultimate protection. And then this happened.

Our three-year-old daughter's hand slipped out of mine momentarily during the Christmas rush at a major shopping mall and she disappeared. The instant I realized it, I cried out to God to find and return her. A few minutes later a security policeman came walking up to me, holding Michelle's hand and asked if this was my child. Relief! After that I strengthened both my grip on her hand and my trust in God. This is the essence of protective security.

Scripture affirms security at every turn. If I experience parental rejection, God says, "If my father or mother forsake me, then the Lord will take me up" (Ps. 27:10). God's presence is secured in the promise, "I will never desert you, nor will I ever forsake you" (Heb. 13:5b).

The disciples panicked at our Lord's announcement of His imminent departure. He responded to their fear with comforting words that have given hope and strength down through the ages. "And I will ask the Father and He will give you another Helper, that He may be with you forever, that is the Spirit of Truth, whom the world cannot receive, because it does not behold Him or know Him, you know Him because He abides with you, and will be in you. I will not leave you as orphans [like Charles], I will come to you" (Jn. 14:16-18).

FELLOWSHIP WITH GOD

Perhaps the most painful result of Adam and Eve's sin was the spiritual separation from God. This was not a physical separation since God is a Spirit and is omnipresent. One of the symptoms of this separation is an inability of man to communicate with God and God with man. Communication is accomplished through the Spirit.

When God desires to communicate with us, it is accomplished through His Spirit. "The Spirit Himself bears witness with our spirit that we are the children of God" (8:16). One of the major benefits of being restored through Christ is that now we can have fellowship with God and "Our fellowship is with the Father and with His Son Jesus Christ" (I Jn. 1:3).

We have also been given the *ministry of reconciliation*. We were first reconciled to God through Christ and then, He, in turn, "...gave us the ministry of reconciliation" (2 Cor. 5:18).

The basic need to be accepted and have communication with God is universal. Even in the staunchest atheistic society, religion flourishes on a personal level. Stalin was an avowed atheist, but at his funeral, his wife made the sign of the cross over him. The need to be able to communicate with God is inborn. By leading others into a personal relationship with Christ, they can have their greatest personal need met which is the doorway to all other needs.

FELLOWSHIP WITH OTHERS

Estrangement from others, which results in superficial relationships, can be reversed in Christ. However, it is not automatic. Many Christians continue their withdrawn habits after conversion, but it does not have to be this way. If we choose to live in accordance with a basic understanding of the Word of God, we are able to have fellowship both with God and with man. This was at the heart of the infant church in the first century. "For they were continually devoting themselves to the apostles' teaching and to fellowship, to the breaking of bread and to prayer" (Acts 2:42).

One of the most unusual dynamics of Christian fellowship is that it does not take weeks to develop. I have spoken in many countries. It never ceases to amaze me how I can instantly begin to fellowship with someone I have just met. By the end of the ministry, I sense a special closeness greater than I may have with my own birth family.

People who feel estranged from others and have little or no family ties can, by being restored in Christ, have a new spiritual family. Bonding takes place through fellowship. As a people-helper, when you restore a person through Christ you potentially meet the second greatest need in his life, that of intimacy with other people.

Superficiality is a cry that people-helpers can identify as an unmet need to have a significant relationship with others. Loners usually believe that no one wants to be their friend. Once they are restored in Christ, they now potentially have a world of friends. Even Jesus called his disciples, *friends* (Jn. 15:15). This is yet another benefit of restoration. But it is not automatic, "A man who has friends must himself be friendly" (Prov. 18:24).

PURPOSE

The swirling snow and long seminar hours did not keep 92-year-old Grandma Harding from attending our People-Helper Conference in Erie, Pennsylvania. After being made aware of her presence, I was curious to see why she was there. While watching her take detailed notes and attentively listen to me for more than six hours, I asked her, "Why?"

Her first response was predictable, "I'm never too old to learn." Her second response was humbling and a personal challenge to me, "This is such good teaching to learn many ways to help others." Then, with the seriousness of a veteran care-giver, she continued, "I am so burdened for some of my friends who are having troubles, and I am praying for them and trying to help them," she paused, then added lovingly, "One of my daily prayers is that the Lord will help me help others, so this meeting means a lot to me." Grandma lived purposefully. Her reasons for living served her well for 92 years.

God gives you at least three reasons for living that continue until you draw your last breath. First, a person who is born again has a character goal that is timeless. "For whom the Lord foreknew, He also predestined to be conformed to the image of His Son ..." (Rom. 8:29). But, being born again is only a start. The fish is caught but not cleaned. God desires that we begin to reflect in word, deed and attitude a likeness of the Lord Jesus.

The second purpose God gives also remains valid for the balance of your life. Before Jesus returned to His Father, He instructed us to, "Go and make disciples by teaching them to observe all that I commanded you" (Matt. 28:19, 20). While you continue to shape your life into a reflection of Christ, He desires that you disciple others to conform their lives into Christ-likeness. How to do this is the basis of the rest of this book.

Finally, a third purpose is that of Christian service. This is not performance to gain something, but to serve one another in love because of what you have already received in Christ. "So, then while we have opportunity, let us do good to all men, and especially to those who are of the household of the faith" (Gal. 6:10). Meeting the spiritual and practical needs of others can exhaust anyone and relieve boredom.

A loss of purpose usually results in boredom. But a restored person with clear purpose may have another problem, that of saying, "No." There will always be more than one can do, but there is also more to do than we are doing. Emerson once said, "It is one of the most beautiful compensations of this life that no man can sincerely try to help another without helping himself."

This may have been one of Grandma Harding's secrets of long life, dedicating herself to minister to the spiritual and practical needs of others. A desire to live often gives a person more days of life, but when the will or purpose to live dissipates, a premature death becomes inviting. This enigma is seen with unfortunate regularity when men and women do not prepare for retirement. If they receive their primary value and purpose from their vocation and the inevitable retirement comes, the absence of purpose results in premature death.

Tucked away in a three-room converted Air Force barrack lived a semi-retired woman with Parkinson's disease. She worked when she could. Her meager social security and Spartan lifestyle kept her comfortable. For all intents and purposes, her vocationally productive years were behind her. Yes, she was limited in what she could do, but in her physical weakness, Nadene was very much alive spiritually. She asked for the details of Linda's and my travel schedule and prayed for us throughout the day. She asked when we were leaving and when we expected to arrive. She wanted to know when I would begin to speak and when I would conclude. Nadene bathed our schedule in prayer. Why? Because this was her purpose for living and it served her well until the Lord took her home.

Her Parkinson's disease drained her strength. In order to concentrate, she had to write out her prayers. Our family's names appeared often. As a restored person in Christ, she lived her limited life to the fullest and never lacked for a reason to live.

TEMPTATION AND NEEDS

Mary excitedly entered my college office. She enthusiastically announced that she was on her way to visit her boyfriend in Chicago. Mary's alcoholic father had been killed the year before when the car he was driving while intoxicated hit a bridge support pillar. Her home life had been abusive and void of any meaningful relationships.

John had showed Mary some personal attention. He had just been asked to leave the college because of repeated inappropriate behavior. Alcohol had become part of his support system. Mary was love hungry and John was co-addicted to alcohol and immorality. Mary told me it was God's will that she find out if John's and her relationship was to be. I heard and understood her cry. She had a natural need to be loved and feel secure. She saw John as an opportunity, weak as it was, to meet that need. I looked at Mary and shared with her that most of our temptations are aroused when we have a legitimate need that Satan or our lust wants to meet illegitimately. I attempted to get her to identify the need, then to see how this trip might be an illegitimate way of getting that need met. I spoke to no avail; she went to .

A year later as I stood in back of the college chapel, a young student that I did not immediately recognize approached me. "Mr. Lynch, remember me?" The change of hair color, style and dress threw me off, "You remember, you talked to me in your office about John?" Half-way through her sentence my memory came to my rescue. "Yes," I replied. "Well, you were sure right. It was a bad experience in . I have since turned my life over to God and have re-enrolled in another Bible college and have my life back on track."

"You were right." The words rang in my ear. I have never felt good being right while watching a person make a wrong choice. It was not so much that I was right, as that a people-helper, operating out of God's Word, can almost predict the results of decisions that are contrary to His Word.

Jesus himself knew what it meant to be tempted at a point of need. "...Jesus, full of the Holy Spirit, returned from the Jordan and was led about by the Spirit in the wilderness for forty days, while tempted by the devil...and when they had ended, He became hungry. And the devil said to Him, "If you are the Son of God, tell this stone to become bread" (Luke 4:1-3). Jesus had a legitimate need. Satan knew it. So, Satan merely suggested that Jesus meet this normal need. Jesus was tempted to meet a legitimate need illegitimately. He responded, "It is written, 'Man shall not live by bread alone.'"

Often you will see only the sin and not the need or the *cry* behind the sin. The sin is wrong and needs to be confessed and repented of on one hand, but there is another issue that needs to be addressed: the need that may have been at the root of the sin.

The first case of incest recorded in Scripture was not motivated out of sensual passion, but a basic need for security. Lot's daughters did not get their father drunk to have sex out of uncontrolled lust, but out of fear that no one would be there to take care of them in their old age (Gen. 19:30-38).

The rampant sexual promiscuity among teenage girls is not because of heightened sexual desire as much as it is out of a deep sense of love-hunger. Women will give sex to get *love*. Men will give *love* to get sex. Yes, we need to teach them to say, "No." But we also need to show them that they can get their empty love buckets filled in appropriate ways and ultimately through Christ.

It is a sobering reality that many of our legitimate needs may not be fully met until heaven. This truth kept Jesus going. Let us "Fix our eyes upon Jesus, the author and perfecter of faith, who for the joy set before Him [in the future], endured the cross, despising the shame, and has sat down at the right hand of the throne of God" (Heb. 12:2).

IDENTIFY THE FIRST CRY

People usually do not advertise their needs so we understand what those needs are. One of the most common ways a need is expressed is by anger. It has many negative expressions, but there is at least one positive benefit of anger. If acknowledged and processed, you could actually welcome anger as a friend. How is that possible?

157

Chapter 8
LEARN TO READ THEIR CRIES

• Choose to listen carefully for the symptoms of the needs.

• Present needs often come from historical roots.

• Sin and separation created most present needs.

• God did not create needy people but an ideal environment and a meaningful relationship.

• God began man's restoration and transformation at conversion.

• God restored our value through expressions of His love.

• Our sense of belonging is reinforced through our relationships in the church.

• Our security is based on our acceptance in Christ.

• Fellowship is now restored with God and fellow-believers.

• We will always be tempted to get our legitimate needs met apart from God.

Chapter 8
SMALL GROUP QUESTIONS

1. What cries do you think you may have misunderstood in the past and how did you come to understand them later?

2. What behaviors have you observed that can be traced back to the fall of man in the Garden of Eden?

3. How would you connect Adam's distancing himself from God to man's fear of abandonment today?

4. What do you think is taking place when a believer feels estranged from God?

5. How have you observed someone attempting to restore his/her worth, value and security apart from God?

6. What do you think believers are attempting to avoid by maintaining superficial relationships?

7. In what practical ways have you expressed your new purpose in Christ?

8. How have you experienced God's restoration process in your life?

9. Of all the things God is restoring in your life, what has been the most significant and how did He do it?

10. In what areas of your life have you been tempted to meet legitimate needs apart from God? How did you deal with them?

Chapter 9
WELCOME THE GIFT OF ANGER

You could cut the atmosphere with a knife. No one was talking to her. Her pastor-husband and their two adult children, who were living at home, were not talking to her either. Her elderly mother withdrew to her own room. These were our hosts in Colombia, South America, where we had come to teach on resolving conflicts in relationships.

Our translator had warned us that loud arguments could erupt at any time. But as we settled in, we sensed a temporary truce must have been declared. Hostilities must have been suspended. Yet, over the next few days it became obvious that Jenny, the wife, was deeply hurt, angry, bitter, revengeful and ready to explode.

She had married a pastor and had been in ministry 27 years. Now at age 47, her life and family seemed to be unraveling. The stress of working full time, serving in the church, raising a family and having her controlling mother in residence kept the stress level high. I knew it was coming and was not surprised when Jenny asked if she could meet with Linda and me, along with our translator, Raquel.

Late in the evening in a secluded part of the house, the four of us met. We asked God to guide our time so that it would be an encouragement to Jenny. She admitted being very angry all her life and I merely asked her to share her life story and to be honest.

ANGER HAS A HISTORY

In prayer, we asked God to give Jenny the freedom to open her heart, feel the hurts and share them freely. A flood of tears poured out. She could hardly speak. We just reassured her to take her time. We would wait. The picture she began to paint for us was not pretty. I took notes to record the history, but I was really listening for something specific. As her story unfolded, I kept track of the hurts she experienced and who caused them. The historical account of past hurts revealed the offenses that we would later process through forgiveness. Using anger to identify needs is one of the most positive benefits of anger!

ANGER HAS A BAD REPUTATION

One of the reasons anger is not viewed in any positive way is that so little is written or taught about it from a positive perspective. Dr. Gary Oliver, the Executive Director of the Center for Marriage and Family at John Brown University states, "In Christian circles, not enough has been written on the positive side of anger" (Oliver, p. 283). He estimates that at least 50 percent of the Christians he has polled view anger from an almost exclusively negative perspective (p. 278).

Anger may be the most lied about emotion, especially in Christian circles. There is a lot of guilt, shame, embarrassment and judgment associated with anger. You will hear believers state, "I'm not angry, I'm just frustrated," to avoid being labeled as angry. Frustration is the Christian word for anger. They fail to realize anger can be registered at various speeds. Peeved is anger at 20 MPH. Irritation is about 30 MPH. Frustration comes in at 40 MPH. Strong anger is clocked at 50-60 MPH. Rage peaks at 80 MPH.

REASONS FOR THE BAD REPUTATION

Jenny spent most of her adult life in church. She heard many sermons on anger. Most of these put anger in a totally bad light and rightfully so. It is labeled as selfish and is identified as fruit of the flesh by the Apostle Paul, who lists the activities of the flesh, placing *outbursts of anger* or eruptions of temper right in the middle of the list (Gal. 5:20).

There are two Greek words used for anger in the New Testament. *Orge* is anger that is an emotion, an internal agitation that tends to be more abiding, stirring, churning. This is the word Paul uses in Eph. 4:26, "Be angry and do not sin" quoting Ps. 4:4. This is a normal, healthy feeling of anger.

The second word for anger, *thumos*, is a burst of rage or a temper that erupts like a volcano. It is more sudden in its rise than *orge* and is found 18 times in the New Testament. In Revelation, seven of the ten times mentioned refers to God's rage in judgment of the godless world. The remaining uses of *thumos* in relation to man are never used in a good sense in the New Testament. God never gives permission to go into a volcanic rage and erupt on others inflicting pain and destruction. Paul is not talking about *thumos* but *orge* in Eph. 4:26.

Jenny also heard sermons that anger is not only the fruit of the flesh (violent temper, not normal anger), but also that it must be removed at all cost. "Let all bitterness and wrath [rage] and anger… be put away from you" (Eph. 4:31). If it was to be removed, then she thought she could not even admit it was there for fear of rejection.

She heard practical reasons to distance oneself from anger. It is one of the most damaging emotions in relationships and the top destroyer both in marriage and with children. James validates this, "For the anger of man does not produce the righteousness God desires in our lives" (James 1:20). Paul warned husbands about becoming embittered against their wives (Col. 3:19). He even warned dads not to provoke [stimulate] anger in their kids by overprotection, criticism, perfectionism and favoritism (Col. 3:21).

Jenny struggled with the fear of being abandoned so when she heard a sermon that angry people should be avoided, especially as marriage partners, it sent her into a panic. "Do not associate [connect] with a man controlled by anger or don't go with [spend time with] a person who has a temper" (Prov. 22:24).

She worked hard to manage her anger until she ultimately exploded. The low-grade anger (*orge*) accumulated and erupted (*thumos*), damaging everyone around her.

ANGER DOESN'T DIE

Anger is never buried dead even if it is stuffed or repressed. Why? Emotions never die. They are recorded chemically and electronically in the brain just like events are recorded. They go deep inside and stay buried and then seep out in life in various ways, emotionally, mentally and/or physically.

God gives you grace when you are offended, but you can choose to resist help from God to deal with the hurts. The writer of Hebrews puts it this way. "See to it that no one fails to respond to the grace of God [which He gives when we are hurt] so that no root of bitterness springing up [like a poison plant] causes [results in] trouble and by it, many be defiled" (Heb. 12:15). Like concentric circles, Jenny's mother's unprocessed historical anger bled over to Jenny, who in turn, spewed it out on her husband and children and even people in the church.

Anger not only damages others, it causes internal personal damage. Psychiatrist Dr. Paul Meier estimates that 95 percent of all cases of depression are caused by repressed [stuffed, accumulated] anger towards others or oneself. Unprocessed anger could result in symptoms of clinical depression: insomnia, decreased energy, irritability, poor concentration, headaches, decreased appetite, thoughts of suicide (Meier, *Jerks* p. 168).

Antidepressant medication will give temporary relief to the clinically depressed by replenishing the brain's serotonin level. Until the root cause of the depression is dealt with biblically, the depression returns within days. In most cases, the root cause of the depression is repressed anger and until the person truly forgives the person(s) who caused the hurt, the brain will continue to be depressed, possibly for life (Meier *Jerks*, p. 170).

Unprocessed anger can get transferred (displaced) from the original object of the anger to a more acceptable and safer substitute (others or self). A husband gets angry at work, comes home and takes it out on his wife, who in turn, takes it out on the kids and the kids kick the dog. If you observed Jenny's rage, you would be tempted to ask yourself what happened to her today to cause this? She is overreacting! There is no such thing as overreaction. It is accumulated reaction often based on one's history.

Anger can be stored up over the years. As it is collected, it raises your normal anger level. When you were born, technically your anger was at *zero*. Mothers would dispute that because angry crying is a common way babies communicate. But as the child grows older, he can accumulate anger from offenses, and the anger level then can rise from *zero* to any level between *one* and *ten*. If you experience a lot of hurt, rejection, abuse or neglect, you could arrive in adulthood stuck at an anger level of *eight* or *nine*. Then if you are offended at a level *one* and you are already stuck at a *nine*, that *one* added to *nine* pushes you to a *ten*. Something small gets reacted to as if it was something big.

This was a perfect description of Jenny. People around her were walking, as it were, on eggshells hoping not to offend her in the least way to avoid a volcanic, angry reaction. Out of fear, they took the responsibility to control her. Even if she was at a *nine*, she could still function in life with a wounded, angry heart, but it is more difficult. It is like living life wearing handcuffs.

SATAN TAKES OVER

Jenny's rage did not look like God. Instead, it had all the fingerprints of Satan. Why? Built up anger allows Satan to take over the management of one's life, relationships and choices. Paul explained how a simple but dangerous situation can result in untold damage in Eph. 4:26-27. "Be angry but do not sin. Do not let the sun go down on your anger and do not give the devil an opportunity." Allow yourself to acknowledge and feel the presence of anger. Don't stuff it! Then choose not to express it in a sinful way. The time frame in which to process the anger is not long: by sundown. For some of us, it may take many moons. We drag it out. That is wherein the danger lies.

The destructive consequence of holding on to anger gives the devil a foothold in your life. Satan would love to intensify your *orge* anger so that it will develop into *thumos* rage and either kill, steal or destroy you and the object of your anger.

It is like a sliding scale. You are in control from *one* to *four*, then gradually you unconsciously release your self-control to the devil. Notice who takes it from there to a *ten*. It's similar to an addiction. It starts with a choice, then develops into a habit (beginning to lose control), then it grows into an obsession that builds into an addiction and total loss of control. A rager does not take hours to get there. It happens in a flash. When Satan has a foothold or *place* of control in your life, the Holy Spirit is grieved that you are not under His control. As a result, under Satan's control, you become bitter, violent and full of anger (Eph. 4:31a).

Sadly, that described Jenny. She often felt ashamed of herself for her outbursts. You may hear a person who has made a fool of himself say, "Why did I do that?" The answer is simple. When we are angry, we do hurtful things and later realize we were foolish and even stupid to have done them. Then shame pours in. Usually when we are angry, we do the next dumb thing and regret it later. Remember, emotions are not subject to truth or reality. They are free to act out if they are not brought under the control of the mind and the Spirit. "A quick-tempered man acts foolishly" (Prov. 14:17). Just ask Moses.

God told Moses to speak to the rock and water would come out and meet the needs of the dehydrated Israelites. Instead, Moses got angry at the people for complaining and in anger, struck the rock and water came out. He got results but at what a cost! Because of his disobedience, God did not allow Moses to enter the promised land of Canaan (Num. 20:11, 12).

WHAT IS GOD'S PERSPECTIVE?

Jenny did not understand that there are at least four reasons to welcome anger as a friend. First, God knows you are going to get hurt emotionally and sometimes physically. Peter warned us it was going to happen and not to react in surprise and shock as though some strange, unfair thing happened to us (I Pet. 4:12).

You can tell this is the core belief of a person in pain who asks God, "Why me?" God could text you back and ask, "Why not you?" The shock reflects the wrong theology that as believers we are exempt or excused from the normal trials, troubles and conflicts of life. Jesus told us the reality that in this world we are going to have tribulation, but He has overcome the world's demonic system (Jn. 16:33). Paul validated this reality himself. "Indeed, all who desire to live godly lives in Christ Jesus will be persecuted" [painfully reacted against] (2 Tim. 3:12).

Secondly, you will experience hurt and God knows that anger can be an automatic emotional response to both present and past hurts, whether you are a Christian or not. You may not have a choice to feel anger, but you do have a choice in what you do with it. The advantages believers have in dealing with the tough stuff of life are biblical tools, the power to use them, training how to use the tools, support while using the tools and rewards for using them.

But just as anger is automatic, our godly response to hurts must also become automatic. How? By utilizing your biblical tools to process them. Because anger is so widespread, even in Christian circles, dealing with anger should be emphasized often in the church. And you just might be the person to do it as you process your anger, learn from it, illustrate *how* to process and then *reproduce* in others what you are illustrating. People will not generally ask you to help them process their anger. They will just tell you their story, but this could be an opportunity for you to share your story and the process you went through to forgive.

Thirdly, God designed anger to be a notifier of needs, fears, frustrations and hurts. Just as physical pain notifies us of physical needs, so anger notifies us of emotional pain. When the red light on the dashboard of your car lights up, it's notifying you of a need. It does not mean you are a bad person because the light turned red. It is alerting you to a need so that you can deal with it and enjoy driving your car instead of being stuck on the side of the road with a breakdown. If you ignore this warning light, the car could experience serious damage. At first it is only warning you of possible damage.

The Psalmist used his depressed feelings to discover a need in his life. He prayed, "Why are you cast down [depressed], O my soul? Why are you disquieted [upset] within me?" (Ps. 42:5a). He gave himself freedom to feel it without shaming himself. Then he asked himself what the need was *behind* this emotion? He used the emotion like a window to see through to determine his need. What did he discover? He had lost his hope in God and it needed to be restored (Ps. 42:5b). The whole point in acknowledging your emotion is to discover the hurt, loss, confusion or need so it can be healed and you can be set free.

Fourthly, Dr. Les Carter would say, "Anger is an emotion that speaks up for personal needs" (Carter, p. 28). It gives pain a voice. Jenny was never allowed to express her emotional pain appropriately so it continued to accumulate. One reason she was not permitted to share her pain is that most people do not know what to do with it. The answer wasn't only to control or manage her anger but to process it with God.

The good news is that God gives you permission to acknowledge your healthy anger without feeling guilt or shame or even second guessing yourself. With that permission, it is your responsibility to process it in a biblical way. God never gives permission to explode in anger and be hurtful, either physically or emotionally, to anyone.

DISCOVER THE LEGITIMATE NEED

Jenny told us her story. I also said, "Don't fight off your emotions, but give them a voice they have never had. Today God is giving you permission to share your history and the emotions behind it." I kept urging her not to stop and that it was okay to feel and express those emotions. Her story broke our hearts. As she shared, I kept track of the specific hurts she endured and the lies that had been instilled in her through those events. Her parents never married, but lived together and had children. No stable home.

- Her birth father was repeatedly unfaithful to her mom, producing nine children by five women.
- He finally abandoned her, her brother and mother for another woman.
- Her mother told her that her dad did not want her, instead he wanted a boy to replace the one who had died.
- Her mother became bitter that dad left. She literally beat Jenny and her brother with a rubber hose every day. She would explode in anger and take it out on her kids. They reminded her of him and his betrayal.
- Jenny emotionally froze at the news that her dad was not coming back.
- She was raped by an uncle at age nine and by other men at 16.
- She had been drugged and raped at age ten.
- She was often molested by relatives.
- She never had her mother's approval and was still attempting to gain it.

Each revelation came through a torrent of tears as we urged her not to stop. Forty-seven years of pain poured out in a safe environment.

DISTINGUISH BETWEEN EXCUSING AND EXPLAINING BEHAVIOR

Jenny would say from time-to-time that she felt badly talking about her mother in that way. We explained the difference between excusing behavior and explaining behavior. We are not excusing Jenny's wrong behavior because of a bad mom or dad. We are not their judge, God is. By sharing her history, she was explaining how she had been affected by their actions. Jenny reacted to them even if she was doing it inappropriately. Often you will hear, "I'm not going to blame my mom or dad for what I'm doing." That sounds spiritual, but there is one small problem with that logic. True, you can't excuse your wrong responses because of parents' past actions, but if you do not assign responsibility to them for their past behavior, you will never forgive them and be free from the past. It is not complicated:

1. If you do not acknowledge the anger, you will not acknowledge the *offense*.
2. If you fail to acknowledge the offense, you will not clearly identify the *offender*.
3. If you do not identify the offender, you will not *forgive* him and be free.
4. If you do not forgive, you remain in the *bondage of bitterness* and torment.

Aristotle once said, "An archer is more apt to hit the target if he can see it." You are more apt to forgive a person if you can clearly identify their offense that needs to be forgiven. Remember, guilt means "worthy of blame." Jenny's mom and dad were worthy of blame for their actions that impacted her. She was responsible to process the hurts her parents caused by using her biblical tools.

WHAT'S NEXT?

Release of emotional pain is a start but not the finish. Expressing anger does not ultimately heal. In psychological clinics, therapists will have the client hit inanimate objects with a rubber hammer to get the anger out. But there is one small problem, research has shown the ineffectiveness of this *therapy*. The anger returns. We will call that *Plan A*. What is God's *Plan B* to stop the reoccurrence of historical anger and to allow the person to live in peace? We will let Fred explain what he did with his list of offenses and how Jenny followed suit.

Chapter 9
WELCOME THE GIFT OF ANGER

- Admit current anger can have historical roots.

- Realize that anger has had a bad reputation.

- Be aware that anger is never buried dead.

- Stop the accumulation of anger by forgiving.

- Be aware that Satan takes over where anger leaves off.

- Understand God knows you will experience hurt.

- Learn that anger is an automatic response.

- Identify the needs behind anger.

- Accept your responsibility to process your anger.

- Distinguish between excusing and explaining behavior.

Chapter 9
SMALL GROUP QUESTIONS

1. Describe a negative experience with a person who seemed to be angry all their life.

2. How have you been taught to view and/or handle anger?

3. In observing people with anger, how has it affected them mentally, emotionally and physically?

4. How do you think Satan can actually take control of a person that is bitter and has a temper?

5. What do you think about welcoming the presence of anger as a friend?

6. In what ways were you not allowed to express normal anger as you were growing up?

7. How do you think your relationships would benefit if anger was acknowledged in a healthy way?

8. Why do you think people are not willing to acknowledge hurts they experienced from family members or friends?

9. What have you experienced being legitimately angry and not able to express it appropriately? What did that do to you personally?

Chapter 10
FORGIVE FROM THE HEART

It's late. I have spent two hours trying to encourage Fred to forgive his alcoholic father for all the physical and emotional abuse Fred endured growing up. We didn't have to pray and ask God's Spirit to reveal the hurts as we did with Jenny. She lived in denial for years. Fred lived in reality daily. What kept Fred from using the forgiveness tool?

REVENGE IS BIBLICAL

One reason Fred found it hard to forgive was because of the depth of the hurt and his deep desire for revenge. Surprisingly, the desire for revenge can actually be the back door to forgiveness. We are often rightfully warned against taking our own revenge so it may be a surprise to learn that the *desire* for revenge is a legitimate, biblical principle. Read some of King David's Psalms regarding revenge (Ps.10:12, 15; 28:3,4; 55:15).

FORGIVENESS DEMANDS PAYMENT

When Fred told me he felt his father deserved to pay for his abuse, I agreed. That shocked him! He even said, "I thought you were a Christian counselor!" It was important for me to agree in principle with Fred who wanted revenge or justice for the hurts. That is biblical. Genuine forgiveness does require payment for an offense, whether it was done intentionally or not. The offense is a bill that is owed. God makes a direct connection between revenge (payment) and forgiveness. "Without the shedding of blood [payment for sin] there is no forgiveness (Heb.

9:22b). Why blood? "For the life of the flesh is in the blood and I [God] have given it to you [to be placed] upon the altar to make atonement for your souls; for it is the blood that makes atonement for the soul" (Lev. 17:11).

Jesus emphasized the need for payment for sin during the Last Supper. "For this is my blood of the new covenant [contract] which is poured out [payment] for many for the forgiveness of sins" (Matt. 26:28). This was the disciples' first clue of the purpose for the death of the Lord Jesus. True, He told them many times that He would die. That was not news. But He had not connected the dots from his death to the *reason* for his death. Now it was clear. His death would provide a ransom (payment) for sin because only His death could atone for sin (Jn.1:29; Rom. 5:8). His blood sets aside all other plans for forgiveness of sin.

DESIRE FOR REVENGE IS NOT REBUKED

Martyrs in heaven cry out for revenge for being tortured and killed for preaching the Word of God and for sharing their testimonies. They shout with a loud voice saying, "How long, O Lord, holy and true, until You judge and avenge our blood on those who dwell on the earth?" (Rev. 6:9-10). What is God's response? He gives them a white robe and tells them to get some well-deserved rest for a little while longer, "until both the number of the fellow servants and their brethren who would be killed as they were, was completed" (vs. 11). The Great Tribulation is not over. But they are not rebuked for crying out for revenge.

WHO SHOULD ADMINISTER THE REVENGE?

In all his letters, Paul described God's grace and mercy but none more clearly than in the book of Romans. Yet he knew the balance between *desiring* revenge and *knowing who* is ultimately responsible for it. He wrote to Timothy that, "Alexander, the coppersmith, did me much harm." Then he went on to say, "May the Lord repay him according to his works:" (2 Tim. 4:14). Paul was an illustrator, personally living out what he wrote to the church of Rome. "Never take your own revenge, beloved, but leave room for the wrath of God [get out of His way] for it is written, 'Vengeance is Mine [My responsibility], I will repay' [justly punish], says the Lord:" (Rom. 12:19; Deut. 32:35). Lot and his daughters had to get out of the way before God could destroy the wicked cities of Sodom and Gomorrah (Gen. 19:16-22).

God does not argue that punishment is due the offender. From the beginning God instilled in His image bearers the desire for justice and the punishment for wrong. Every known culture has revenge laws in its society, even with no exposure to Judeo-Christian teaching. A desire for justice is born in us.

LOGIC BEHIND REVENGE

I finally asked Fred why he could not bring himself to forgive his dad. "If I let him off the hook [by forgiving him], he gets off scot-free!" He thought his offenses would go unpunished. Technically, his dad was never on Fred's hook. To think a person is on your hook or is controlled or punished by your lack of forgiveness, is a fantasy. Withholding forgiveness is a subtle form of revenge. If we have been hurt and become bitter, we are hooked (bonded) emotionally to the offender. They have hooked us and are controlling us instead. Remaining bitter to punish them is like drinking poison, hoping to harm the offender. It is also a self-protecting tool that often fails. When you feel the need to take your own revenge, you have probably removed God from your thinking.

Where does it lead? Dr. Paul Meier explains that physically our brain runs on the chemical serotonin like a car runs on gas. We can run out of gas mentally and emotionally. When we remain bitter, our brain dumps the serotonin into the blood stream and it is broken down into by-products that are lost in the urine. When this occurs, we could suffer from classic symptoms of depression. (Meier, *Jerks* p. 170)

Fred seemed to be depressed most of the time. He could not sleep, had difficulty staying focused and often expressed his desire to die. That is life on the hook. Fred's dad was not on Fred's hook. Fred was, in reality, on his dad's hook and he had been dead for ten years. He controlled Fred from the grave. Forgiveness is not for the benefit of the offender. He may never acknowledge what he did or see the need to change it. The primary benefit of forgiveness is for emotional and spiritual healing of the offended. It can improve cardiovascular function, diminish chronic pain, relieve depression, boost one's quality of life and lower blood pressure. Once you reach middle age, forgiveness produces better overall mental and physical health than in those who do not forgive. Dr. Paul Meier maintains that the majority of mental health problems can be avoided by becoming skilled in the use of the forgiveness tool. (Meier, *Jerks* p. 168).

FEELINGS ARE ACKNOWLEDGED

Where was Fred stuck? What was behind his reluctance in letting his dad go? Revenge? Yes, but much more. He wanted his dad to feel the pain he and his sister and mother felt during the years of his father's alcoholism and physical abuse. His deceptive logic was, "I can't forgive him because I want him to feel the deep pain we have endured." There is at least one problem with that logic. Most offenders cannot or will not fully feel or understand your emotions. Does that mean you are stuck with those emotions with no hope that anyone will feel or acknowledge them?

God knows that human need. He sent His Son to earth, not only to die for our sins, but also to experience the worst human pain (emotionally and physically) that anyone could endure. Why? So, when you approach the Lord Jesus, our great High Priest, you are assured that He knows exactly what you are going through. He was hated, despised and accused of being controlled by demons and that was just a start. The physical abuse He suffered was brutal. The emotional pain even caused Him to sweat drops of blood. He was verbally assaulted every time He turned around. Talk about rejection, He got it from all sides. He was misunderstood, lied about, falsely accused and abandoned by His family, friends and disciples. He begged His Father for a *Plan B* to avoid the cross. He was declared innocent seven times and killed. His Father had to separate Himself from Jesus when the sin of the world was placed on Him. So, why did He endure it all? Hebrews explains it this way, "For we do not have a High Priest who cannot sympathize with our weaknesses but was in all points tempted [tried] as we are, yet without sin" (Heb. 4:15). The word, *sympathize*, means *to feel or suffer with*. It is instant identification with your pain and loss.

As I mentioned before, it amazes me how a woman who has been sexually abused can spot another woman who has suffered that painful humiliation. While speaking at a marriage conference, a former alcoholic friend came up to me and asked, "Do you know you have five alcoholics in the auditorium?" She had been one and she could spot one. It is something she sensed almost immediately without a word being spoken. That is the response you receive when you go to Jesus. He knows what physical and emotional pain is like. And so do you! That is why you are so valuable to someone who is experiencing what you have worked through using your biblical tools. You have learned a lot; now you are a trophy of God's grace, ready to share how you were healed.

How do we know God feels our pain? Saul was abruptly stopped in his tracks by the Lord Jesus in a blinding light from heaven when he heard, "Saul, Saul, why are you persecuting [hurting] Me?" Jesus did not ask, "Why are you persecuting My church?" The union between Christ and the church is one. "You hurt the church, you hurt Me." The bewildered Saul, out of shock asked, "Who are You, Lord?" He did not recognize Jesus, but he knew it had to be a supernatural being. Then he heard, "I am Jesus, whom you are persecuting" (Acts 9:4,5). "You hurt my people, you hurt Me." Jesus not only understands, but absorbs your pain Himself. He does weep with those who weep (Rom. 12:15).

When you release your offender from the obligation to feel your hurt, you are then free emotionally and mentally from his control. You are off his hook. If your offender was to live a hundred years, he would never feel the depth of your hurt. But Jesus did, and now you are free to let Him carry it. How? Forgive the offender, acknowledge your personal loss, choose to accept the loss and thank God for how He will use it for your personal benefit and to help others as a result of it.

UNFORGIVERS ARE KNOWLEDGEABLE

Fred knew his Bible from cover to cover. He was a Bible scholar in his own right and a gifted apologist as a defender of the faith especially with prominent cults. Many, like Fred, who cannot forgive or give up their desire for revenge, may know a lot of biblical theology. Dr. Mason, the president of the prominent Bible college mentioned in Chapter six, had an earned doctorate in theology and biblical languages. He received the highest honors when he graduated from seminary. But his academic knowledge did not automatically translate into real life experiences and maturity for him.

Fred knew that God had already paid the sin bill through the death of His Son (2 Cor. 5:21). All the charges against us were nailed to the cross with Jesus (Col. 2:13,14). In fact, the payment for sin was big enough to include the offenses of all people (I Jn. 2:2). In his mind, Fred knew that taking his own revenge was, in a sense double payment, but not justice. Forgiveness only makes sense because of Christ's death on the cross for us. Apart from His payment for sin, forgiveness is illogical because it leaves justice unsatisfied.

I tried another approach with Fred. "Let's suppose we had your dad in my office and we stripped off his shirt and beat him with a whip tipped with jagged glass. If we beat him ten times would you forgive him?" (Luke 22:63).

"NO!"

"How about twenty times?"

"NO!"

"Forty times?"

"NO!"

I suggested we take a rod and beat him on the head (Matt. 27:30). He crossed his arms as if to say, "I know what you're doing." I didn't stop. I described how we could press thorny branches into his skull (Jn. 19:2). Spit in his face (Matt. 26:67). Drive railroad spikes into his hands (Jn. 20:25). It was obvious I was getting nowhere.

FORGIVENESS CLEARLY DEFINED

It became increasingly clear that the major roadblock in Fred's thinking was that he had separated revenge from forgiveness. The need for justice is at the heart of genuine forgiveness. You see this clearly in the meaning of the Greek word for forgiveness in the New Testament. It is made up of two words, *away* (*apo*) and *to send* (*hiemi*). Together they mean *to send away*. Historically, in the first two centuries believers understood forgiveness meant to send away. But later it came to include the release from punishment for some wrongdoing. (Detzler, p. 168). A true understanding and use of the original meaning of forgiveness is the biblical tool many have used to gain freedom in Christ.

Have you heard people say that to forgive you just have to release it or *let it go*? There is one small problem. If you let it go, you can pick it back up again. The Bible does not equate *release* with *forgiveness*.

The New Testament verb (apoluo), *to loose from*, is translated, *forgive* in Luke 6:37 but the reference is to set a person free as a legal act. The verb does not mean *to forgive*. (Vine, p. 251). To tell someone to *just let it go* is not an accurate picture of the literal meaning of forgiveness. It can be a form of denial ("Just forget it. Don't let it bother you").

The Old Testament gives us a clue as to the meaning of forgiveness. Once a year, on the Day of Atonement, the High Priest would take two goats. He would kill one and sprinkle its blood on the altar. Then he would take the second goat, place his hands on the goat's head and confess the sins of the nation over it. It was then sent away into the desert as the scapegoat (lit. the goat of removal). It was sent away, then released.

The process of forgiveness can be compared to taking a letter with a list of sins and placing it in an envelope with a postage stamp and mailing it. It is *sent away* to the Lord Jesus. Once it is sent to Jesus it cannot be retrieved. Sadly, non-Christians have no place to send theirs or others' sins. However, faith-followers of Jesus can send the sin done to them or by them to the Lord Jesus and picture it nailed to the cross (Col. 2:14).

PUT HIM IN THE JESUS JAIL

I was desperate! Fred was not willing to forgive his dad. Then a thought crossed my mind that in most societies, legal revenge (punishment) is carried out in jail or prison. That is the location for *punishment* for a crime. So, the idea came to me, since Jesus is responsible to take revenge on all evildoers, picture in your mind that He has a *jail* which we symbolically call the *Jesus Jail* (Rom. 12:19).

Then, I told Fred a story and asked him to imagine he was the sheriff of a small town. He had no deputies but he had caught a bank robber and had put him in his small jail. Now he was responsible for him 24/7, his food, clothes, sanitation, exercise. If he wanted to go on vacation he had pull a mobile jail behind his car. Then he received an email from the large county prison offering to take charge of his prisoner. When he transferred his prisoner, he also had to bring his conviction papers.

WHAT IS A KEEPER?

The choice comes down to two options: he is a *keeper* or a *sender*. A keeper is one who chooses to keep the offender in the prison of his own heart with two devastating results.

First, a bitter person cannot express love to others because he is emotionally frozen. No one feels genuinely loved by an angry person. Second, he cannot receive love and as a result, he does not feel loved. Fred was tortured all his life because he did not feel loved, even though he had an affectionate wife and two kids. The bitter person is stuck emotionally and cannot function relationally. Bitterness also prevents love from getting through to him. He will even minimize others' expressions of love for him. That is what living in darkness feels like (I Jn. 2:9).

The keeper assumes God's responsibility for *collecting* the debt the offender owes. He deceives himself into believing that it is possible for the offender to pay him back for all the hurt he has caused. The keeper can still function in life, but it takes much more energy to do it. He can still work, marry, have kids, manage a home, attend church or be involved in the community. But in reality, he is stumbling around in darkness, stubbing his toe with each step he takes.

WHAT IS A SENDER?

He understands that the hurts he has experienced need to be punished (Rom. 12:19). He gives himself permission to feel the anger from the hurts, as we did with Jenny. Then he identifies the specific hurts and the people who hurt him. In prayer, he sends both the offense and the offender to the Lord Jesus Christ and puts them in His *jail* (jurisdiction for punishment). The sender trusts God to deal with the offender as He sees fit because he knows that God is a righteous judge. Jesus had to do it (I Pet. 2:23). The Apostle Paul had to trust God to punish Alexander, the coppersmith (2 Tim. 4:14). It is not complicated! There may be a thousand ways to sin or be sinned against, but there is only one way out. It is through the door of forgiveness.

I hardly finished telling Fred the Jesus Jail story and explaining the choice to keep his dad in *his* jail or send him over to the Jesus Jail, when he slid off the couch and there, on his knees, he began to pour out a lifetime of emotional pain. Fred's desire for revenge became the back door to forgiveness. He was finally willing to let God deal with his dad His way and in His time.

FREEDOM IN COLOMBIA

For almost two hours Jenny shared her pain and was able to name all the offenses and offenders. It was a good start. But now came the crucial step in her journey to freedom. I simply asked her to join me in prayer and to either picture herself talking to the Lord Jesus or just sensing His presence. I urged her to go deep into her heart and feel the depth of the pain she had experienced all these years. She had never given herself permission to do that. Instead, she would push it down and it would inevitably resurface in many harmful ways. I personally believe this is what is meant to forgive from the heart (Matt. 18:35) where all the emotional pain is stored and must be acknowledged as you forgive. That is why most people have a great deal of emotional release when they feel the pain, name its source, and send the offender over to the Lord Jesus. One woman told me she lost 635 pounds. How? That was the total weight of all those she forgave.

In prayer, Jenny went down the long list and named each of the offenders and their sins against her. As the tears flowed, it was like lancing an infected wound and cleansing it in preparation for healing. She finally transferred all the *prisoners* out of the prison of her heart and sent them to the Jesus Jail. Now she was free.

After Jenny forgave those who hurt her, something unusual took place. She told us she now felt more like an adult than a helpless child. This is a normal feeling for one who has worked through forgiveness for a very painful experience. She had been stuck emotionally like a child in her thoughts and reasonings, but through forgiveness, she could put away her childish perspective and began to think and reason as an adult (I Cor. 13:11).

In two hours Jenny went from responding as a child still controlled by her mother, to emotionally responding as an adult. She could now relate respectfully with her mother on an adult-to-adult level, not as a dependent daughter. Weeks later we heard that they were getting along much better, and Jenny and her husband had moved back into the master bedroom. She was also thrilled to learn that we wanted to tell her story in this book.

TIME FOR A REALITY CHECK

Jenny's restoration with her mom may be more an exception than the rule. Forgiveness does not always result in the restoration of relationships. Jesus forgave those who were killing Him, but they did not stop (Luke 23:34). Stephen forgave those who were stoning him, but they did not stop (Acts 7:60). Paul forgave Alexander, the coppersmith, but nothing changed in their relationship (2 Tim. 4:14,15).

Another step must often take place after forgiveness. If you have been repeatedly hurt by someone, yes, you do have to forgive them seventy times seven times (Matt. 18:22). Forgiveness is what *you grant* but trust is what *they* must *earn*. You may have to casually associate with a forgiven offender (mom, dad, former spouse), but you are not obligated to have intimate fellowship with them if they continue the hurtful behavior or deny their responsibility to make it right. Forgiveness is the judicial or legal part of the relationship. A criminal who has served his sentence is now judicially free and now must rebuild trust. Rebuilding trust is the restoration part of the relationship. But the forgiver does grant the offender the opportunity to rebuild the trust one step at a time.

Jesus, in the Sermon on the Mount, told the offender to go and be reconciled to the one he offended (Matt 5:24). It is the only time this particular Greek phrase, *be reconciled* (*diallasso*), is used in the New Testament. It means there is mutual acknowledgement and forgiveness. Both parties must be involved in the reconciliation. However, the word that refers to our reconciliation to God is a different word, (*katallasso*). God does not need to be reconciled to us (2 Cor. 5:20), He has not offended us, we have offended Him.

God knows that it may be necessary to break off association or fellowship with an offender (I Cor. 5:9-13). You may need to protect yourself or your family. A married daughter who was molested by her father must forgive him, but she is not obligated to allow her young children to be with him, especially unsupervised. Forgiving an offender does not mean you can release them from the consequences of their offenses. King David was forgiven for murder and adultery but he still experienced many losses as consequences of his sin (2 Sam. 12;10-14).

The *sender* knows he may lose something in time (on earth) but he will win for eternity by his godly response (Matt. 5:11,12). The offender may get away with his sin on earth but will lose in eternity. If he is a believer, he will lose his rewards forever (2 Cor. 5:10). If he is not born-again, he will experience much deeper pain and agony forever in the lake of fire (Rev. 20:12-15).

NOW WHAT?

I believe that acknowledging and feeling the pain of the past and forgiving from the heart may be the easy part. Living with the consequences and losses may be the hardest part. Many well-meaning suggestions are given to deal with the consequences, "Put it behind you" or "Don't think about it," but they are not biblical and do not work. What can you do with the losses and scars to be totally free? Let Nancy answer that question for you.

Chapter 10
FORGIVE FROM THE HEART

• Understand revenge is biblical.

• Forgiveness does demand payment.

• God does not rebuke the desire for revenge.

• Allow God to take responsibility for revenge.

• Realize withholding forgiveness is a form of revenge.

• Bitter people are controlled by the offender.

• Accept the fact that only God completely understands your pain.

• Sending an offender and their sin to Jesus is forgiveness.

• Choose to put your offender in the Jesus Jail.

• Distinguish between being a *keeper* or a *sender*.

Chapter 10
SMALL GROUP QUESTIONS

1. When have you wanted to take revenge and if you have, what was the result?

2. How have you let others *off your hook* after you have been hurt?

3. What practical emotional, physical or spiritual benefits did you experience after you let someone off your hook?

4. How does it affect you to know that Jesus does feel your pain? What did you go through to get to that point?

5. How has what you have gone through helped you identify with others' pain? How has it given you the ability to spot another's pain?

6. What are some ways you have heard people use to explain forgiveness? How do those definitions compare with the concept, *to send away?*

7. What struggles have you experienced before you could put offenders in the *Jesus Jail*? What finally brought you to that point?

8. After you forgave your offender, what legitimate power and control returned to your life?

9. How are you able to be around someone who has deeply hurt you? What is it like?

10. How have you rebuilt trust or has someone rebuilt trust with you?

Chapter 11
LEARN HOW TO LIVE WITH
THE MEMORIES

"I can't believe I'm sitting here. I should have settled this long ago. It's about my dad. I think I have forgiven him, but I must not have because I live with the memories every day." I asked Nancy why she felt she had not forgiven him. She said she had done it many times. Her answer describes one of the hardest aspects related to forgiveness. How do you live with the memories and losses as a result of offenses?

"If I have forgiven him, I should be able to *forgive and forget*. So, if I can't forget, I must not have forgiven him." Where did she learn this? Her father was a pastor and Nancy regularly heard from the pulpit that if you have genuinely forgiven, you will be able to forget. My response startled her. "I hope you never forget!"

"But that is what you are supposed to do, isn't it?"

Or is it?

One of the many obstacles to forgiveness is the false teaching that forgetting is part of the actual process of forgiving. And since one is not able to forget, he logically concludes he can't forgive. It is one thing to forgive (send the offender to the Jesus Jail) and another to learn to live with the memories and consequences: physically, mentally and emotionally. Although the painful events are in the past, the consequences and losses from them can continue into the present and affect one's quality of life.

The well-meaning counsel often given to those who have been offended is, "You need to forgive and forget" or, "Don't let it bother you." It's as if you have a switch on your chest that you could just flip and, poof, it's gone or a *delete* button in your memory bank. My mother used to say, "Turn the page, son." What people really want for you to do is to repress your emotions. One problem is that the emotions will resurface another way, physically or emotionally.

Another approach is, "You shouldn't feel that way" as if shaming a person is going to remove the memories. You are made to feel guilty because you are not able to block out of your mind the offending person and the events. Then, you begin to feel, "What is wrong with me that I can't forget, but others can?" One of the reasons you're told to *forgive and forget* is because people do not know what to do with your memories.

FORGIVENESS IS NOT FORGETTING

Why would I tell Nancy I hope she never forgets? Because forgiveness has nothing to do with forgetting, God designed your brain so that all memories are stored both by electronic impulses and chemical transference. You are capable of recording 600 memories a second which works out to 1,419,120,000,000 bits of information in 75 years. The brain stores all that is recorded so it is almost physically impossible to forget.

Though the memories are there, the brain hates pain and it can block it out through denial, suppression, repression, disassociation or splitting off in the mind. These coping strategies can prevent you from dealing with what was done to you, by you or around you. But pain is never buried dead! Sadly, the brain's strategies inhibit you from using your biblical tools to work through the issues so you can learn from them, illustrate how you processed them and build a foundation to reproduce the process in others. The greater loss in burying pain is that it robs God of His glory. He wants others to see your good works (like forgiving your offenders) and glorify Him (Matt. 5:16).

God, in His mercy, may allow your memories to be blocked until you are able to deal with them. They may be triggered later in life and bring up an issue you have suppressed all your life. Many women have completely blocked out memories of being sexually abused as a child. If God uses some current event to recall a past hurt, it is His way of saying now is the time to process that hurt biblically for your benefit and His glory.

It is very important to note again, memory is not a function of the spirit, but a biological function of the brain. You were not born again in your brain; your brain is a physical organ. You were born again in your spirit. Jesus explained the difference, "That which is born of the flesh [physically] is flesh and that which is born of the Spirit is spirit (Jn. 3:6).

Christians' brains function physically the same as non-believers' brains. This is a surprise to theologians who think something mystical happened to the memory function at salvation or after some deeper life experience. However, the mind needs to be continually renewed [changed] after salvation through repeated exposure to the Word of God (Rom. 12:2) coupled with obedience (Jam. 1:25).

The Greek word, *transformed,* (Rom. 12:2) is reflected in the English word, *metamorphosis,* which describes the process of a caterpillar spinning a cocoon and emerging as a butterfly, totally changed from the inside out (2 Cor. 3:18; 4:16). Our change into Christ-likeness is a lifelong process. The Apostle Paul puts the responsibility on you "to work out [the benefits] of your own salvation [into everyday life] with fear and trembling, for it is God who works in you both to will and to do for His good pleasure" (Phil 2:12, 13). Theologically, it is called progressive sanctification. The biblical tool of forgiveness does not destroy the brain's physical function of memory that God designed;

instead, God gives you biblical tools to deal positively with memories and grow spiritually.

GOD CAN'T FORGET

Nancy grew up in the church and attended Sunday mornings, Sunday evenings, and Wednesday nights. One of the reoccurring themes she heard was how wonderful it is that when God forgives your sins, He forgets them. That is why Nancy responded to my *never forget* statement with such a strong reaction. "But Chuck, God forgives and forgets and we are to forgive others just as He does."

I asked her a simple question, "What are the attributes of God?" With a bewildered look, she began, "God can do anything." That is the attribute of omnipotence. "For with God nothing will be impossible" (Luke 1:37). She added, "God is everywhere" which describes His omnipresence. She continued, "God knows everything." That is His omniscience. "The eyes of the Lord are in every place, keeping watch on the evil and the good" (Prov. 15:3). Then I asked her, "How can an all-knowing God forget?"

Recently, I heard a prominent preacher state, "We cannot forget, but God is able to do what we cannot do, forget." He was half-right. We cannot forget. But to state that God can forget reflected a shallow understanding of God, especially His omniscience. An all-knowing God cannot forget.

I reminded Nancy that Jesus is living in Heaven in a glorified body with the memories of the cross. He did not forget how and why He was killed. Those in Heaven are constantly praising the Lord Jesus for who He is and what He did on the cross. "Worthy is the Lamb that was slain to receive power and riches and wisdom and might and honor and glory and blessing" (Rev. 5:12). Over 25 times in the book of Revelation alone, Jesus is referred to as the Lamb

But remember Jesus' words on the cross while being slain: "Father, forgive them for they know not what they do" (Luke 23:34). Is Jesus walking around Heaven now asking the saints and angels why He is called the slain lamb? No, He still remembers who, how and why He died.

But Nancy knew her Bible and pointed out these verses. Jer. 31:34 "...for I will forgive their iniquity, and their sins I will remember no more." Ps. 103:12 "As far as the east is from the west, so far has He removed our transgressions from us." Where is east and west to an omnipresent God? Micah 7:19 "...He will tread our iniquities underfoot. Yes, you will cast all their sins into the depth of the sea." In the New Testament we read, "Their sins and their lawless deeds I will remember no more" (Heb. 10:17).

GOD USES HUMAN ILLUSTRATIONS

I explained to Nancy that God uses human analogies to explain spiritual realities. He utilizes human experience to give us an idea of what takes place in the spiritual world. God is Spirit and we normally relate to Him through something physical, though they are *not* totally equivalent. King David compared God to things he was familiar with. "The Lord is my rock and my fortress and my deliverer, in whom I take refuge, my shield and the horn of my salvation, my stronghold" (Ps. 16:2). These word pictures helped him relate to God as his source of protection and security. Jesus referred to Himself as the light of the world, the door of the sheep pen, the good Shepherd and the vine; all tangible things to help explain spiritual realities.

As to forgiveness, God uses our human memory system as an illustration, but not an exact comparison. We forget things as if they never happened. And the older we get the more forgetfulness occurs. In a similar way, God says He won't remember our forgiven sins. That doesn't mean He forgets them; rather, He will remember them against us no more. He makes a choice not to bring them up against us again. Forgiveness would be easy if afterward, our memory was erased, but the reality is that it is not erased.

FORGIVENESS IS AN ACCOUNTING TERM

Biblical counseling is the process of discipleship and that is exactly what we were doing with Nancy. For her, it involved learning the technical explanation of forgiveness. In the Old Testament, God uses the principle of accounting to describe forgiveness. King David put it well, "How blessed is the man to whom the Lord does not impute [put on their bill as due] iniquity" (Ps. 32:2). Paul described the same concept in the New Testament. "God was in Christ reconciling the world to Himself, not counting (imputing) their trespasses against them" (2 Cor. 5:19).

When God forgives, He does not hold the sin bill against us anymore because it is paid (Rom. 8:1). But it does not mean the debt never existed. When Jesus declared on the cross, "It is finished," He was stating, "paid in full." The same words were found in papyri receipts for taxes with "paid in full" written across them (BKCNT p. 340). For Jesus, it meant His redemption work was completed and the sin bill has been paid in full. Now He offers that paid-in-full pardon for our sin if we are willing to confess (agree) that Jesus is now Lord of our life and that He was raised from the dead as proof that He is God, Savior and Lord (Rom. 10:9,10).

EZEKIEL SAID IT BEST

The Old Testament prophet, Ezekiel, best illustrated what God actually chooses to do with His memory of your forgiven sins. Ezekiel referred to a wicked man who turns from his sin, "None of the transgressions which he has committed shall be remembered against him." (Ez. 18:22). The sin is not forgotten but God chooses not to bring it up against him ever again as due (owed) (Rom. 8:1).

This is a key relational tool. When you forgive someone, you are not to bring it up to them again; however, forgiveness and trust are two separate issues. You must forgive your offender, but he must rebuild trust which may take months, if not years.

I've had couples who after they gave and received forgiveness of each other, discussed what happened and why for understanding sake, but not for blaming, shaming or revenge. Conflict that is resolved can provide a rich source of intimacy as a couple grows closer together through healthy reconciliation.

God expects us to forgive as He does. When He forgives, He does not forget but chooses not to bring it up against us again. The Apostle Paul explained it this way, "If anyone has a complaint against another, even as Christ forgave you, so you also must do" (Col. 3:13).

WHAT TO DO WITH MEMORIES

Choose to live with *paid bills*. My wife, Linda, keeps an organized file of our paid bills. If I ever wonder whether we paid the electric bill last month, she can pull it right up and show me the receipt. Memories are like paid receipts for bills that were owed but are now paid. They are reminders of the forgiveness you granted (their bill is paid.) or the forgiveness you received (your bill is paid.). Memories are designed to remind you of the biblical tool of forgiveness you used for your healing and freedom and for God's glory. It is a choice!

The Apostle Paul remembered the great hurt Alexander, the coppersmith, caused him, but he also remembered what he did with Alexander's sin. "The Lord will repay [revenge] him according to his deeds" (2 Tim. 4:14). Paul transferred (sent) Alexander over to God and left the responsibility with God to do as He saw fit. Paul did not believe revenge was wrong, but he knew Who was responsible for it (Rom. 12:19). The key here is that Paul didn't just focus on the memory of Alexander's hurt but connected it to his forgiveness of Alexander and turning him over to Jesus.

DRAW BOTH GUNS

I grew up in Southern California and westerns were the big thing on television. It always seemed strange to me that the good guys had two guns in their holsters and the bad guys only had one gun. In nineteen countries and on five continents, I have illustrated what to do with memories of forgiven sin in a visual way using the two-gun analogy.

After choosing someone in the audience to come up on the platform, I asked him to point his index fingers like two guns. Then I taped the two fingers together and designated the left finger the memory of the offense and the right finger the memory of the forgiveness given or received. Now, the fun part. I told him, "Now put your guns in your holsters (pockets)." He moved his taped fingers left or right but could not undo them so he ended up putting both guns in one holster.

Next, I asked him to bring out only the gun that represented the offense. He struggled to undo the tape but finally held out both fingers taped together. "I told you to bring up only the gun that represents the offense." He just shrugged his shoulders. I explained that God wants you to connect the memory of the offense with the memory of the forgiveness you granted or received.

What can you do if the memory of a forgiven offense keeps coming to mind? Use that memory as an opportunity to praise God for the forgiveness. He wants you to connect the offense (the left gun) with the forgiveness (the right gun). Why? For your benefit and God's glory. The alternative is to keep replaying the forgiven offense in your mind which stirs up anger, and worse yet, can lead to bitterness and depression.

You will hear people tell you not to dwell on the past. That is partially true. I would add that when painful memories come up, fix your thoughts also on the forgiveness you gave or received. While teaching, I bring up my past (an alcoholic father, abandonment, divorced parents) and how I came to forgive my father. I'm an illustration of an adult son of an alcoholic who is not limited by my past, but I am grateful to God for using it to encourage others in difficult relationships. The past that has not been processed biblically does not bring glory to God. But when you process and learn from it and use your life as an example of how it is done, this brings glory to God and gives others hope that they, too, can do the same with their past.

Most of the on-going pain from a past hurt done to you or by you is a failure to remember that you have forgiven your offender and sent him/her to Jesus. Choose not to dwell on the offense, but, when it pops up in your mind, immediately connect it to the forgiveness you granted or received. What has happened in the past does not define you. Your identity in Christ alone does.

ACCEPT THE LOSS

Loss can keep you stuck. You can do the right thing and forgive an offender, but you still have to live with the loss as a result of the offense. How could anything good come from your loss and pain? Just ask Joseph. He was kidnapped by his older brothers at sixteen, sold as a slave in Egypt, falsely accused of sexually violating his master's wife and languished in prison for years. He was finally released to serve Pharaoh and become second in command in Egypt (Gen. 41:40,41). He lost his youth, family, home and reputation before being vindicated by God.

When Joseph's brothers came to Egypt many years later to buy food during the severe famine, Joseph had a prime opportunity to get revenge. He chose not to, instead, he explained God's purpose for all his losses. "But as for you, you meant evil against me, but God meant it for good in order to bring about as it is this day, to save many people alive" (Gen. 50:20). This did not undo all the pain and humiliation he experienced from his brothers or from the Egyptians. Nothing was undone, but everything had to be accepted with a determination to live at peace with his losses.

Acceptance of your losses and living with them is the hardest part of forgiveness.

- Loss of a happy home growing up
- Loss of physical affection
- Loss of verbal affection
- Loss of adequate food, clothes, necessities
- Loss of a happy marriage
- Loss of loving support
- Loss of reputation
- Loss of accrued assets
- Loss of being a father or mother
- Loss of becoming what one wants to be
- Loss of security
- Loss of innocence
- Loss of confidence
- Loss of learning life skills

Nothing will undo the sexual violations experienced as a child nor the physical or emotional abuse, rejection, abandonment, favoritism, criticism, accidents or divorce you endured. But forgiveness restores your power of choice to accept and to grow through the losses and be an even better person in Christ than you might have been had these things never happened. The alternative is to live in bitterness or regret. Either way, you *will* live with the consequences.

WHAT ABOUT MY OWN SIN?

By confessing your sin to God (I Jn. 1:9), you remove the weight of sin and shame from your shoulders and transfer it over to Jesus. Then thank Him! "But what if I still feel like it is not forgiven?" First, stop re-confessing past sin that you have already confessed. Each time you re-confess that sin, you reinforce the lie in your mind that you were not forgiven. This feeds the sense of false guilt and depression for past forgiven sin.

God makes it clear, it is your responsibility to confess your sin. Tell Him, "I was wrong for..." It is God's responsibility to affirm that He is faithful and that He is just. His justice was satisfied for sin by Jesus' death on the cross. Not only are you forgiven but He will "cleanse you from all unrighteousness," a word picture of the inward washing from all confessed sin and its contamination. He is the only one who can wash you clean through the blood of the Lord Jesus Christ (Rev. 1:5).

Your memories of past forgiven sin are not designed by God to promote re-confession. If you confess the same sin a thousand times, that is 999 times too many. It only reinforces the lie over-and-over again that God did not do what He said He would do; forgive you. Scripture does not say, "If we *re*-confess our sins." ONCE is enough!

WHAT ABOUT GUILT FEELINGS?

It is your responsibility to distinguish between true guilt and false guilt. Why? They feel the same! True guilt means I am worthy of blame or conviction. If I have sinned, I should feel guilty. That conviction is the responsibility of the Holy Spirit and can also come through people (Matt. 18:15) and God's Word (Ps. 119:10).

False guilt is feeling that you are still worthy of blame even after confessing your sin to God. False guilt can even feel truer than legitimate guilt because feelings are not subject to truth.

199

False guilt means you are still taking moral responsibility for attitudes or actions that you have confessed and been forgiven (Rom. 8:1). Now, it is up to you to test your feelings with truth and historical fact. How? Do what the Apostle John told his listeners to do, "Beloved, do not believe every spirit, but test the spirits [with truth and realty] to see whether they are of God, because many false prophets [and false emotions] have gone out into the world [or turned loose in your mind] (I Jn. 4:1).

Just as we are to test every teaching with the truth of God's Word, we are also to test every feeling with truth and reality because emotions are not subject to truth. You can feel God does not love you in spite of verses that state just the opposite (Jn. 3:16).

Emotions are not bad, God designed them. But emotions were never designed to give you objective direction. God does not lead through emotions, He leads through His Spirit to our spirit (Rom.8:14).

When there is a conflict between our "feeler" and our "thinker," that creates anxiety. The Greek word for anxiety is *merimma*, which is made of two words, *merizo*, to divide and *nous*, mind. It is a divided mind (James 1:8). The division is between feelings and fact. Your task is to test the feeler with truth, then, choose to think and act based on truth.

DO I NEED TO FORGIVE MYSELF?

No place in Scripture ever teaches or illustrates self-forgiveness. The root of this false teaching comes from the inability to identify the lie embedded in the emotions that you are not completely forgiven. What part of God's forgiveness and cleansing from *all* unrighteousness is not clear? You may not feel worthy to be forgiven. Well, you are not! You are not forgiven because of your worthiness, but because God said so (He is faithful), and He has satisfied His justice through Christ's death for our sins (I Jn. 1:9). Humbly accept that fact!

Many writers, preachers, teachers, counselors and friends assert you need to forgive yourself because you are experiencing guilt. It is their sincere attempt to help you deal with false guilt, but it avoids the fact that you have already confessed your sin and God has forgiven you. What can you do when you still *feel* guilty? Identify the lie behind those emotions and confront the lie with the truth that it *IS* forgiven. Finally, firmly renounce the lie, affirm the truth, and purpose in your heart to live out the truth. The belief in the lie that your sin was not totally forgiven can destroy your quality of life more than the actual sin and lead to depression. The battle is a conflict between the *feeler* and the *thinker*. You can never get rid of guilt by self-forgiveness. You can try to cover the lie temporarily, but it returns again and again.

DON'T CONFUSE SADNESS AND GUILT

If you feel sadness after you have confessed past sins, hurts and offenses, it is a normal emotion that is a part of life. Regret, too, is normal. Both sadness and regret can motivate you to humility which is pleasing to God (Jam. 4:6). The sooner you can move from sadness to acceptance, the sooner you will be at peace. King David came to this point after his full recognition of his adultery and murder. He realized there was nothing he could do to undo his sins. "For you [God] do not desire sacrifice, or else I would give it; you do not delight in burnt offerings." Then he acknowledged God's desire. "The sacrifices of God are a broken spirit, a broken [crushed] and contrite heart – these, O God, you will not despise" (Ps. 51:16, 17). You and I must have a spirit that is broken of all self-righteousness and excuses. We were guilty, now forgiven and free to walk humbly with gratefulness before God and people.

DISTINGUISH BETWEEN A GLANCE AND A GLARE

It is appropriate to glance at the past from time to time. It is like glancing in your rearview mirror but keeping your eyes primarily on the road ahead. If you drive staring in the rearview mirror, you will ultimately crash. Likewise, to keep focusing on bad things in the past can result in depression or even a mental breakdown.

Remember who you are! You are a trophy of grace and an illustrator of one who is processing your past biblically and learning about yourself, God and others. People need to see your example so they, too, can use the biblical tools to become free. As you show them how, you are reproducing yourself – that is focused discipleship.

BUILD A TROPHY CASE

Build a trophy case in your mind of all the occasions you received grace and mercy, then destroy your hall of shame. What's the difference? The hall of grace and mercy remembers your forgiven sin but it is covered by grace and mercy. Your hall of shame recalls the same events but without covered grace, mercy or forgiveness. The Apostle Paul used the memory of his sin of blasphemy, persecution and abuse of Christians before he was converted as an example of God's mercy and patience. He was a trophy of grace and an illustrator of God's patience to those who would believe in Him for eternal life (I Tim. 1:12-16). His memories came from his hall of fame, not his hall of shame. Like King David, Paul used the memories of his sin as a major source of appreciation for God's grace, rather than lingering guilt over his forgiven sin. Grace is freedom to remember what guilt tries to forget.

Paul acknowledged to the Corinthian believers that he often felt unqualified to be called an apostle. How could he feel that way? Why he wrote most of the New Testament and established more churches than all the other apostles. But he never forgot his murderous attacks to destroy Christians or the sound of screaming children begging him not to take their mommy and daddy away and the terrified look of men and women as they were dragged away. Those sights and sounds were etched deeply in Paul's mind, but he used those horrific memories as a daily reminder of who he was. "I am who I am by the grace of God" (I Cor. 15:10). His past was the backdrop which displayed his present life as a trophy of God's grace.

Paul may have appeared to have bragging rights when he listed all his achievements in Judaism. But he relegated them to a manure pile compared to the surpassing value of knowing Christ Jesus (Phil. 3:5-8). He refused to be absorbed or controlled by his Jewish heritage or worldly status.

GOOD VERSE MISUSED

Has someone ever exhorted you to forget the past and to move on based on Phil. 3:13? "...but one thing I do, forgetting those things which are behind and reaching forward to those things which are ahead." Paul was not referring to forgetting his past sins but rather to his past achievements in Judaism, yet at least twice Paul referred to his past sins to highlight the basis for his deep appreciation of grace.

Remember, you are an illustrator of how to process the sins or hurts you experienced. Frankly, your life cannot be as greatly appreciated by others if they do not know what shaped you to become who you are today. Your past is the frame around your life that highlights your life story. Don't forget what you've been through. Share it appropriately. The only thing worse than a mistake is an uncorrected mistake. Don't forget it. Use it. Share it!

THE GREATEST MOTIVATION TO LOVE GOD

A prostitute slipped into a dinner party that Jesus was attending at Simon the Pharisee's home (Luke 7:36-50). She knelt at Jesus' feet which were extended as He lay on a couch, the traditional posture for eating. She began to wash Jesus' feet with her tears. Simon had failed to have his servant perform the customary task of washing the dinner guests' feet before the meal. She took her hair and wiped his dirty feet. But she did not stop there; she kissed those dirty feet. Simon was in shock! Righteous people would not allow *sinners* to even touch them because that would contaminate them and disqualify them from going into the Temple. The fact that Jesus allowed her to do that proved to Simon that Jesus was not a prophet.

Jesus' response to Simon is one of the most classic responses on forgiveness. "For this reason I say to you [Simon], her sins, which are many, have been forgiven for she loved much; but he who is forgiven little, loves little" (Luke 7:47). What would motivate a woman to humiliate herself by washing, wiping and kissing Jesus' dirty feet? Gratefulness! Her love for Jesus was in direct proportion to the memory of her forgiven sin! That is why you should never forget what you have been forgiven. When the memory comes up, take these simple steps.

Thank God for the memory.

Thank God for the forgiveness.

Love Him out of gratefulness.

Use your memory of forgiven sin as a motivation to love God and to serve others. Loving and serving are not from a motivation to repay to God but out of appreciation for His forgiveness. You could not live long enough or do enough to repay God or anyone else for your sins; nor could others live long enough to repay you for their sins against you.

FORGIVENESS DOES NOT END CONFLICT

Forgiveness does not automatically restore relationships; but there is a biblical pattern to resolve conflict or to give you peace even if others do not change.

Chapter 11
LEARN HOW TO LIVE WITH
THE MEMORIES

- Forgiving is not forgetting.

- Memories are permanent.

- Memory is not a function of your spirit.

- God does not forget.

- God uses human illustrations to explain spiritual realities.

- View forgiveness as an accounting term (paid in full).

- Recall the offense and what you did with it.

- Accept the loss and grow through it.

- Test guilt feelings with truth and reality.

- Self-forgiveness is based on a lie.

- Don't confuse sadness and guilt.

- Distinguish between a glance and a glare at the past.

- Build a trophy case of your past victories.

- Use forgiven sin to motivate you to love God.

- Forgiveness does not automatically restore relationships.

Chapter 11
SMALL GROUP QUESTIONS

1. If you have been told to *forgive and forget, just move on or put that behind you,* how did it make you feel? How do you think they wanted you to accomplish it?

2. When painful memories come to mind, how do you deal with them?

3. What has been your experience of being told God does not forget? Describe your response when you learned that God does not forget.

4. What physical things remind you of God attributes of or how He relates to us?

5. Share how you have forgiven someone and disciplined yourself not to bring it up against them again.

6. What losses have you lived with because of someone else? How have you dealt with the losses? What benefits have you identified for yourself and others because of these losses?

7. How did you stop *re*-confessing a past confessed sin?

8. How do you deal with false guilt? How do you distinguish true from false guilt?

9. If someone told to forgive yourself, how would you actually do it? Why would people tell you to do that?

10. How would your life be different if you only glanced at your past (that was processed) and focused on who you are now in Christ?

Chapter 12
WORK OUT YOUR CONFLICTS

Many believers are surprised that they still have conflicts in relationships after they become Christians. The contemporary church attracts visitors with music led by a praise band, multi-colored lights and the pastor dressed in Levis with his shirt tail hanging out. The people are friendly, seem happy and appear to have open hearts. Visitors would like to have what they see so they commit their lives to the Lord Jesus as their personal Savior. What an experience! Then they drive home.

Before long an argument breaks out. It gets loud. The kids run for cover. Shame sets in and mom and dad are devastated by what they have done - again. Sadly, their past patterns continue and the thought soon enters their minds, "I guess this Christian thing doesn't work for us." Not only new believers are plagued with thoughts like this but long-term believers feel embarrassed when they come for counseling. One survey of 1,700 university students revealed that 79 percent believed that Christianity works for others but it doesn't work for them (Anderson, p. 10). Something is not working for them. Neither did it for Christian friends of ours who divorced after being married 50 years.

GOD KNOWS CONFLICTS HAPPEN

The myth that underpins many fellowship groups is that bad things don't happen to good Christians. *Every day with Jesus is sweeter than the day before* sounds spiritual, but often it is not reality.

Christian spouses have conflicts. The Apostle Peter was married and may have experienced marriage conflicts first-hand. He shared a few keys that apply to all relationships. When someone does something *evil* to you, do not escalate the situation by hurting them back in return. If they insult you, do not return insult for insult (I Pet. 3:8,9). But he does not stop there. Think of a way to bless them instead. That does not mean patting them on the head and saying, "Bless you." No, he means do something good for them, something that would benefit them from their perspective. Why? Because that is what God called you to do and you will receive a blessing by doing it.

God also knows that even as a believer, you can become bitter in your marriage. The Apostle Paul urged husbands, "Love your wives and do not be bitter toward them" (Col. 3:19). Yes, Christians can become bitter. It starts with unprocessed anger and develops into bitterness. Bitterness is the house that anger built; it is not a condominium, but a prison.

God documented the conflicts some of His greatest servants had in their marriages. Moses and Zipporah had harsh words over the need to circumcise their older son that Moses had failed to circumcise as a child. She accused him saying, "Surely you are a husband of blood to me" (Ex. 4:24-26) because she had to circumcise their son.

David engaged in a heated argument with Michal, his wife, over the way he enthusiastically danced before the Lord and the people without his royal robes while celebrating the return of the Ark stolen by the Philistines. Michal met David as he returned home with a sarcastic greeting, "How glorious was the king today in the eyes of his servants' maids as one of the foolish ones shamelessly uncovers himself" (2 Sam. 6:20). This fight did not end well. David separated from her and she never bore children (vs.23).

Conflicts arise between Christian parents and their children. Very little is written in the New Testament about parenting. But two verses that convey the same idea are addressed to dads, "Fathers, do not exasperate [provoke to anger] your children that they may not lose heart [become discouraged and give up]" (Col. 3:21). This can happen through unreasonable strictness, favoritism, criticism, perfectionism, inappropriate discipline, shaming or unfavorable comparison. Eph. 6:4 adds bring them up in the training and teaching of the Lord. But Paul first dealt with the father's anger before instructing him in the positive approach to raising children.

Believe it or not, major conflict can arise among those in Christian ministry. In Paul's letter to the Philippians, he paused to ask for help on behalf of two Christian women who could not get along. He urged Eudia and Syntychi to change the way they related to each other and to begin to live in harmony (Phil. 4:2). Paul asked an unnamed friend to help these women. They had ministered with Paul, Clement and others and he wanted them to continue to do so. But it would take a third party to come along-side them and help them work through their conflict. From Romans to the first part of Revelation, Scripture records one relational, doctrinal and ethical conflict after another. God knows there is conflict among believers. He does not overlook it or sanitize Christian ministry in the New Testament.

CONFLICTS ARE PAINFUL

Nothing can make you feel more helpless or hopeless than a conflict in an important relationship that appears irreconcilable, whether it is your spouse, kids, parents, in-laws, church or ministry. Hopelessness explains why Della walked into our office demanding to see a counselor now! I had an open hour and the receptionist asked if I would see her.

Della was ushered into my office, sat down and looked me in the eye and said, "I have a plan." That was a veiled way of saying she was suicidal and had a plan to kill herself. I calmly asked why she was here and if there was a particular reason that she wanted to do this. She felt trapped in a physically and emotionally abusive marriage. Her pastor had told her she had no biblical grounds to separate from her abusive husband because he had not had an affair.

I turned to I Cor. 7:10-11 and explained she had three options, not just one. She could stay in the marriage with no change (vs. 10), she could separate and remain unmarried or she could separate and be reconciled (vs. 11). I believe she had other options but these were three clear ones. She did have a choice. She was not trapped.

At the end of the hour she walked out of my office, looked around the lobby and expressed to the receptionist that she would like to serve here someday, and she did. She volunteered as a receptionist and later became our lead prayer warrior. I learned much later that she did come into my office that first day with a purse full of pills.

Painful conflicts, whether real or imagined, reveal needs for growth into Christ-likeness in relationships. One of the reasons God allows conflict to continue is to reveal dysfunctional, selfish patterns in relationships and to encourage people to consider biblical alternatives for a better quality of life.

CONFLICTS CAN BE COMPLICATED

The good news is that untangling complicated interpersonal conflicts is possible, though not easy. It is somewhat like untangling a plate of spaghetti. The number one question people ask when discussing a complicated conflict is, "What can I do?" Why do they ask that? One reason may be because what they have been doing has not worked and they do not know what to do differently. In interpersonal relationships, the absence of biblical truth is usually not the problem. Rather, it is the lack of practical wisdom to apply the truth to specific conflicts. Della has read I Cor. 7:10-11 dozens of times in her 75 years but she never saw the practical ramifications of the choices offered there.

Solomon expressed it this way, "There is a way [of speaking, acting, thinking] that seems right [appropriate] to a man, but the end [result] is the way of death" (Prov. 14:12). Death means separation. There is physical death which is the separation of the body from the spirit. There is spiritual death which is separation between God and unbelieving man. Finally, there is relational separation which could lead to divorce. All of these are painful.

BIBLICAL TOOL OF PERSONAL RESPONSIBILITY

Our book, *You Can Work It Out*, is based on one verse that teaches an important aspect of dealing with conflict. "If possible, so far as it depends on you, be at peace with all men" (Rom. 12:18). This answers two very important questions in conflict, "What can be done," and "Who should do it?"

"So far as it depends on you," can be paraphrased, as much as it depends on your circle of responsibility. Most conflicts fail to identify who is responsible for what. There is the ever-present failure of not taking personal responsibility. Jesus expressed the same idea when He said, "First take the plank out of your own eye [circle of responsibility] then you will see clearly to remove the speck from your brother's eye" (Matt. 7:3-5). Both people have responsibilities that they must identify and assume.

What are the four practical keys in Rom.12:18 to work through conflict?

1. *Identify* what actually happened (facts).
2. *Assign* responsibility for all the parts of the conflict.
3. *Assume* responsibility for the assigned parts (own them).
4. *Fulfill* what is in your circle of responsibility.

211

WHAT DOES THAT LOOK LIKE?

IDENTIFY THE FACTS

No surgeon will perform hip surgery without first getting a clear x-ray. Kathy slipped on the ice and landed on her hip. What should the orthopedic surgeon do? Should he replace the hip or insert a rod to hold the bones together and let the body heal? A clear x-ray helped make the decision and allowed for less invasive surgery.

In resolving a conflict, the first step is to honestly identify what happened (or is happening). At this point you are only gathering the facts. Sadly, this is usually the first place where counseling can begin to fail. "He who answers a matter before he hears it [completely], it is folly [foolish] and shame to him" (Prov. 18:13). A very simple mistake is to believe everything you hear and to fail to look deeply into the matter (Prov. 14:15).

We can listen faster than a person can talk. In arguments we tend to talk over the person speaking and we fail to listen for understanding. Not smart! "Do you see a man hasty [quick] in his words? There is more hope for a fool than for him" (Prov. 29:20).

WHY IS TRUTH IMPORTANT?

God only gives grace for the truth. Jesus based His ministry on grace and truth, not just grace and not just truth (Jn. 1:14, 17). God desires truth in the depths of our hearts (Ps. 51:6). But truth is usually the first casualty in a conflict. God never gives grace (favor, divine assistance) for denial, ignoring reality or lying. Christian denial is an attempt to deny God access to a hurt (conflict) that He wants to heal for your benefit and His glory (Matt. 5:16). You can only heal what you acknowledge. Denial prevents you from enjoying your relationship with God or others.

212

Acknowledging the truth brings glory to God. This is exactly what Joshua said to Achan, who, during the battle of Jericho, stole a number of forbidden items that God strictly said must be destroyed. "Now Joshua said to Achan, 'My son, I beg you, give glory to the Lord God of Israel, and make confession to Him, and tell me now what you have done; do not hide it from me'" (Josh. 7:19).

WHAT ARE FOUR OBSTACLES TO TRUTH?

Picture a room with one large door and inside the room is the issue. Standing guard outside the door are four heavily armed guards preventing anyone from entering the room to deal with the issue in a conflict. As a discipler, you may face these same four guards that have to be disarmed before you can get to the real issue. Often the issue is not the issue. It has been Dr. Larry Crabb's experience "that we have a quiet unwillingness to look deeply and honestly at some ugly problems and internal pain hidden deeply in us" (*Understanding*, p. 65).

(1) **Fear of Reality:** The first guard blocks a reality you don't want to admit. Jenny did not want to face the fact that she was not wanted, never loved and was an imposition to her parents. Just because a couple has had sex, does not mean they want children. A husband may be unwilling to admit he is having a physical affair or a wife may hide her emotional affair. There may be a denial of a drug, alcohol or pornography issue. Who wants to admit they are physical or emotional abusers? It would take a lot of grace to acknowledge you are critical, judgmental, selfish, irresponsible, disrespectful or bitter. The brain hates pain, especially guilt and shame, so it has at least 40 ways to avoid facing that reality. Denial is only one of them.

(2) **Fear of Feeling:** Why did Jenny spend most of her life denying her painful past? Simple. If you do not acknowledge it, you think you will not have to feel the negative emotions. But

they will invariably come up one way or another. The whole goal is not to feel the guilt, shame, fear and anger that will arise. One evidence of this is hearing a person say, "I don't want to go there." Why? To face the reality of not being loved or wanted, or feeling inferior or inadequate can be overwhelming and devastating.

You may have met Amber in our first book, *I Should Forgive, But* (p. 95). After we opened our counseling session in prayer, she blurted out, "I don't want to hate him." I assured her that no one in our office would encourage anyone to hate someone. She then acknowledged her grandfather molested her as a child. She did not want to admit that reality because she would feel a deep sense of hatred toward him. Yet, in a short time she was able to forgive her grandfather and to cherish the memories of the good things he did with her on the farm. It is not uncommon after a person processes the hurts to come to love the offender.

(3) **Fear of Responsibility:** If you disarm the first two guards, a fear of facing reality and a fear of feeling painful emotions, you are face-to-face with the third guard, a responsibility you do not want to assume. But with God's help, you can do it. Amber chose to forgive her grandfather. Jenny forgave a host of offenders, put away her childish thinking of being powerless, and chose to communicate with her mother adult-to-adult with respect. Fred finally forgave his father and accepted the loss of his childhood.

Assuming personal responsibility takes many forms. If one is critical, he must stop and replace criticism with praise and appreciation. If there is an affair, the adulterer must stop it immediately, confess the sin, ask for forgiveness and rebuild the trust. You may have to accept someone that you have rejected or love someone that seems unlovable. The hardest task may be to admit you were wrong and ask for forgiveness. Restitution may be in order. God only gives grace, strength and direction to be responsible. The power of personal responsibility is found fulfilling what is in your own circle.

(4) **Fear of Motives:** The fourth guard is a motive you don't want to acknowledge. Ulterior motives hate being exposed and are fiercely protected. Who wants to admit they are proud, selfish, envious, jealous, or covetous? Protecting pride is probably the strongest of the four guards. It is hard to admit reality, feel the negative emotion and assume one's responsibility. That is humiliating. But God never gives grace to protect pride. The opposite is true. He will humble you, but He would prefer that you humble yourself, then, He will lift you up and exalt you in due time (I Pet. 4:6).

DEFEAT THE GUARDS

With Fred, I did not argue that he should forgive his alcoholic dad. I just asked him to lay aside, for a moment, the fact he should and tell me why he couldn't. Fred felt if he forgave his dad, he would get off scot-free. Once we explained that God would deal with him, Fred was willing to assume his responsibility to forgive his dad.

We explained to Amber that if she forgave her pedophile grandfather, she would not be obligated to allow her children to be around him, especially unsupervised. Forgiveness and trust are two separate issues. Often, fears can be addressed biblically to a person's satisfaction and they are then willing to enter the room of truth and reality.

ASSIGN RESPONSIBILITY

The second key to resolving a conflict after identifying the truth of what is taking place, is to separate and assign responsibility for all the parts, "As far as it depends on you" (Rom. 12:18). Literally it can be translated, "As far as it proceeds from you" in yours or others' circles of responsibility.

When people tell me about a conflict, the tangled details appear to be like the previously mentioned plate of spaghetti.

215

As they begin to unravel the details, I draw for them a big circle on my note pad and have them draw an identical circle on their note pad. Then I draw a stick figure in the circle to represent the one talking to me. For a couple, I draw two stick figures. If they mention an adult son, mother-in-law, or anyone else, each person gets a stick figure in the circle. Then I take each person out of the big circle and put them in their own circle. I have even done this drawing in restaurants on paper napkins.

The idea of having one's own circle of responsibility may be new thinking for some. Since the brain does not like pain (guilt, shame), people tend to shift things out of their circle and place it in others' circle. People tend to shrink their own circle and enlarge the other person's. This projection is seen in criticizing a fault, habit or attitude in someone else when it is really in themselves. They will shrink their own circle of responsibility in order to avoid the fear of seeing a truth they do not want to recognize in themselves, to avoid feelings of guilt or shame, and to avoid all personal responsibility. Projection is cemented in pride, selfishness and defensiveness. God is not concerned with how big or little your circle is but what you do with what is your responsibility. He only blesses personal obedience (Jam. 1:22,25).

The conflict is complicated only if you fail to identify truth and assign to each person their responsibility. Here are three questions to ask. First, what words are they using that are hurtful, demeaning, critical or judgmental? This also includes tone of voice and body language. Second, what activities, habits and hurtful behaviors are being displayed? Third, what negative attitudes are present in the conflict? Attitudes control words and actions. An entitled, prideful attitude is highly destructive in a relationship. It needs to be acknowledged and confessed in order to take responsibility to correct it.

PARENTS' RESPONSIBILITIES

The number one responsibility God assigns to parents is to refrain from provoking their children to anger. They do that by making unreasonable demands, enforcing petty rules, showing favoritism, spewing criticism, displaying perfectionism, ignoring them, or failing to spend quality time doing things that are important to the children (Lynch, *God's Peace in Your Home*). A daughter needs to be loved and cherished and given appropriate physical attention. A son needs to be admired and respected and instructed for manhood. They both need physical and spiritual care in an atmosphere of training or discipleship which includes appropriate discipline, correction and guidance in the Lord (Deut. 6:6). It is important to focus on discipleship, not just discipline. To the degree you disciple, you will have less need for discipline. The opposite is also true.

CHILDREN

The command for children to obey their parents in Eph. 6:1-3 is referring to younger children, not adult children. Loving but firm boundaries give children security. The rules must be few, fair and consistent. Both over-correction and under-correction produce the same negative results. Obedience to parents will hopefully prepare children to obey God in the future. A child's first impression of God is through his parents.

ADULT CHILDREN

Parents will always be the parents, but as children enter adulthood, the parents' function changes from parenting to friend, mentor or advisor (Jn. 2:1-5). Adult children must relate to their parents, adult-to-adult, no longer parent-to-child and likewise, parents to their adult children. The adult children must always remain respectful, but they are no longer responsible to obey their parents. Respect is an attitude of the heart, not obedience to parents' wishes or commands (Lynch, *Mending Fences*, p. 21-44).

Allow adult children to learn from their mistakes. Parents must evaluate if they are enabling them which actually disables them emotionally, mentally or financially. Give advice when asked and leave the decision to them. Not following parents' advice as an adult is not a sign of disrespect. It is a sign of adulthood. Avoid looking to your adult children for your emotional happiness. More keys can be found in the book on how to build better relationships with adult children, whether or not, they are still in the nest (Lynch, *Mending Fences Healing Hearts*).

COUPLES

There is much literature available on marriage for any couple who is motivated to have a happy and meaningful relationship. A husband is to study the life of Jesus and learn how to love his wife. As the primary leader of the family, he is to follow the example of Jesus with a towel around his waist as the lead servant. God designed his wife to be loved and cherished by him all her life. Love is unconditional. He is to grant her honor as a co-heir of the grace of life (I Pet. 3:7).

A wife has the privilege of respecting and admiring her husband. Respect is an attitude of the heart. She may find it hard to believe that he has a greater need for respect than for sex. And as with love, respect is unconditional. She may have to distinguish between his position and personality. But respect does not grant permission to be abused or treated as a doormat. Jesus never treated the church that way. He came to serve, not to be served (Matt. 20:28).

IN-LAWS

I'm married to a mother-in-law and she is fantastic! What is the circle of responsibility of in-laws? Communicate with adult children on an adult-to-adult level. Give them advice IF they ask for it. If they don't, ask for permission to share. This will open the door of their minds. Clarify each other's mutual expectations.

Maintain a clear slate through forgiveness. Do not build your emotional security around your child and his spouse. Love them with respect. Establish healthy boundaries. Learn to dispense your resources wisely, and grandparent wisely. Resolve all conflicts biblically, if possible. Respect their family rules and traditions. Resign any effort to control; that is God's responsibility.

EVALUATE OTHER RESPONSIBILITIES

It is important to define responsibilities if a child is born outside the marriage or to your single adult child. There could be custody issues and ex-spouses still have legal responsibilities. It is important in blended families to define roles and responsibilities. Failure to do so can create more conflict than necessary.

RESPONSIBILITIES CHANGE

While my dad was home in my early years, he provided for mom and us three boys. Years later he abandoned the family. Fifty plus years later he was in desperate condition as an alcoholic.

One year I sent him a Father's Day card after I found out where he lived. All I could say was, "Thank you for being my dad." I got a phone call immediately when he received that card. I made him an offer. If he would leave San Diego and move to Kansas City, I would take care of him on one condition: he would do what I say. I realized it was my responsibility to take care of my dad who was now in his 70's. The roles were reversed. I became the responsible adult.

He arrived drunk. I put him in the detox unit of the hospital for three weeks. He came out sober and moved in with us. I got him a volunteer job at the college where I served and a room in the single men's dorm. He began to thrive and reported that those were the best days of his life. I realized it was my responsibility to take care of my dad who was now in his 70's.

He was treated with dignity, but I was in charge. He was a very grateful man.

Job changes, debilitating illnesses, accidents, financial setbacks, tragedies and death are some of the reasons the responsibilities may need to be modified. If the kids divorce and abandon your grandkids, you may now have to raise them. Many retired couples have had to change roles to parent their abandoned grandchildren. Before you assume these responsibilities, there are at least five key questions you should honestly ask yourself before you assume others' responsibilities:

1. Do I have time to help this person or to work this problem out with them?
2. Do I have the authority necessary to help (legal, medically)?
3. Do I have the ability (physical, emotional, spiritual) to help?
4. Do I have the resources (financial) to help them out?
5. Am I helping them to do what they are fully capable of doing for themselves? Enabling them is the same thing as disabling them for life.

As for my dad, I had the time, ability and resources, but I did not have the authority. It had to be given, which he gladly gave. My brother did the same for our mother until she passed away at age 93.

Sometimes the circle of responsibility has to be firm; at other times, it must be flexible. Only God's Spirit and practical advice can lead you to be firm or flexible. There is always a need for shared responsibility. My wife would prefer not to cook AND do dishes. If she cooks, I do the dishes. If we have company coming, I ask her what she wants help with. That usually means I vacuum the house. But I have not been successful in getting her to mow the lawn.

AVOID TWO TRAPS

In assigning responsibility, there are at least two traps you may encounter. The first trap is blame-shifting. The blame-shifter's goal is to redirect his responsibility and project it on to others to avoid accountability, perceived failure, loss, guilt or shame. People will shrink their circle to the size of a golf ball and inflate others' to the size of a basketball. This is usually accompanied by manipulation, *false* guilt and shame. They take the attention and responsibility off themselves in order to avoid guilt, shame and loss of pride. Blame-shifting is like seeing your dirty face in a mirror and then washing the mirror. Jesus rebuked Peter for attempting to shift the focus off himself and on to John (Jn. 21:21,22). Blame-shifting is not new. Adam tried this with God regarding his responsibility for his sin in the Garden. He blamed his wife; then he blamed God for giving her to him (Gen. 3:12).

The second trap in assigning responsibilities is taking someone else's blame. If you are wrong, admit it, but if you are not wrong, reject accepting the blame. Often taking unnecessary blame is done to keep peace, but this kind of peace is only temporary. Chronic peace-keepers are susceptible to this trap. Women will tell me that they take the blame that is not theirs so that they can fix the relationship However, in time, they slowly become angry, resulting in bitterness, which may be more destructive in the end.

ASSUME RESPONSIBILITY

It is one thing to identify the needs and even assign responsibility for the parts of a conflict. Many believe if they accomplish this, the job is done. But here is the set-up for failure. We see this often in preaching.

If I were to speak on Father's Day on four important jobs of a father, I could see the faces of the men tracking with me. Then I close the message in prayer and receive appreciation for that timely message. The men go home and there is no change.

What did I fail to do? I failed to get a tangible commitment from them to assume their responsibility. Telling them they have the responsibility does not automatically translate into ownership and action. You can tell your kid he needs to clean up his bedroom. You have assigned it, but there is no commitment from him to do it. He may even know it needs to be done, "I know, Mom," is the normal response. But you can add "Can I count on you to get it done in the next two hours?" If he says, "Yes," you have assigned, and he has assumed.

At the end of my Father's Day sermon, as I close in prayer, I could ask the men if they will assume this responsibility by looking up at me, coming forward or signing a commitment card. Any of these would be appropriate. Often we preach that you should, ought or must do something, but it rarely happens because there is no commitment to assume what has been assigned.

In marriage counseling, I do the same thing. We identify the issues and responsibilities for the parts. Now comes the hard part: getting a verbal commitment from the couple that each one will assume what has been assigned. He may know he has failed to love her, and she to respect him. Now they know what they should do, but I must hear, "I will do what is in my circle to love her / to respect him." When one fails to assume his responsibility, he also forfeits the personal power he needs to work out the conflict. You cannot help a person who does not want to be helped, nor can you help someone who will not assume responsibility for his/her own attitudes and actions (Anderson, p.200).

ASSUME WHAT IS YOURS

Assume only what is legitimately in your own circle of responsibility before the Lord. Joshua is a classic example of this principle. Israel, as a nation, was going in the wrong direction away from the Lord. But Joshua stood tall as the leader of his family and boldly stated, "As for me and my house, we will serve the Lord" (Josh. 24:15). Anyone in his family or extended family who did not want to do so, had the freedom to leave. "My family, my rules." Joshua had fully understood what was involved and he was determined to follow through.

This is difficult for a person who gets his dysfunctional identity from fixing people. Some men marry women whom they want to rescue and fix. Often the rescuer loses interest in the marriage, then has an affair with another needy woman, and the cycle continues.

Controllers have the same problem. A controller will draw a large circle around himself, then manipulate others into his circle taking responsibility for them all, telling them what not to do, what to do and how to do it. Controllers become relational vacuums, sucking everyone and everything into their circles. He is *Lord of the Ring*.

At the root of the controlling pattern is fear and the need to prevent abandonment by others. This is coupled with an inordinate view of his own importance cemented in pride, "My way or the highway." This results in outbursts of anger when the controller cannot control or change things around him that he has no power over.

You can respectfully reject others' attempts to make you assume their responsibility, with a simple, "This is not my responsibility," "This will not work for me," or "I'm not willing to assume this responsibility." In the case of your boss, you can state, "I am willing to do this, but I cannot do both tasks. Which would you prefer me to do?" He may fire you and find someone else willing to expend themselves to please him. However, with a respectful servant's attitude, you may be surprised just how well this works. I experience this often with my office manager. There are many projects I want done so I pass them on to her.

Out of her maturity she tells me she is willing to do anything but physically cannot do everything. She respectfully asks me to prioritize. This works for her and it works for me. Something may come up that changes my priorities and she will ask, "Is this a new number ten?" Even in her flexibility, she cannot assume responsibility for everything I give her. Yet I am amazed how much she gets done when the priorities are clear.

Other than your boss or spouse, you owe no one an explanation for why you will not do something that is not your responsibility (Cloud, p. 97). You should not give an explanation if doing so could result in an argument. Your reasons could then become bullets in the other person's gun to be used against you. You can simply say, "I'm just not able to do this at this time." If they ask why, repeat the same statement with respect. They may respond sharply, "Just tell me why." You know now there is an argument about to erupt. They may try to guilt-trip or shame you. That is their choice. But you have the power in your own circle to say, "No." It is freeing to know that God gives you power *only* for your own personal responsibility.

People who assert that they cannot say, "No," are emotionally handicapped. Behind this character weakness is the fear of rejection, disappointment or even abandonment. When a person tells me they cannot say, "No," I ask them if they think they are responsible people. The answer is, "Yes." In fact, they tend to be over-responsible. Pleasers cannot say, "No," because of a lifetime of seeking human approval and a fear of disapproval. Chapter 15 explains how to correct this weakness.

A person's angry response to your, "No," may be a signal of their blame-shifting, manipulation or a refusal to assume their own legitimate responsibility. Blame shifting is not new. Cain shifted blame away from himself when God confronted him about his brother's murder (Gen. 4:9).

REASONS TO SAY NO

There are at least nine reasons to respectfully resist assuming others' responsibilities in order to hopefully try to accomplish the following:

- To make peace. This will only postpone the war.
- To avoid guilt feelings which only return later.
- To maintain a childish perspective which avoids growing up.
- To gain acceptance when enough is never enough.
- To avoid rejection which will only come back to you in another form.
- To please, but you can never please enough.
- To protect yourself only to be hurt worse later.
- To help others when they are fully capable of helping themselves. It will temporarily make you feel good but will only contribute to their irresponsibility.
- To give them what they want because you think that shows love. Love gives a person what he needs, not necessarily what is wanted. Fear gives a person what he wants but not what he needs.

When making a commitment of your word, Jesus simply said, "Let your *yes* mean *yes* and your *no* mean *no.*" "For whatever is more than these is from the evil one" (Matt. 5:37; CF Jam. 5:12).

To assume your legitimate responsibilities can be painful to your pride, especially when there has been a past habit of blame-shifting. Jesus pointed this out at the beginning of His ministry. If you are in the process of offering your sacrificial gift at the altar and there you remember that your brother has been offended by you, stop, leave your gift before the altar, go your way and be reconciled to your brother, if possible, and then return and present your gift" (Matt. 5:23,24). That is tough!

This is the only time this Greek form of the word, *reconcile,* is used in the New Testament. It implies a two-way reconciliation that will take work from both-parties. Assuming your part may be difficult especially if the other person is partially at fault or may have misunderstood you.

To humbly assume your responsibility and even admit when you are wrong greatly increases your feelings of being favored by God because "He opposes the proud [who rejects responsibility] but gives grace [favor, value] to the humble" [who assume responsibility] (I Pet. 5:5).

FULFILL YOUR RESPONSIBILITY

You have identified what the issues are. You have assigned the legitimate responsibilities. You have assumed your part, whether the other person did or not. Now comes the most important key to resolving conflict. Fulfill what is in your circle of responsibility. Obedience is the ultimate determination of failure or success. What will also work for our disciples is not what we do for them, but what *they* do themselves. James urged us to put into practice what was taught and not just be listeners, deceiving ourselves that listening is doing. Why? Because your obedience will be blessed by God (Jam. 1:22-25). No amount of church attendance, Bible study, mission trips or giving can replace obedience. Nancy (in Chapter 10) at the end of our counseling sessions, summarized the basis for her spiritual healing in one word, *obedience.*

When people say they do not believe counseling is helping, I simply ask what things that they agreed to are not working? In most cases, it is not the counseling, but their failure to fulfill what they agreed to do.

BENEFITS OF DOING

What are the benefits of fulfilling your circle of responsibility? When you clearly identify what is in your circle, you will have something to focus on for direction. You will know the next right thing to do. With this focus you now have a purpose in life. You lose your purpose when you do not understand your responsibility.

Another benefit is that you now have something tangible to do and you will begin to feel you have accomplished something each day. A sense of accomplishment is important to us. Otherwise, we will do a lot but feel we are not getting anywhere. You can say to yourself, "I have accomplished my responsibilities for this day." This gives a sense of security and contentment because you are at peace with yourself, *even if* nothing or no one around you changes.

RECONCILIATION IS NOT GUARANTEED

As you focus on and fulfill your responsibility, there is a good possibility that relationships will heal but healing is not a guarantee. Paul described for Timothy what people will be like before Jesus returns (2 Tim. 3:1-5). One characteristic is that they will be *irreconcilable.* The literal translation of this Greek phrase is, *without a libation,* or a drink offering. It is a word picture of two generals at war who decide to stop fighting and to make peace. They establish the conditions and seal the treaty by each pouring a cup of wine over an altar while facing one another. One general pours out his drink offering on the altar, but the other general decides he does not like the terms of the treaty and pours his drink offering on the ground. There is no drink offering (libation) to seal the agreement. They are irreconcilable.

Likewise, you can do all that is within your circle but the other person may refuse to do his part and reconciliation fails. Paul instructs a spouse who is married to an unbeliever to live with him. But if the unbeliever leaves, the spouse is free to let him go because God has called us to peace" (1 Cor. 7:15).

Some believing wives are bitter toward God because He did not change their husbands after all their hard work at reconciliation. They fail to remember that God has given people the power of choice. Is it His will the marriage stays intact? Yes. But not everyone wants to do the responsible thing to save a marriage. They still retain the power of choice, even if it means the destruction of the marriage.

Keep focusing on your circle of responsibility; then having done all that you could humanly do, stand firm (Eph. 6:13). Keep entrusting yourself to the sovereignty of your heavenly Father who judges righteously (I Pet. 2:23). Thank God that He will judge you only for your own circle of responsibility (2 Cor. 5:10). It may seem unfair if you are the only one being responsible, but life is unfair because Satan is temporarily in charge of this world. He definitely does not play fair (Eph. 2:2). Jesus was declared innocent seven times, then, killed.

FULFILL AND FORGIVE

You can be free by forgiving others for their failure to act responsibly. Send them and their sin over to the Lord Jesus and say, "Good bye." Forgiveness is for your benefit, not theirs. When you accept your responsibility and the consequence of their failure, then God can even use their failure to bless you. It may not happen in time, but you will have God's blessing for your obedience in Heaven forever.

One of the biggest contributing factors in a conflict is communication. Almost every couple I see will say from the start that their biggest problem is communication. However, it is not communication, per se, but *how* they communicate. How can you learn to communicate AND fight fairly? Let's see!

228

Chapter 12
WORK OUT YOUR CONFLICTS

• God knows conflicts will happen.

• Conflicts can be painful.

• Conflicts can be complicated.

• God established the principle of personal responsibility.

• Identify what actually happened or is happening in the conflict.

• God only gives grace for truth.

• Honestly face the four guards hiding reality.

• Assign responsibility for the parts of the conflict.

• Realize responsibilities do change.

• Avoid the traps of blame-shifting and blame-taking.

• Assume your responsibilities.

• There are nine reasons to say, "No."

• Fulfill what is in your circle of responsibility.

• Realize the benefits of being responsible.

• Reconciliation is not guaranteed.

Chapter 12
SMALL GROUP QUESTIONS

1. How have you worked through conflict with others? When did you come to a point in the conflict where you did not know what to do next?

2. In past or present conflicts, how difficult is it to discover the truth and discuss it?

3. Why do you think it is so difficult for people to assign legitimate responsibility to others for their part in the conflict?

4. What experience have you had with a person who constantly shifts blame off himself on to others?

5. What have you done when others attempted to place responsibility on you that is not yours?

6. How have you assumed a responsibility that belonged to God? What did you do when you realized it? When others attempted to do what was in God's circle of responsibility, what was the result?

7. What is the hardest responsibility you have had to assume? How painful was it for you to assume it?

8. How have you felt personally empowered when you did fulfill what was in your circle of responsibility?

9. What relationship have you restored or maintained by fulfilling what is in your circle of responsibility?

10. What personal benefits did you experience by fulfilling your personal responsibilities?

11. How have you done everything in your power to heal a relationship and it was not healed? How did you respond? How has your life been different since then?

12. What losses or consequences have you experienced by doing the right thing? What did God teach you through that?

Chapter 13
ESTABLISH FAIR FIGHTING RULES

If you were a fly on the wall in my office you would hear words like, "We just can't talk," "There is no talking to him," "We always get into a big fight," "He just walks away," "We can't have a civil conversation," "She just gets angry." These are statements from those caught in a web of verbal conflict who feel there is no escape.

I love it when a couple starts off by stating that they just cannot communicate. They have been married 25 years and it is hard to believe they have not talked in 25 years. They do communicate, but their communication style fails to get their words heard and understood. The solution is not complicated. They are playing the same game, but each one has a different rule book.

Every relationship is bound to have conflicts including arguments in the home, on the job, in the church or with extended family. Dr. John Friel states that couples who never fight are in as much trouble as couples who fight destructively. Why? Because we are human beings with different needs, wants, values, tastes and beliefs and, therefore, fighting will occur. In truth, there are no couples who do not fight. Some couples just do it so covertly and craftily that we cannot see it, and they are not aware of it. If you put any two people together for any reasonable length of time, conflict will arise (Friel, Adult Child's Guide, p. 169).

There is no such thing as a compatible couple. Relational studies indicate that happy and unhappy couples have a similar number of irreconcilable differences. They argue about the same things (money, sex, household chores, work obligations, kids, priorities, vacations). Most of the issues are never resolved and many surveys on marital problems list communication as the *most common problem*.

WHY SO MANY CONFLICTS?

GENDER DIFFERENCES

Gender differences contribute to frustration in communication. Men tend to emphasize logic and minimize feelings. Women tend to use feelings to express themselves. The longer women talk about an issue, the better they feel, whereas the longer men have to talk, the more they feel the relationship is in trouble. Neither form of communication is wrong. A healthy relationship tries to understand and appreciate each other's way of expressing themselves.

CULTURAL DIFFERENCES

Different cultural backgrounds can contribute to communication conflicts. An Italian family may communicate with strong volume and emotion. Those with an Asian heritage may talk in soft tones with emotional control. North Americans may speak more directly, Germans friends tend to be very frank while Latins are more indirect. Direct talk could be interpreted as rash, disrespectful, even arrogant.

These are not necessarily wrong ways to communicate, but each culture has what it considers normal. When marrying cross-culturally, one must understand they are marrying a culture, not just a person. Failure to recognize the individual communication styles may result in marital conflict rather than mutually blending and celebrating the best of both cultures.

BIRTH FAMILY DIFFERENCES

Suppose a wife's family of origin talked openly about everything but her husband's family was more private and emotions were avoided. In a dysfunctional family, there are three very important rules: Don't talk (keep secrets). Don't trust (you'll get hurt). Don't feel (expressing emotions is not acceptable).

Life experiences in the birth family can make communication difficult. She may have experienced abuse and rejection, like Jenny, and carried a lot of emotional baggage into the relationship. He, on the other hand, may have experienced warm acceptance in his family. Whatever you experience growing up is what you tend to think is normal, and you might reproduce it in your present relationship, though it may be hurtful to the other person.

ESTABLISH THE RULES

Regardless of the differences, every relationship needs to establish and agree on fair communication rules to communicate well. In marriage, this should ideally be decided before you say, "I do." It is a must for premarital counseling. God sets forth His plan for marriage in His Word, not to inhibit pleasure but to increase marital enjoyment. Marriage was His idea. These same rules work in every relationship: parent to child, brother to sister, employer to employee.

All games have rules which the players agree on before they play. The Apostle Paul commented to Timothy, "If anyone competes in athletics, he is not crowned unless he competes according to the rules" (II Tim. 2:5). The Ten Commandments were God's *game plan* for Israel to establish and maintain a relationship with Him.

If a relationship is going to be mutually satisfying, you cannot just make up your own rules to suit your agenda. Wedding vows are the rules that were mutually agreed upon.

When a couple is in conflict, they should remember what they promised each other at the wedding. This is why rules are provided for a game *before* it is played. Paul stated, "Fulfill my joy by being like-minded, having the same (standard for) love, being of one accord, of one mind" (Phil. 2:2).

I have four grandchildren and five great-grandchildren. At times they like to change the rules in the middle of the game. If they are young, we let them, but as they get older, we play by the rules. Adults sometimes attempt to do the same thing the grandkids did, especially if they are angry or believe they are losing an argument. "There is a way [to communicate] which seems right to a man [at the time], but the end [result of that communication style] is the way of death" [more distancing and withdrawing] (Proverbs 14:12). It is the fool who thinks he is right all the time (Proverbs 12:15a). He believes he is entitled to talk, argue or debate any way he wants.

DEFINITION OF INSANITY

If you continue to communicate in the way you always have, you will always get the same results. This is insanity and also reflects immaturity. Most couples who are at a point of divorce are usually deeply involved in highly repetitive and dysfunctional patterns of communication (arguing). It is not the fact that couples argue that determines whether the future is bleak or bright. Researchers can watch a couple arguing and predict in 15 minutes with great accuracy who will or will not be together in five years. Four of these negative patterns are as follows:

- Blame-shifting instead of taking personal responsibility.
- Patterns of escalation in volume and intensity instead of controlling emotions without raising one's voice.
- Invalidation (name-calling) instead of maintaining mutual respect without expressing disgust or efforts to demean the other person.

• Withdrawing (avoidance) instead of staying engaged in the discussion.

Building relational harmony must start with your conscious decision to choose to communicate differently than you have in the past. I agree with Dr. Paul Meier, "happiness is a choice," in choosing to communicate differently than you have in the past (Rom. 12:18). Changing a few communication patterns and understanding the thinking behind them can make a huge difference in relationships.

What are ten basic communication rules (tools) that can get you talking in a more healthy, positive way? Prepare to add your own rules that reflect Scripture in principle or precept.

I. STOP INTERRUPTING, START LISTENING

When Greg and Sandi made their appointment, they were desperate. They felt they could not go on. This was their last stop before divorce court. I've heard the same thing hundreds of times. "We just can't talk without it growing into a full-blown fight." I expressed appreciation to them for taking the big step in getting some serious coaching. However, they even began to get into a fight while telling me why they can't talk to each other.

I quickly injected myself into their *dialog* and explained that in my office we communicate respect-to-respect. Our first communication tool is: "Stop interrupting, talking over each other or cutting each other off. Start concentrating on listening to understand what is actually being said."

"Impossible!" was written all over their faces. I read two verses to set the stage, "Be kindly affectionate to one another with brotherly love, in honor, giving preference to one another (Rom. 12:10). "Let every man be swift to hear [and understand], slow to speak" (Jam. 1:19). Because actions come from the heart, there must be a change in the heart (attitude) first. So, I asked if they would commit themselves to obeying God's Word from the heart and start with granting mutual respect. Success in any counseling or discipleship effort is based on one word, *obedience*.

They are Christians and surely they would say, "Yes" because they are supposed to. But what they did not know is that I would remind them of their commitment many times. It would not be easy to keep, but their affirmation of where they wanted to *Be* in their communication, was a start. Now I needed to explain some details.

Talking is not Listening. Talking over someone is an indication that little or no effort is being made to understand. Instead, it may be a desire to win an argument, to defend, to control the conversation or to punish in anger. Talking over someone is such a crucial issue that James addressed it in the first New Testament book written, "Be swift to hear [and understand], slow to speak" (Jam. 1:19). The word, *swift*, means quick, speedy, and in this case, to accelerate listening efforts. Concentrate on understanding what is actually being said.

Good communicators are good listeners. The first step of good communication is to become a good listener with the goal of understanding: getting the facts straight, seeking to learn, maintaining an open mind, trying to understand the other person's feelings or point of view.

Most of us can listen faster than people talk. That is because God wants us to put some mental energy into slowing down our response and our effort into understanding what is being said. When it is your turn to listen, *really listen*. This demonstrates to others value and acceptance. Interrupting conveys disrespect and rejection.

One Talks, One Listens. The American Indians, in speaking to each other in a group, would allow only one person to talk at a time. To make this happen, they developed the *talking stick* tool. The one holding the stick had permission to talk and all others had to listen. When it was another's turn to speak, the first speaker would pass the stick to the next person. It is God's goal to get the talking stick out of your hand as fast as possible in order to listen. "Be quick to listen [pass the stick] and slow to speak" [hold the stick] (Jam. 1:19).

Waiting for a person to complete his thoughts takes a great deal of patience and self-control (Gal. 5:23) and demonstrates respect and honor for others. It would be a practical way of showing love, honor and preference to one another (Rom. 12:10).

Patience and self-control are fruit of the Holy Spirit (Gal. 5:22,23). If you are filled (controlled) with the Holy Spirit, both these qualities will be evident in your communication. Impatience and impulsive talking is indicative of the flesh in control which results in the deterioration of relationships (Gal. 5:19-21).

Jumping to a conclusion is the most dangerous jump you can make in relationships. Your task is to stop making quick assumptions. "Do you see a man that is hasty [quick] in his words? There is more hope for a fool [getting it right] than for him" (Prov. 29:20). The number one complaint in communication is that the other person is not listening, only reacting.

Tolerating is not Listening. Failing to appropriately respond to a reasonable attempt to talk is the opposite of interrupting. A passive person will do this to control or to punish. Giving an appropriate nod from time to time communicates you are listening and making an effort to understand. It is important to look at the speaker and to communicate that you are engaged.

Tolerating (stonewalling, shutting down, withdrawing) is one of the four indicators that can predict the end of a marriage or significant relationship. Three other negative patterns are criticism, contempt and defensiveness.

Not only are you to pay attention to the words spoken, you must also learn to read body language. Sandi would tell Greg, "It looks like you are angry" and he would respond, "No, I'm not." She would insist, "Yes, you are." She was listening to his tone of voice and watching his facial expression which confirmed his anger.

Tolerating fails to acknowledge the other person's perspective. Acknowledging another does not mean you are agreeing but it allows you to acknowledge his perspective which is his reality. This gives you the opportunity to learn because words are only seven percent of communication.

Preparing a Defense is not Listening. Because we can listen faster than the other person can talk, that ability should be redirected to listening and understanding. Do not allow yourself to think about what you will say before you have listened and confirmed that what you understood was correct. You clarify by mirroring back what you believe you heard. This is not easy. It will require effort and concentration.

If you may need a moment to think about what is being said, then say, "I need a minute to think about this." "A person [parent, spouse] who answers a matter before listening [and understanding] it is folly [foolish] and a source of shame to him" (Prov. 18:13).

Defenders tend to lose because they are not good listeners, and out of fear, are focusing on their defense instead of listening to understand. Rarely are points scored by defenders. Usually the only things being defended are pride and the need to win or control.

If an explanation would be helpful for the other person's understanding, offer to explain either now or later the reason for your action or decision. Let the other person choose the time to hear your explanation. An offended person may not be open to hear your explanation at that moment. Occasionally, when you give him the choice, his curiosity may prompt him to ask for the explanation right then.

Mature, secure people listen to understand, and immature people interrupt in order to control or to gain more advantage because of fear and selfishness. The Hebrew word for understand is *hearing*. Listen to King Solomon's prayers as he began his reign, "Therefore, give your servant [Solomon] an understanding [lit. hearing] heart to judge your people, that I may discern between good and evil. For who is able to judge this great people of yours?" (I Kin. 3:9)

By learning to listen and understand you will learn to talk *with* people and not *at* them. Choose to avoid lectures, monologues, forced late night arguments and marathons. These are forms of control and verbal abuse which often result in invalidating others' opinions or perspectives. Talking at others is self-centered and conveys that their opinions are not significant to you.

Your task is to make each sentence simple, clear and direct, speaking calmly, clearly and confidently. What distracts you from listening to others is a focus on your own point, deciding that you already know what the other person is about to say and twisting the other's conversation to fit your own expectation. You can show that you are listening by being silent, pausing before speaking, making eye contact, physically turning toward the person, uncrossing your arms and nodding when appropriate (Mason, p. 131).

Our teenage daughter asked if she could talk to me while I was reading the newspaper. I said, "Sure, what's up?" She responded, "Dad, put down the newspaper." I could have listened and looked at the paper. But to her, I was not listening. In reality, she was right. You show respect to the person talking to you by looking at them and not the cell phone, TV or other distraction.

2. STOP NAME CALLING, START ENCOURAGING

Calling each other negative names tears down the person's worth and value. Instead, use words that reflect mutual respect, value and love. You may disagree with their opinion, but you are responsible to respond in honor and respect. You are talking to someone who is as valuable in God's sight as you are. Honor is an attitude of the heart, not necessarily agreement with them (I Pet. 3:7; Rom. 12:10, 13:7).

Calling each other negative names is an obvious sign that the initial issue has been abandoned, an argument is escalating and the relationship is deteriorating. This is usually the time when couples come for counseling because it is very hard to rebound. The Apostle Peter, who was married, may have known from personal experience why the Holy Spirit led him to write, *Be sure each one of you agree on how you are going to relate to each other, being sensitive to each other's feelings like you would with a brother or sister you deeply love. Be tender with each other with mutual respect. How? Do not return an evil verbal response when you are given one but figure out how to bless the other by doing or saying something beneficial to them. You are called by God to inherit a special blessing from God if you do* (I Pet. 3:8,9 paraphrased). If this one principle was kept, most arguments would cease and relationships would be transformed.

What if you don't use this tool? As the argument and relationship escalate, both parties have unintentionally turned themselves over to Satan and they will then begin to do Satan's destructive work for him. "Be angry and do not sin; do not let the sun go down on your wrath, or give place to the devil" (Eph. 4:26,27). When you give yourself over to be the mouthpiece of Satan the words that come out are designed to kill, steal and destroy (John 10:10). You become a verbal terrorist. "There is one who speaks like the piercing of a sword to cut someone down" (Prov. 12:18).

Calling each other names is a defensive tactic designed to avoid facing the current issue and bringing it to closure. It is a distraction from the real issue. That is why Greg and Sandi never settled an issue. They would start with one issue, then resort to calling each other names. The issue was not really the issue. Destroying the other person was.

Name calling is usually done when one has a weak position, feels he/she is losing in the discussion or is angry and wants to inflict emotional pain. God is clear about the sin of calling each other destructive names, "Let no corrupt [unwholesome] word proceed out of your mouth" (Eph. 4:29). The word, *corrupt*, means rotten like rotten fish or fruit. Rotten words come from what is in the heart. "A good man, out of the treasures of his heart, brings forth good; and an evil man, out of the evil treasures of his heart, brings forth evil. For out of the abundance of the heart, the mouth speaks" (Luke 6:45). The source of the damaging words is the heart, not the lips. The lips do not have a brain. Just changing the behavior, and not the heart (control center), is a temporary fix that will revert sooner or later to what is in the heart.

There are at least three stages of an argument that if continued, will result in the end of the relationship:

• An argument starts with an issue that never gets resolved.

• The argument degenerates to picking on each other, jumping from one issue to another, name calling or bringing up history to hurt the other person.

• If the argument escalates, they start questioning the relationship (separation or divorce) and insecurity and distancing step in.

Calling each other negative names can be a selfish attempt to control by shaming. It is unjustified shame because Jesus took our shame (Heb. 12:2).

Name calling is a form of verbal cannibalism or terrorism. "But if you bite [with your words] and devour one another, take care that you are not consumed by one another" (Gal. 5:15). Verbal cannibalism explains why relationships can become ugly. Literal cannibalism was done with the belief that if they ate their enemy, they could get their enemy's power. It goes back to a power struggle for control.

When you view the other person as an enemy, you will try to crush him. Now Satan can walk away and let people turned enemies hurt and destroy each other. They will do Satan's dirty work for him (Smalley, p. 156). "The tongue is a fire, a world of iniquity. The tongue is so set among our members that it defiles the whole body and sets on fire the course of nature, and it is set on fire by hell" (Jam. 3:6 NKJ).

In contrast, "Pleasant words are like a honeycomb, sweetness to the soul and health to the bones" (Prov. 16:24). "A word spoken in season, how good it is" (Prov. 15:23). Your choice is to be a builder of people or destroyer of lives with your words.

3. AVOID ISSUE-HOPPING, STAY FOCUSED

One reason arguments continue for hours is that a couple may begin with, "You keep losing the car keys," then, "Look who leaves drinking glasses all over the house," to "Look who is never ready on time." They hop from one issue to another. It happens with spouses, kids, friends, co-workers, in almost every relationship. This also includes going to the history channel. "Do you remember when you....?" Or blame-shifting, "Look who's talking!"

Issue-hopping avoids staying focused on the issue at hand out of feelings of guilt, the fear of losing an argument or the desire for revenge. Often people cannot remember what started the original argument because they hopped from one issue to another. This results in 20-30 years of accumulated unresolved issues, never bringing any one to a satisfying settlement.

When discussing an issue, if another topic is brought up, acknowledge it and write it down. Then, make a commitment to return later to address it. Avoid the trap of getting distracted from the current topic. Issue-hopping is a debate tool to remove focus from oneself on to someone else One way to reduce this dysfunctional behavior is to make an effort to verbally acknowledge the other person's position but stay focused on the current issue. Many long arguments are an attempt to get one person to acknowledge the other person's position. Acknowledgement does not mean agreement, but it communicates that you have at least heard the other's perspective. Simply acknowledging the existence of their position is a very positive step forward. You can simply say, "I acknowledge your position and I will seriously consider it." "You have really given me something to think about." "I would like to think about this and get back to you."

People who are controllers refuse to acknowledge another's position because they believe it gives the other person power they do not want them to have. No one can take away your personal power of control because self-control is a fruit of the Holy Spirit (Gal. 5:22,23). God's Spirit will keep you from losing your personal power. A communication tool referred to by many writers is to paraphrase (or mirror) in your own words what you heard someone say without judging, evaluating, correcting or interrupting. Repeating the key points back to the speaker shows that you want to understand what is being said.

Dr. David Augsburger explains what this looks like. "I want to hear you accurately so I'll need to check out what I heard at crucial points to be as sure as I can that my meanings match your meanings. I get an idea of what your meanings are from your words, your tone of voice, your facial gestures and body movements. But it is only an idea. I must check it out at times by replaying what I heard for your approval, until you agree that you have been heard. I want to hear deeply, accurately, clearly enough that I am able to some real extent, feel what you feel, hurt a little where you hurt" (Augsburger, p. 23). Dr. Mike Firmin would say, "Help me see this the way you see it." But it is important that you do this with an open, accepting face, not with squinted eyes or furrowed brows. With your facial expression, you want to sincerely honor another by clarifying what he is saying.

What are some simple statements you can make to reflect this tool?

"Am I hearing you say....?"

"Am I hearing you right?"

"Did you say ...?"

By allowing the listener to repeat the speaker's words, the speaker can affirm that the listener heard him correctly.

Speaker to listener: "Yes, I believe you heard me correctly."

When I have used this tool with couples, parents and kids, or feuding relatives, the results have been amazing. What I often hear is, "I did not know you felt that way." Why? They were either talking over each other or issue-hopping and escalating emotionally, not thinking rationally enough to hear the other person.

Reflective listening helps the speaker to continue to clarify his statements and reduces lecturing which is ineffective because there is little or no opportunity to clarify and settle the issue. If you were to listen to conversations around our office, you would often hear, "Am I hearing you say....?" This one tool has greatly reduced potential conflict because of misunderstanding.

4. STOP OUTBURSTS OF ANGER, STAY IN CONTROL

Loud, angry outbursts tend to shut down the flow of communication. At the point when anger escalates, the relationship begins to degenerate. Instead, focus on keeping control of your own emotions and continue to speak in mutually respectful tones. "A soft answer turns away wrath, but a harsh word stirs up strife" (Prov. 15:1).

The most common reasons for the outbursts of anger are to control, change, manipulate, avoid responsibility, avoid guilt feelings, remove perceived obstacles or exact revenge.

When someone raises their voice to communicate a point, drop your voice to just above a whisper. They will have to drop their voice in order to hear you. They may even feel shame for their outbursts when you remain calm, accepting and willing to listen. You will be amazed who is really in control of the conversation. No one else can make you give up your power of self-control.

Anger can result in making bad decisions that we regret later. People refer to out-of-control anger as a *dumbing* emotion. Moses lost the privilege of going into the Promised Land because he was angry at the people for complaining that they had no water. God told Moses to speak to a rock and water would flow out. But in his anger toward the people, he struck the rock twice. In reality, he probably wanted to strike the people (Num. 20:10; Deut. 32:48, 50-52). It is like an angry man punching a hole in the wall with his fist, seriously damaging his hand and wrist. Psychologists call that behavior displaced anger. They want to hit the person but they hit the wall instead.

Anger injects fear in the listener which shuts down the mind and prevents hearing and responding. When parents yell at their children it instills fear which causes the child's brain to shut down to protect itself. James warns that the anger of man (or parents) does not produce the righteousness of God (Jam. 1:20). Dr. Scott Stanley points out that all people, happy or unhappy, argue, but the future of the relationship does not hinge on *what* they argue about but *how they* manage their negative emotions such as anger and fear.

245

5. AVOID PUSHING HOT BUTTONS

Hot buttons are like triggers that inflict emotional pain. Pushing a person's hot buttons is meant to hurt them in a sensitive area. Avoid escalating an argument by blurting out sweeping generalizations that are intended to push hot buttons.

- You ... "You think you know better."
- You always ... "You are always playing your computer games."
- You never ... "You never carry your load."
- You must ... "You must think you are always right."
- If only ... "If only you would not have done that."
- You shouldn't ... "You shouldn't feel that way."

The word *you* in this context is a shaming word. No one feels good when they are shamed. If you want distance in the relationship, this will do it. To have a mutually fulfilling, meaningful relationship, stop this practice now!

Hot buttons can be used to remind the other person of his past failures, weaknesses, forgiven sins or lingering grudges. If the past issues have been forgiven, you have no business going to the history channel and bringing up old issues against the person again. Forgiveness is not forgetting, but it is a commitment not to bring up forgiven issues again. Ezekiel wrote concerning a forgiven person that, "None of the sins he has committed will be remembered against him" (Ezk. 33:16). It would be appropriate if it is mutually agreeable, to discuss a past event for understanding, clarifying or affirming forgiveness.

Bringing up a forgiven event instills false guilt in the person whom God has forgiven and cleansed. The forgiven offender is responsible to rebuild trust, but in doing so he is not to be manipulated or reminded of his forgiven offense. That is like holding a club over his head and threatening to harm him emotionally if he does not do what you want. *Clubs* are ineffective on those who understand forgiveness and their position in Christ as a saint, a holy one, chosen and set apart for God. Believers are referred to as saints at least 60 times in the New Testament. That is our identity, not our past failures.

If a past issue has not been dealt with biblically, select a time to discuss it and do whatever it takes to settle it. Denial of an issue is not a healthy choice. Some issues take longer to process than others, adultery being one of the most difficult, but it is not impossible. Shelia, who is one of our counselors, had to process the deep pain of her husband's affair. They both would acknowledge there are still issues they deal with, but these are much less painful than they were 20 years ago.

The alternative is to use others' hot buttons to stimulate fear, guilt or shame in them which causes distancing in the relationship. Some of those fears are:

- Fear of rejection
- Fear of abandonment
- Fear of not being loved
- Fear of not being heard or validated
- Fear of failure
- Fear of ultimatums (threats of divorce or leaving)

These fears reduce one's ability to give and receive love. Love drives out fear, and fear drives out love (I John 4:18). No one feels loved who is managed by fear.

It is the responsibility of the one possessing the hot buttons to disconnect them. If a person brings up a past, shameful event, and it pushes your hot button, he did not create it. How can you cut the wires to that button? By processing the past event so that the memory of it does not control or define you. Then others can push it all they want, and it should not affect you negatively. If something gets thrown up to you again that has been forgiven (at least by God), you are free to say matter of factly, "Yes, that was wrong," and drop it.

Because you are thoroughly cleansed by the blood of Christ, you are totally forgiven and are now sparkling clean (I John 1:9). Others can say you are still *dirty*, but you know the truth and you stand spotless before them. They may remind you that you were *dirty*, but you need to remind yourself of the two-gun analogy we discussed about living with memories. Others will be tempted to bring up the left gun representing the sin, but you have tied the two guns together, and you remember what you did with that sin. It is confessed, forgiven and thoroughly cleansed. The hot button has power if you bring only the memory of the sin and fail to bring up what you did with it. If you put this two-gun principle into practice, you have just cut the wires, and the button of manipulation no longer works.

Spending a lot of energy trying to prevent others from pushing your hot buttons is a waste of time! You have the power of self-control, not people-control, which frees you to be led by the Spirit of God (Rom. 8:14) and not by the manipulation of others. Yes, others should live out their biblical truths, but that is their choice. You are not powerless when they fail to use their tools.

6. STOP SIGNS OF DISGUST

Without even saying a word disgust can communicate disrespect. Disgust is the opposite of honor. Dr. John Friel indicates that body posture, tone of voice, facial expressions and gestures make up at least 80 percent of emotional communication between people (Friel, p. 129). How have physical signs of disgust affected you?

- Deep sighs
- Rolling of the eyes
- Frowning
- Hands on hips
- Finger pointing
- Crossing arms

- Throwing up hands
- Avoiding eye contact
- Abruptly walking away

This dishonoring behavior may be done so naturally, you do not even know you are doing it. Once you realize it, take responsibility to confess it as sin and purpose to show honor which is an attitude of the heart. It does not mean the other person deserves it. Just as love is unconditional, so is honor. In choosing to honor and respect, you can disagree and even say, "No" respectfully.

7. STOP WITHDRAWING, STAY ENGAGED

One of the most painful things especially for women, is when someone they care for withdraws, pouts or uses the silent treatment. This dysfunctional behavior may be designed to protect from being hurt again or to punish emotionally by withdrawing love, care, admiration and fellowship.

Although we hurt God by our sinful behavior, He never withdraws His love. Naturally, He is grieved by our sin (Eph. 4:30), but He does not take away His Holy Spirit from us. King David experienced that fear in when he prayed, "Do not take Your Holy Spirit from me," (Psalm 51:11) after his adultery with Bathsheba. In the Old Testament, God gave His Spirit to accomplish a specific task, but in the New Testament, His Spirit comes into our lives as a permanent resident (1 Cor. 3:16).

God disciplines us when we sin, but that is intended to correct behavior, not to punish behavior (Heb. 12:6). The reproofs of life are designed to teach us. They are learning experiences (Prov. 6:23). God will let us experience the consequences of our behavior (Gal. 6:7) which are the results of choice.

Wives and daughters have a strong need to be with and stay connected to their husbands and fathers. Withdrawing emotionally and relationally causes deep wounds and is usually done to punish, inflict pain or gain attention. This is sin!

Suppose a mother gets upset with her married daughter and to punish her, chooses not to call as regularly as she has done in the past. What should the daughter do? She can call her mother as if nothing happened (Christ-likeness) or wait until her mother calls and answer with a cheerful greeting. She can say she missed hearing from her and ask how she has been. If the daughter is happy and cheerful, she has not rewarded her mother's immature behavior that was intended to hurt or manipulate.

Manipulation only works if there is a hook inside of you for acceptance and approval. If you are secure in your personal relationship with Christ and clearly know who you are in Him, the attempt to manipulate will fail. Behavior that is not rewarded tends to diminish. The mother may try something else to manipulate, but a clear understanding of one's position in Christ will disarm any further attempts of emotional manipulation. In effect, the hot button has been disarmed.

On the other hand, the daughter could go to the mother and speak to her adult-to-adult and respectfully ask what is behind her behavior. The daughter is not pleading for her mother's acceptance or love. It is not a matter of the daughter panicking because her mom is upset. She is seeking to understand what is behind the behavior and if there is an offense that needs to be dealt with biblically (Matt. 18:15).

8. STOP WALKING AWAY

To walk away from a discussion without reaffirming your return is a form of abandonment and shaming (Friel, p. 130). It is different if one fears for their physical safety.

Do not follow the other person around from room to room if they have called for a time-out. Following from room to room is often done by one who cannot stand to leave an issue unsettled or because the person pursued is rarely willing to revisit the issue later; thus, it does not get settled. Following someone around or just dropping the issue without settling it is not healthy and does not reflect spiritual maturity.

When a person is done talking, he is done talking. You must respect his boundary. Domestic violence is sometimes triggered by the failure of one person to allow the other to call a time-out. He feels trapped and comes out pushing, biting or hitting, which is wrong.

Declaring a temporary time-out can be a helpful tool to prepare your heart and mind to return to the discussion in a calmer frame of mind. It gives you an opportunity to cool off and rethink what is taking place and what is important. It is your task to plan a *reconciliation conversation* after a period of cooling down. Often the issue is not the issue. There may be something deeper behind the current situation. Discovering this is not easy, but it is very important.

Taking a time-out can help you calm down and allow yourself to return to clear thinking. If you remove yourself, state, "I need a time-out to calm down so I can think, but I will come back." Some couples can agree to take a break and revisit the issue at the next mutually convenient time, perhaps the next evening after the kids are in bed. Anger may block the rational thinking process and words said in anger are usually damaging, so it is important to honor the other person's need for time-out and space.

Commit to yourself to deal with the issue. Failure to do so will allow the issue to either grow into a monster or accumulate unbearable baggage. You may need to designate a specific time (a fight night) each week to handle sensitive issues. Avoid the *all-the-time and any-place* approach to resolving arguments. This makes it difficult to relax out of fear that another argument will erupt any time and continue indefinitely.

Mutually agree on a time and place to meet to discuss things that bother you. Do not do this on a date night, family night or any other socially enjoyable occasion, and especially not during a time of intimacy. These times should be off limits for conflict resolution. While working through an issue, it is always a healthy activity to celebrate and remember what attracted you to each other in the first place.

There may be a need to bring in a third party to help with the reconciliation process. The Apostle Paul encouraged the church family in Philippi to do this for Euodia and Synthche to help settle their differences (Phil. 4:3). He tried to enlist help from a wise brother in Philippi to arbitrate between those going to court with a fellow believer (I Cor. 6:1-7).

Surprisingly, conflict can deepen relationships and even foster a better quality of intimacy with couples when they stay engaged in the process and choose not to walk away. Greater understanding gained by working through a conflict can draw people closer together.

9. STOP ALL PHYSICAL ATTACKING

It cannot be stressed enough not to allow any shoving, biting, poking, throwing things, slamming doors or physically restraining another adult. One husband pointed his index finger at his wife and she bit it. Both acts were wrong, as would be taking another's car keys or preventing them from walking out the door. They are adults and their power of choice needs to be respected.

10. MUTUALLY AGREE ON THE RULES

Purpose to agree on these and any other communication rules that you may add. Scripture urges us to be of *one mind* or in agreement on important matters. "Fulfill my joy by being like-minded, having the same love, being of one accord, of one mind" (Phil. 2:2).

Take these rules seriously with heart-felt conviction and review them when things are calm. It is important to acknowledge and confess when you have violated your rules and to ask for forgiveness. But first state, "I was wrong for ...."

Allow the kids to know you have established your own communication rules. Ask them what they think of them and how they would adjust or add to them. Attempt to guide your kids to understand them or you can call a family meeting and share you feel the need to establish some communication rules and ask for their input. You will be surprised how many of their suggested rules will mirror yours. Then you can share your rules and blend them together.

Post the rules in a visible place, perhaps on the refrigerator door, as a constant reminder of what you agreed to, just like board game rules. Once you have established and adopted your rules, learned from them, and implemented them in your relationships, you become equipped to share with others how they work and how beneficial they are towards a better quality of life.

START SLOWLY

Be patient with yourself. It is better to select one or two communication keys and do them consistently rather than to try to do all ten and apply them only halfway. When you fail to keep them, simply state, "Excuse me, I was wrong for...." Then, resume using the tools. These will help you experience a more meaningful quality of life.

Conflicts can raise a whole range of emotions that are negative. How do you end the control of the negative emotions that have been so much a part of your life? It is possible. Now, learn how to do it.

Chapter 13
ESTABLISH FAIR FIGHTING RULES

• Choose to communicate in a healthy way.

• Stop interrupting and start listening.

• Stop name calling and start encouraging.

• Stop issue-hopping and start focusing.

• Acknowledge each other's perspectives.

• Mirror back what you have heard.

• Stop outbursts of anger; start controlling yourself.

• Stop pushing hot buttons; start focusing.

• Stop showing signs of disgust; start honoring.

• Stop withdrawing; stay engaged.

• Stop walking away; start reassuring.

• Stop inappropriate physical contact; start caring.

• Mutually negotiate the rules.

• Post your fair fighting rules visibly.

Chapter 13
SMALL GROUP QUESTIONS

1. How has it been difficult to communicate with someone who is important to you because of personality, gender, cultural or birth family differences?

2. What communication styles have you used in the past that you have found that were ineffective? What made you change them?

3. What have you done that has helped you to prevent interrupting or talking over someone? How did you learn to do that?

4. How have you been hurt in the past by someone who has called you a negative name?

5. What was the most positive thing someone said to you? If appropriate, what was the most negative thing said to you and how did it affect you?

6. How would staying focused on one issue at a time improve your relationships?

7. What hot buttons have you had and how have you disconnected them?

8.- What non-verbal forms of disgust have you used and what have you done to correct them?

9. How has someone withdrawing from you affected you? How did you respond? If it was corrected, how did that pattern change?

10. How has a third party helped you with a conflict with someone?

11. How do you think your relationships would improve if you and others agreed on these or similar communication rules?

Chapter 14
GAIN CONTROL OVER
NEGATIVE EMOTIONS - PART I

LEARN FROM THE SHUTTLE

On February 1, 2003, the Space Shuttle *Columbia*, disintegrated over Texas, USA, during re-entry into the earth's atmosphere. All seven crew members died shortly before it was scheduled to conclude its 28th mission. Of all of Columbia's debris that was scattered over three states, the one thing officials wanted most to recover was the *black box* or flight recorder. By analyzing it, they hoped to determine what went so terribly wrong before it blew up. They wanted to answer the big *Why* question.

God has designed a *flight recorder* in us. He calls it the heart (lit. mind). You are warned to "keep [protect] your heart [mind and what you believe] with all diligence for out of it spring the issues of life" (Prov. 4:23). You must filter and protect what you choose to believe for many good reasons.

SKIP THE BRAIN

If you ask most people why they do what they do, they will say it is a response to circumstances. Most people believe that behavior and responses are direct results of some action of another (offense) or an event (circumstance). We think we are just responders. It is as if we instantly jump from the current event to our behavior or emotional response.

Current events   Behavior or
or actions   Responses

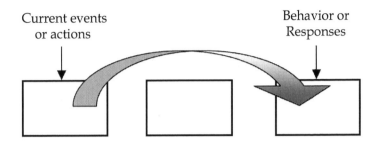

FIRST STOP

It feels as if our response skips our brain and we automatically respond because it happens so fast. But all the data from our senses first goes to the brain, the process center. We refer to this as the core belief center or the heart. It is our flight recorder and has recorded everything we have ever experienced. It is out of this recorded data that we respond. Events may not cause your response but how your mind interprets the events will.

Actions/Events   Core Beliefs   Behavior/Responses

Jesus explained it this way, "For out of the heart proceed evil thoughts, murders, adulterers, fornications, thefts, false witnesses, blasphemies" (Matt. 15:19). All these behaviors are results of processing that took place in the heart. You are what you think (Prov. 23:7). All your speech emanates from your core belief system before it is uttered by your lips (Matt. 12:34). Again, that is why God warns us, "Keep [protect] your heart [mind and what you believe] with all diligence [with all your strength] for out of it springs the issues of life" (Prov. 4:23).

258

WHAT'S IN THE BOX

The core belief system (heart) contains our thoughts (truths and lies we believe); the memory of things done to us, by us or around us; and the memory of the emotions we experienced during those events. These events help form our core beliefs. Out of our core beliefs come negative emotions which control our behavior and responses. Dr. David Ferguson asserts that "human personality consists of roughly four-fifths emotion and one-fifth intellect. This means that our decisions are made on the basis of 80 percent emotion and 20 percent intellect" (Ferguson, p. 3).

The heart is the processing center. It houses all your beliefs based on truth (reality) or lies (deception), stores your memories (conscious or subconscious) and negative emotions (guilt, shame, fear, etc.). God created emotions and can even use negatives ones as a warning that something is not working right in one's life. When a red-light flashes on the dashboard of your car, it does not mean the car is no good, it just notifies you of a need. The heart also contains entitlements, privileges, motives and rights that you give yourself that may or may not be deserved.

A SAD REALITY

Negative emotions can manage your life more than positive ones and control your thoughts, goals, behavior and relationships. That is why God said that whatever you do, protect what you believe (think) about God, others and yourself because your emotions are products of your thoughts. The sad reality is that negative emotions can also control your spirituality, ministry, finances and career.

When you have a conflict within or without, you must go to your *flight recorder* to find out what emotions are behind your behavior. If you do not deal with (understand and process) your emotions, your emotions will deal with you. You can deal with physical pain and still experience mental peace and joy because they are the fruit of the Holy Spirit, not circumstances (Gal. 5:22,23). It is your emotional health that most likely determines whether or not you are happy in life.

Many people work hard to disprove the lies they believe about themselves. They soon discover that no amount of achievement changes those lies. If they believe they are a failure, they may respond by being an over-achiever to prove they are competent, valuable or talented. The disillusioning part is that enough is never enough to disprove the lies or to change the negative emotions. What is an over-achiever to do? He must go to his flight recorder and discover the source of those lies or negative emotions and deal with them.

You can still function in life even though you are emotionally handicapped with negative managing emotions. It just takes more effort and they drain your energy which can result in depression. The emotionally handicapped person feels hopeless to change these life patterns because they wrongly believe, "It's just the way I am" or "It's just the way others are" and they feel hopeless and resign themselves to the pain.

DEFINED BY YOUR COMFORT ZONE

Negative feelings can not only manage your life and relationships, they can define your sphere of safety, security and comfort. These spheres of comfort are called *comfort zones* and are usually defined by fear and/or lies you believe about yourself, others or God. They are not characterized by faith. The emotions of guilt, shame and fear can also force you to create a comfort zone. Why stay in this zone? Your mind will do anything to protect you from physical or emotional pain. Remember, your mind has at least 40 defense mechanisms to protect you from experiencing emotional pain. You may not mature if defense mechanisms are not identified and removed.

COMFORT ZONE LOSS

Comfort zones defined by negative emotions can prevent you from experiencing at least three things. First, they can prevent you from enjoying a better quality of life in Christ. Joshua had to step out of his comfort zone to cross the Jordan River at flood stage to enter the promised land. God told Joshua to have the priests, wearing heavy robes and carrying the ark, to step into the river at flood stage. They could quickly be sucked under and drowned by the raging river. It would seem to be certain death. They had to leave the safety of the river bank and step into the churning water before God would part the river for them to walk across on dry ground (Josh. 3:13). At the Red Sea Moses only had to lift up his rod and the sea parted (Ex. 14:16). That was easy for the Israelites, but not so for Joshua and the priests.

Second, negative emotions also hinder you from pleasing God because they are based on fear, not faith. It takes an expression of faith to please God. Picture yourself standing in an area surrounded by yellow caution tape, a visual reminder of your zone of fear. You think you are in control, but that is a delusion imposing a false sense of emotional security. There are no safeguards against loss inside the zone of fear. What lies outside the zone of fear? It is faith. You see, "Without faith it is impossible to please Him for he who comes to God must believe that He is [exists] and that He is a rewarder of those who seek Him" (Heb. 11:6). The men and women in Hebrews 11 pleased Him by stepping out of a zone of fear into one of faith that had potential loss, risk and pain. God placed each one in His Faith Hall of Fame as those who pleased Him.

Third, comfort zones defined by negative emotions will prevent you from further growth and experiencing life as God intended. The life God planned for Israel had every conceivable benefit one could imagine waiting for them in the land of Canaan. They were to cross the Jordan River and conquer the land. Although it would take human effort, total victory was promised.

Moses sent out an advance team to survey the land, report back and then move forward. The twelve spies brought back the same report: great abundance and great danger. Ten spies focused on the danger (fear), and two spies focused on the abundance (faith). The ten were more persuasive because their report fed into the people's fear. Two focused on the God of faith, not denying the danger but picturing what He would do. A whole generation died in the desert from unbelief and missed the blessing God had for them (Deut. 1:27,28; 32,33). Joshua and Caleb had to suffer with them 40 years before they could experience what they saw 40 years before through the eyes of faith.

LET'S BE HONEST

Living outside the comfort zone is not the safest place to live. All you have to do is read what Paul experienced in the faith zone. He was beaten, imprisoned, stoned, shipwrecked, threatened by robbers, hunted by his own countrymen, lied about by false brethren, exhausted, sleepless, hungry, thirsty, cold and stripped of his clothes. At the same time, he carried a deep concern for all the churches (2 Cor. 11:25-28).

Potential physical, psychological, emotional and spiritual pain could be your experience in the faith zone. Peter and some of the apostles, having been beaten and threatened by the Jewish leaders, departed from the presence of the Jewish council "rejoicing that they were counted worthy to suffer shame for His name" (Acts 5:41). What did they do then? They immediately went back to the temple where they had been arrested and "did not cease teaching and preaching Jesus as the Christ" (vs. 42). How could they do this? Paul answered it best when he left Ephesus for Jerusalem where he faced certain imprisonment and death, "But none of these things move me; nor do I count my life dear to myself [why?] so that I may finish my race with joy and the ministry which I received from the Lord Jesus, to testify to the gospel of the grace of God" (Acts 20:24).

THE PRISON OF NEGATIVE EMOTIONS

What are some of the top negative emotions that, if not dealt with, will control your quality of life, stunt your personal growth and disappoint the Lord, who deeply loves you? Let's examine some of these Emotion-Prisons.

Fear of Failure: Dr. Mark was about to lose his wife and his relationship with one of his two teenage daughters. He showed favoritism to one daughter over the other. He was an absolute clean freak conducting white glove inspections of the house when he came home from the hospital. Things, and the order of things, were much more important to him than relationships.

I inquired about his home life as a child. His physician father was constantly putting him down and often told Mark that he would never be a doctor, that he would only mess up anything he tried to do. "You are a failure just waiting to happen" was drummed into him daily.

Dr. Mark did well at the university, in medical school, on the medical board exams and as a highly skilled anesthesiologist. Where was the failure? There was none, but he had an inordinate fear of experiencing it. If you have a few setbacks in life, they do not prove you are a failure. No, they prove you are normal.

Fear of failure is the number one fear men experience to a lesser or greater degree. No one likes it. When you acknowledge your humanity and realize we are all less than perfect, then you can accept the grace God gives you and learn from life experience. Present fear creates a dread that you might reexperience your childhood emotions in adulthood. Typically, there was a very critical person in one's past who instilled this fear.

Imagine the great loss to the kingdom of God because believers stay in their prisons of fear. To prevent stepping out of this supposed *safe* zone, we will defensively excuse ourselves by saying, "That is outside my comfort zone." Translation: I don't trust God with that because of my fear of failure and possible rejection. Fear of rejection can also be a prison.

Fear of Rejection: The fear of rejection means we believe others have the power to devalue and disregard us. The English word for rejection means *to be cast back, to disregard.* This is exactly how God described Israel's rejection of Him, ..."and you have cast Me behind your back" (I Kings 14:9).

Past experiences of rejection could be overt or covert. Dr. Mark's dad was overt. He made it clear that Mark had no worth, value or potential. As far as his dad was concerned, it would have been better had he not been born. But covert rejection is the result of not giving the normal nurture a child needs. He is just tolerated, ignored, never affirmed or cared for and left to raise himself emotionally with little or no investment from the parents. The brain puts a meaning on all this and concludes, "I'm not wanted," "I am rejected," "I am just a nuisance." With the fear of re-experiencing these emotions, one stays in the comfort zone of fear of rejection and avoids close relationships. One of the reasons couples live together and avoid a marriage commitment is to have an easy out if they sense rejection coming. "I can leave you before you leave me."

Fear of Losing Control: When people have experienced a lot of emotional, and possibly physical pain, they may vow to themselves that this will never happen again. So they take absolute control of their environment to avoid re-feeling past pain or to acquire the power that they observed in a controlling parent. Pride and power feel good.

The controller manipulates others around him to draw them inside his circle so they will behave as he dictates. He must control people, places and things on the outside because he is out of control with fear and pride on the inside. This is the flesh's replacement for self-control by the Holy Spirit (Gal. 5:22,23). Flesh control keeps him from being vulnerable and ensures that no one could ever hurt him again, especially emotionally. It is important not to call it control because control is only the result, not a cause. He is not a controller; he is scared and arrogant and control is the result.

Diotrephes is a classic New Testament example of a prideful, insecure controller. He cut off all outsiders from his little church kingdom and removed insiders if they did not avoid the outsiders he rejected. He believed he knew best and robbed fellow believers of their power of choice which is a key characteristic of a controller (3 John 1:9,10). Peter made it clear that this flesh pattern was a violation of God's instruction to elders (pastors) not to lord (boss) it over the members, misusing their position of authority (I Pet. 5:2,3). Those being controlled on the outside are not free to be led by the Holy Spirit on the inside (Rom. 8:14).

Opinionated people are information controllers who are prideful, argumentative and critical with a need to be right. Anger is usually the emotion used to control others. They also use threats of rejection and abandonment and tend to misuse the concept of submission in relationships. They twist Scripture to reinforce their control, emphasizing one scripture to the exclusion of another. Ultimately, they make others responsible for their emotional security in order to avoid growing up and trusting God outside their fear zone.

Fear of Abandonment: Why would a woman stay in an emotionally or physically abusive relationship and hate it? Why would a man totally control his wife's every action, belittle her every thought or constantly accuse her of having an affair? These actions are not logical unless you check out their black boxes to discover the errors in their core beliefs. You will discover the abused wife and abusive husband have the same mental malfunction. They are afraid of being abandoned and alone. A woman once told me that even if her abusive husband tried to kill her, she would not leave him. She was locked in her fear of being alone. Ten years later her oldest son and his wife were in my office for marriage counseling, and guess what he was doing to her? The pattern he learned from his father and mother had become his normal. The mother unintentionally conveyed to her son that the abusive behavior was normal and appropriate.

Why does a wife tolerate abuse? There are at least two competing fears. One is the fear of the abuse reoccurring. She can tolerate that. But there is a deeper fear of being alone. This is the deepest negative managing emotion. The discomfort of being alone is the only negative thing mentioned during the six days of creation (Gen. 2:18). God knew the value of companionship. One reason God gives us the Holy Spirit is to be our Comforter. The word *comforter* literally means *one called alongside of.* He fills the void left by people abandoning us.

This fear of abandonment is often seen in codependent relationships. The word, codependent, comes from the alcoholic recovery literature. A wife may be dependent on the husband emotionally or financially, and he may be dependent on alcohol. Later the definition of codependency was expanded to include any two people depending solely on each other for their mental, spiritual, emotional and/or physical security.

What is a codependent relationship? One person makes another person act in the place of God on their behalf. If you listed the characteristics of a codependent person in one column and the attributes of God in another, you would soon discover they are the same. A codependent person would say, "You should know how I feel." She must have the divine attribute of omniscience. "You must always be there for me and let me know where you are at all times." That would be the attribute of omnipresence. "You need to fix this." Now she must be omnipotent. Codependency is a relationship substitute for God. It is often expressed as, "I need someone with skin on to be there for me." Immature people seem to have the same need for a teddy bear they had as a child.

Fear of Not Being Loved: Susan Smith strapped her two young sons in the back seat of her car and let the car roll into a lake, drowning both of her children. Everything inside of us screams, "How could she do that?" There is a logical answer. Her boyfriend wanted her, but he did not want her two boys. In her mind, this was her only opportunity for a chance to be loved. Susan was later convicted of murder and sent to prison. There she eventually realized what she had done and she went insane.

Related to not being loved is the accompanying thought, "I am not loveable." Why would a beautiful Christian girl have sex with four guys at the university? If you have a core belief that you are not loveable, you will do irrational things attempting to disprove the lie (in the core belief).

She knew it was sin and confessed it as such. Yet her father, in a passive way, had failed to show her love and appropriate physical attention. The meaning she placed on his failure was that she must not be worthy of love. That emotion was devastating. She knew Christ demonstrated His love toward her while she was a sinner and died for her (Rom. 5:8), but the emotion of feeling unlovable was often stronger than the biblical truth. She was ultimately able to come out of her fear zone, trust a young man and marry.

Fear of Inadequacy: Inadequacy is a neighbor to the fear of failure. If you believe you are inadequate, you will try nothing. Men seem to demonstrate this fear more than women. Scripture is full of accounts of great men of God who had to battle this fear.

• Moses	Exodus 3:11; 4:10
• Gideon	Judges 6:12,13
• Jeremiah	Jeremiah 1:6
• Saul	I Samuel 10:21,22
• Solomon	I Kings 3:7-9
• Paul	I Corinthians 2:3

One characteristic of the fear of inadequacy is the need for constant affirmation. This is a child-like perspective, not an adult one. You may *know* Paul's affirmation that you can do anything God expects of you through Christ who gives you His strength to do it (Phil. 4:13). But when you *feel* inadequate, truth and reality get pushed back in the recesses of your mind. The *inadequacy lie* in the core belief needs to be identified, renounced, and replaced with truth, and a commitment made to live out the truth. This will be explained in Chapter 15.

Feelings of Worthlessness: It is painfully difficult to live with feelings of being defiled, dirty, defective, worthless or of little value or that, "I'm just no good." These feelings are close to the fear of rejection. As a believer, you may *know* that God has blessed you with every spiritual blessing in the heavenly realm (Eph. 1:3), but this fact does not over-ride feelings which are not subject to truth.

People can be very creative in attempting to gain a sense of worth and value from homes, cars, clothes, jewelry, tattoos, achievements, work, adult toys, positions, kids, education, etc. Enjoying these things in balance is not a moral issue; however, it becomes a moral issue when one looks to these things for his primary source of value. Our ultimate worth and value is wrapped up solely in our personal relationship with Christ and our adoption into God's family (Rom. 8:15). On the negative side, it is understandable that people who are engaged in self-destructive habits come to the wrong conclusion about themselves and thus stop caring.

Guilt and Shame: These are related, yet different emotions. Guilt feelings come from wrong actions. Guilt results from things one has done, whether actual or perceived. It makes you feel you are worthy of blame. You can be made to feel guilty when you have done nothing to deserve it. Guilt is the master tool of manipulators.

Shame is the controlling attitude that I am flawed and defective as a human being. You may feel like a failure, a loser, a disappointment. Shame also comes from things we have done, things that were done to us or from events that happened around us. The New Testament word is made up of two words, *no* plus *honor.* To be shamed is to lose any sense of honor.

You can be tormented by feelings of shame if you grew up in poverty, your mom had many relationships with men and your dad was an alcoholic or the neighborhood adulterer. Being sexually abused or forced to participate in sexual activities can leave you feeling worthless, dishonored, empty and lonely. You will find shame at the root of addictive behaviors, people-pleasing, eating disorders and self-mutilation.

Fear of Not Being Perfect: Perfectionism is probably the most common and damaging characteristic of dysfunctional families (Friel, *An Adult Child's Guide*, p. 97). Perfectionists are usually black or white thinkers who believe they are either totally good or totally bad and project the same unrealistic standards on others. They fail to acknowledge that the Christian life is a growth process in *becoming* like the Lord Jesus (2 Pet. 3:18). Instead, perfectionists demonstrate human effort to be God (Gen. 3:5). They feel they never achieve their perfect goal and are driven by thoughts of, "I ought," "I should," "I must." Things and the order of things are more important than people and relationships because they tend to be self-absorbed in trying to get everything right (perfect).

This behavior is based on three controlling emotions in their comfort zone: guilt, shame and fear. The fear has three levels: fear of discovery of a flaw, rejection because of the flaw and fear of abandonment for the flaw. Thus, they harbor a host of negative emotions. They form whole religious groups that are characterized by legalism or extreme behavioral patterns which are exhibited in present-day Pharisees (Matt. 23). People in legalistic churches perceive themselves as sinners in the hands of an angry God, but in truth they are saints in the hands of a loving God (Anderson, p.10). Legalism is the religion of self-righteousness. Perfectionism is a character disorder, not a character quality. Excellence, on the other hand, is a character quality and is not motivated by fear.

Anger: Unprocessed anger can turn into a negative emotion that affects everything you do and every relationship you have. It can come out in explosive outbursts, damaging everyone nearby or anger can be swallowed and come out in subtle, passive ways. It is like guerilla warfare and causes a person to avoid any outward conflict and contact with people. Those with unprocessed anger usually have a short fuse that can be ignited even by small things resulting in over-reactions that the events do not warrant.

THEY DIDN'T DISAPPEAR

It comes as a surprise to many believers that their negative emotions did not vanish when they became a Christian. Conflicts among believers in the New Testament confirm that these emotions do not automatically disappear at salvation. The Apostle Paul described the behaviors of believers in the church at Corinth. Though the Corinthians were called saints in the first chapter (vs. 2) and were enriched in speaking and knowledge, they did not lack any spiritual gift (vs. 5-7), yet they had divided themselves into exclusive groups following various leaders. But notice why.

These factions boasted, "I am of Paul," or "I am of Apollos," or "I am of Cephas," or "I am of Christ." What were they saying? Their identity came from following a man. It was an identity crisis, the attempt to feel important by associating with someone regarded as valuable. Why? They were still being managed by feelings of inferiority rather than their relationship with Christ. Similarly, teenagers idolize rock stars or sports figures to make themselves feel significant.

The reality that our negative emotions do not disappear at salvation can be a source of discouragement and bitterness toward God. It feels as if "Salvation did not work for me." It is a myth that everything changed at salvation. For some, there are drastic changes but that is not the experience for most believers. This is one more reason that you, as a people-helper, are needed in an active discipleship ministry, especially with new believers.

Change is the goal, not necessarily a present reality. You must grow into Christ-likeness and mature in your core beliefs. Paul warned about identifying with the secular world system; instead, you must go through a growth process from the inside out by replacing your old belief system with a new biblical belief system. Paul did not emphasize just behavioral change but changing the thinking behind the behavior (Rom. 12:2). He compared the difficult change in bringing about this transformation to birthing a baby (Gal. 4:19). Why is transformation so hard? Simply because you were born again in your spirit, but not in your mind (John 3:6). As valuable as the new birth is now and for eternity, it is not a shortcut to end the control of negative, damaging emotions.

WHAT PASSED AWAY?

Doesn't scripture indicate that "if anyone is in Christ, he is a new creature; the old things passed away, behold new things have come" (2 Cor. 5:17)? Yes, you are now free from the control of sin and your power of choice is restored. You can choose to yield to temptation, but you do not have to. You have a new identity in Christ (Gal. 2:20) and are no longer in Satan's sphere of darkness. You are a child of God, a saint, an ambassador of Christ. Also, you are a royal priest and so much more.

Salvation did not erase your mind, your black box where all your memories and past emotions are stored. They can affect your present emotions which control your behavior, responses and relationships. Eighty percent of what is in the mind including thoughts, feelings and motives cannot consciously be recalled at any given moment unless God brings them back for the purpose of healing. Memories can be triggered by sight, sound, touch, people or events.

THEY ARE NOT LOGICAL

Negative emotions are not always logical or reasonable, but they *feel* like they are. In your mind, you may know the truth, but your negative emotions can be an embarrassment to you. You can *know* in your head God loves you but you may not *feel* His love. This creates a conflict between what you *know* and what you *feel* which results in anxiety. A girl who was raped in childhood can still *feel* powerless and vulnerable in adulthood even though now she has the power to resist that feeling.

Feelings are not managed by facts for a very logical reason. Feelings are not subject to truth. A jealous husband can be very controlling of his wife because he feels she may leave him like his mother did. He feels, "All women will leave sooner or later." Although his wife has given him no grounds to mistrust her, yet he *feels* it's only a matter of time. He is responding to reality as he feels it in his core belief. Present events can activate childhood emotions. You know you should not feel that way and it is embarrassing when it happens.

MORE POWERFUL THAN TRUTH

Negative emotions seem to have more power in our lives than biblical truth. People in the Bible were frequently controlled by negative emotions in spite of their vast exposure to truth. Peter is just one example.

The Apostle Peter's fear of rejection by representatives of prominent Jewish leaders had more power over him than all that Jesus taught him during their three years together. God used Peter at Pentecost when 3,000 were saved (Acts 2:41) and later, 5,000 (Acts 4:4). He was used by God to open the door of the gospel to the Gentiles with the conversion of Cornelius (Acts 10). Yet, look what happened when he faced possible exposure and rejection from his Jewish peers visiting from Jerusalem. "But when Cephas [Peter] came to Antioch, I [Paul] opposed him to his face because he stood condemned. For prior to the coming of certain men [emissaries] from James, he used to eat with the Gentiles; but when they came, he began to withdraw and hold himself aloof, fearing those who were of the circumcision." Why? It was not because of a change in theology (truth) but simply the fear of rejection by those who insisted on the necessity of circumcision. "And the rest of the Jews joined him in hypocrisy, with the result that even Barnabas was carried away by their hypocrisy" (Gal. 2:11-13).

Why did Peter remove himself from the Gentiles? Simple. Peter had a core belief that if those Jews knew he was associated with Gentiles who were not circumcised, they would reject him. That fear of rejection ran deep in Peter. Jesus' ministry, privileges and powers that Peter experienced could not erase that fear. It is the same illogical fear that perfectionists have, "If you knew the real me (human flaws), you would not like me and would reject me." If what we believe does not reflect truth, then what we feel does not reflect reality.

273

WHAT IS THEIR SOURCE?

Usually we are more aware of our negative emotions than we are of the historical source behind those emotions. The source may have originated early in life through events or actions of others, either done to us or around us. There are at least two kinds of trauma or hurts that could create them. Type A trauma (active) are hurtful things that deeply affected us physically or emotionally growing up or in adulthood. Type B trauma (passive) is the result of the absence of good things that we all need; to be loved, affirmed, validated, kept safe, nurtured (Friesen, p. 8).

My alcoholic father never hit our mom or us kids. He was a perfect gentleman. We never saw him drunk, but he had Vodka bottles hidden all over the house. He just started staying out later and later. He would be gone a day or two or more. Then he never came back home. My dad failed to give me all that I needed as a boy, a teenager and young adult. He never wrote, called or sent money for our support. It was as if we died.

Abandonment is ten times more painful than a beating. The beating is over quickly, but abandonment is for the rest of your life and affects graduations, marriage, children, grandchildren — a total loss. I never heard my dad praise me or say he loved me. When he was home, he was still absent. Remember Fred in Chapter 9. He begged his dad on his deathbed to tell him just once that he loved him even as an adult. His dad said, "I don't have time," then, rolled over and died. That crushed Fred.

Emotional memories can be likened to a boxcar on a train that was left on a track siding. The main train (our body) has gone on into adulthood but the emotions (box car) are still stuck on a siding in the past. They can still send signals to the train and control its performance. Sometimes you will hear a person referred to as, "stuck in the past." Some men respond to their wives as if she were their mother and some women respond to their husbands as if he were their dad. These are parent-to-child relationships instead of adult-to-adult relationships. One of the spouses is stuck emotionally in the past.

UNUSUAL REACTIONS TO FEELINGS

There are various reactions to strong negative feelings. We blame the devil for them, and he may indeed have injected the lies behind the feelings we experience. He also falsely accuses us to God daily with lies (Rev. 12:10). We can also blame ourselves for our poor attitudes or our reluctance to admit our hurts because we see them as signs of weakness or spiritual immaturity.

Another response is to blame someone else or project unpleasant traits, behaviors or feelings by attributing them in an accusing way to someone else. A jealous husband could project his feelings onto his wife out of fear of being replaced.

We can also respond to our negative feelings by turning to addictive behaviors: drugs, alcohol, sex, work, kids, TV, social media, religious activities, hobbies, relationships, shopping, gambling, pornography, hiding behind a veneer of Scripture verses or theological platitudes. We may even pray that those negative feelings would be taken away. But without discovering where they are coming from, we will continue to be plagued by the lies we have believed: "I'm no good," "I can't do anything right." "I'm a failure." Feelings are God-designed notifiers of the pain and lies that He wants us to work through biblically to discover how they were instilled, to renounce and to replace with truth.

Our brain, to defend itself from further pain, may go into denial. It will shut down the emotions so we do not feel. Remember, denial is one of the 40 ways our brain protects us from feeling pain. When we discount even the smallest hurt, we then miss the opportunity for that hurt to be healed biblically. Ignoring hurts never makes them go away. Neither does shutting them down (which is similar to denial).

GOOD NEWS

The good news is that you can change. You are not doomed to live your life controlled by powerful negative emotions. Freedom and healing are a biblical process and as you learn from the process, you will become an example of one who has gained this freedom. You will be in a great place to help others gain the freedom they long for. Now, welcome your emotions as friends and watch how God uses them to build emotional maturity in your life.

Chapter 14
GAIN CONTROL OVER
NEGATIVE EMOTIONS - PART I

• Notice the brain records everything.

• Your responses come from the heart, not the events.

• Negative emotions can control much of your life.

• Negative emotions establish our comfort zones.

• Be aware you will experience losses outside your comfort zone.

• Negative emotions did not disappear at salvation.

• Only our spiritual status was made new, not the mind.

• Negative emotions are not logical.

• Negative emotions are based on lies.

• Identify and correct the normal reaction to controlling emotions.

Chapter 14
SMALL GROUP QUESTIONS

1. What negative emotions have you experienced?

2. What are ways you have dealt with those negative emotions?

3. How were you taught to deal with them in a healthy way?

4. How have you been affected by someone else's negative emotions. How did you deal with those people?

5. How has your quality of life changed since you dealt with your negative emotions?

6. How would you describe your comfort zone? What emotions manage your comfort zones?

7. What experience have you had with others attempting to control you? How have you responded?

8. When you were taught, *old things passed away*, but they did not for you, what was your response?

9. How did you feel when you experienced a negative emotion that you knew was not based on truth?

10. How have you experienced encouragement to discuss the presence of negative emotions and realize they can be changed?

Chapter 15
GAIN CONTROL OVER
NEGATIVE EMOTIONS - PART II

Jenny took major steps to freedom and maturity using her emotions to identify her needs. Emotions used in this way can be one of your best friends. Negative emotions can serve as a window into your life's storeroom of pain, hurts, loss and lies. They can point to the source of these things so that they can be processed biblically so you can have a better quality of life. Negative emotions can serve you in at least two positive ways.

HOW DO YOU SEE LIFE?

The first benefit is that they reveal to you how you look at life. All of us look at our world through the window of our own emotions whether it is clear or distorted. Jesus used a slightly different analogy with the function of the eye. "The lamp of the body is the eye. If therefore your eye is good your whole body will be full of light [truth] but if your eye is bad, your whole body will be full of the darkness [lies]. If therefore the light that is in you is darkness, how great is that darkness" (Matt. 6:22,23). Think of it, what you think is light (truth) could be darkness (lies).

The kind of light (information) that goes into the body (mind) controls how you are going to respond. If the light is pure and true, your life will thrive but letting in what is impure or false brings painful darkness.

The Apostle John referred to it this way, "If we walk (live) in the light (of truth) as He is in the light, we have fellowship with one another..." (I Jn. 1:7). Your quality of life depends on the quality of light (truth) you let into your life. All the information coming into Jenny's life was distorted by anger, bitterness, self-loathing and rejection. Her core belief system was completely skewed. Looking through her emotional window we could see the painful sources that God wanted to heal. Her darkness felt like light to her because she did not have anything to compare it to. It was just her normal reality. Like Jenny, your negative emotions can notify you of what needs to change in your core belief system. They can alert you to a past or present hurt or a distorted reality of God, others or, especially, yourself.

When I gave Jenny permission to feel her legitimate anger, she pulled back the shade of her memories so we could look through the window of her emotions. We saw the dreadful darkness of what had been done to her and her perception of God, others and herself. This information would not have come to light (reality) in a casual conversation. Jenny had carried those negative emotions for 47 years. The light of God's Holy Spirit shone through her emotional window and exposed her world of pain and her need for Later, we will illustrate how to use emotions in a positive practical way on a daily basis.

HOW OTHERS SEE LIFE

The second benefit of negative emotions is to reveal to you how others may view life. This is a major key to helping people. In a normal conversation, what Jenny went through would never have come up. If a person casually mentions their struggle with anger, guilt, unworthiness, loneliness, perfectionism, failure or a need to control, normally the conversation would continue about the symptoms of the emotions. We will explain how to listen to others who need encouragement to process their negative emotions and experience a better quality of life in Christ. Remember, if you do not know how to understand and deal with your emotions, they will deal with you, but understanding both negative and healthy emotions will return power to your life. What are the steps to emotional freedom?

STEPS TO FREEDOM

How did Jenny and Fred make major changes in a few short hours? A psychotherapist friend in Poland explained her system to bring emotional freedom. She said in the past it would take two years to accomplish but now it takes only six months. Then she asked me how long it would take with my system. I answered, "About two or three hours." Shock!

She quickly asked, "Would you show me how to do this?" I was hoping she would ask. "Sure, I would be happy to. Would you find a friend who is struggling with their temper and see if they would allow me to take them through the process with you looking on?" We agreed on a schedule; then came the surprise. The friend she asked happened to be our hosts. Hona and her husband, both doctors, had been very kind to us and were exemplary hosts.

IDENTIFY THE MANAGING EMOTIONS

After the children were in bed, the four of us met in Hona's living room. We began our time with prayer, asking God to direct our every step. This is a spiritual exercise, not a psychological therapeutic tool. This exercise is taking a step forward in spiritual growth in Christ.

Her therapist summarized her experience with Hona and described some of the events she had witnessed herself. I then thanked Hona for being willing to allow us to lead her through this spiritual process trusting God to direct us as we go. Then I asked her to share how she had been expressing her anger in her daily routine. It was important that she had identified and acknowledged the emotion. I drew a simple picture of a window with two stick figures on the left of the window, one indicating her and the other me. Then I wrote the word, "Anger," under the window. I encouraged her to feel the anger, which was a way of looking through the window to discover the events that were the source of her anger. Remember, emotions are a result, not a cause. We would use her emotions to show us their source.

ANGER

Next, I asked her, just as we did with Jenny, to prayerfully allow herself to feel the anger. For years she had attempted to hold back the anger, push it down or outright deny it because of the fear of the unknown. Denial is like placing the lid over a trash can to eliminate strong odors or placing duct tape over the red warning light on the dashboard of a car to ignore its warning.

Various efforts have been used to silence these emotions. Why? Emotional pain can be intense, overwhelming which makes you feel like you are losing control. This results in the thought, "I guess that is just who I am." The strategies we use to hold down negative emotions are called self-defense mechanisms. These are ways we react by deceiving ourselves about our real needs, desires and goals. They are efforts to protect our pride and to avoid anxiety. Suppression is the primary defense mechanism on which others are based (Meier, *Jerks,* p. 103).

Sometimes we remember the emotion of a memory better than specific events. It is important to know that God will give you the strength, energy and hope you need to feel the emotions in order to understand where they are coming from (I Cor. 1:4). One of Satan's biggest lies is to convince you that you can experience an emotion or recall a memory so painful that God cannot comfort you in it. Therefore, you may first have to deal with the fear of feeling it. Dr. Ed Smith calls this a fear that comes from a guard standing at the door that leads to an issue to prevent entrance to the pain for healing and praise to God for the healing. This is one of four guards we summarized in Chapter 12 that would prevent you from working through a conflict: fear of a reality you do not want to acknowledge, an emotion you do not want to feel, a responsibility you do not want to fulfill or a motive you do not want to admit.

Some have suggested that you identify the intensity of the emotion you feel, ten being high and zero being low. I asked Hona to feel the intensity of her anger and she instantly said, "Ten." A practical benefit of this tool is that after the process is over, you can ask the person to report the intensity level now. Often it goes very low, if not down to zero. I strongly encourage honesty about the reality of the anger level. A person once told me that her level went down to one. After further inquiry, she confessed it went down to zero but it was hard to believe it herself! Yes, this scale is a bit subjective, but it can offer a barometer to gauge the decrease in emotional intensity after the process.

IDENTIFY THE WOUNDS

In prayer, while feeling the anger, we asked God to reveal the source(s) of Jenny's anger. We allowed God to take her back to the historical events while feeling the anger.

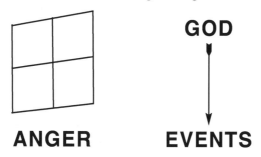

Events and thoughts feed the emotions in the heart. You have heard people say, "The more I think about this (mentally), the angrier I get" (emotionally). You may start to replay in your mind historical events that produced your negative emotions. It may be just a glimpse or perhaps a fleeting image. At this point, ask God what the memories are all about.

Here is a strong warning, do NOT tell a person what you think the memories mean. That is the responsibility of the Holy Spirit, not you. Many counselors have made that mistake and found themselves in legal trouble because of the power of suggestion. You may have a good guess based on past experience, but this is a spiritual exercise, not psycho-therapy. As a general rule, the more abuse one experienced, the less he will be able to remember because memory is like an iceberg: ninety-eight percent of it is below the surface and invisible. Do not be surprised if he has not thought of these events for years because they may have been suppressed for a very long time. When they come up, do not minimize them to yourself or others. You are searching for truth and reality.

Sometimes I will hear a person who is recalling a memory say, "This is stupid," "I'm embarrassed," or "What's the big deal?" This is an adult evaluating an event experienced by a child. A man was still terrified as an adult when he recalled watching his dad, as a boy, shoot his dog because it was afraid of the gun's noise and would not hunt with them. "This happened 45 years ago. I should have been over it a long time ago, but it feels like yesterday." He was stuck emotionally on a railroad siding in an emotional boxcar but continued to grow up physically. This minimizing is an adult's perspective of a child's painful memories. It was a big deal to the child at the time of the event, so it is important to remember that because it happened to a child, it may seem silly or insignificant now as an adult. Yet it could very well be that the childhood memories of the past are still feeding the emotions that manage the adult's life today.

Recall our goal: identify the hurts, deal with them biblically, then put away the childish things and grow up into adulthood. You cannot put away what you do not acknowledge. Many refer to these past events as baggage. The Apostle Paul referred to a similar exercise when he told of his own experience growing up, "When I was a child, I spoke like a child, thought like a child, reasoned like a child. When I became a man, I did away with childish things" (I Cor. 13:11). The phrase, *did away with,* is a verb tense that means it is something he did in the past once, but the results are continuing on into the future. This is what you are doing: you identify what has held you down so you can release it like a beach ball held under water that when released, springs to freedom on the surface.

Realize only you are going back, God is already there, not *was* there because He exists outside of time. God created time for man, but He is an eternal being (Gen. 1:1; Deut. 33:27). There is no past, present or future to God. He is timeless and eternal (Rev. 1:8).

God views time differently than we do, "With the Lord, a day is as a thousand years and a thousand years is as a day" (2 Pet. 3:8). God's eternal existence answers some very practical questions. Can God heal today? Yes. Can God heal tomorrow? Yes. Can God heal yesterday? Yes. He can heal pain of historical events in your life today. He will not change history, but He can end the control of the history. You can see this in the life of Joseph recorded in Gen. 37-50. Technically, he never forgot what his brothers did to him in the past, but it did not control him in the present.

This is the point where you use your emotions to identify your past history so you can process it in the present. As the Holy Spirit brings to your remembrance the hurtful events and the people who hurt you, journal or list them. Why is listing them important? If you do not acknowledge the emotion, you will not identify the hurt and those who hurt you and that would prevent you from being able to forgive them. The emotion would continue to control your life and rob you of the peace that is available in Christ (Matt. 18:34,35). This control is a spiritual, mental stronghold that needs to be torn down. "The weapons we fight with [i.e., forgiveness] are not the weapons of this world. On the contrary, they have divine power to demolish strongholds. We demolish arguments [in our minds] and every pretension that sets itself up against the knowledge of God and we take captive [control] every thought to make it obedient to Christ [truth]" (2 Cor. 10:4,5, NIV). Strongholds are habitual words, thoughts and actions that control us.

PICTURE STANDING WITH JESUS

Hona was able to feel her anger and to list many of the same hurts that Jenny experienced with her mother. Then I suggested that she picture herself standing before the Lord Jesus or just sense His presence and picture her mother standing next to her, but she could say or do nothing to hurt her.

Jesus invited us to come to Him personally, "Come to Me, all who are weary and burdened and I will give you rest. Take My yoke upon you and learn from Me for I am gentle and humble in heart, and you will find rest for your souls. For My yoke is easy and My burden is light" (Matt. 11:28-30). Why picture Jesus in your mind? This lays down new memory traces in the brain right next (parallel) to the past hurts. Memory traces are the normal electronic and chemical functions of the brain. They are like the old single blade garden plow: you plow one furrow the length of the garden, then turn around and plow a second furrow right next to it. The first furrow is the memory of the offenses, and the second furrow is the reminder of the forgiveness that was either given or received. This is exactly what the Apostle Paul did with Alexander the coppersmith (2 Tim. 4:14). Do you have to picture Jesus? No. You can just sense coming into His presence as He has invited us (Heb. 4:14-16).

While Hona pictured her mom standing next to her before the Lord, I encouraged her to acknowledge verbally the specific sins her mother had committed against her. By naming them, she did not have to describe them, (especially in cases of sexual abuse).

WHAT TO AVOID

There are three things to avoid when acknowledging your offender's sins. Do not plea bargain their sins away, "I've done bad things too." Do not minimize their sin, "It really was not that bad." Do not excuse their sin, "They did the best they could," or "They were just acting out from their own wounds too." Excusing or rationalizing is the same. It is an attempt to justify unacceptable attitudes or behaviors by inventing excuses for the behavior (Meier, *Jerks*, p. 108). When we confess our sins to God (I Jn. 1:9), we cannot plea bargain, minimize or excuse them away. The word, *confession*, means to say the same thing God would say about the offense, "It was wrong."

Do not defend wrong behavior. "Well, my dad's parents were hurtful to him, too." That is expressing understanding, not forgiveness. You were wounded by their woundedness. It is still a wound that needs to be healed. Do not attempt to explain away their behavior, "They had a hard life." This may be true; they may not have intended to hurt you. Whether you are shot in the shoulder intentionally or accidentally, your body does not know the difference, and you treat it the same way. It is the same with your emotional wounds. You use the same biblical tools whether you were hurt intentionally or unintentionally. It is important to remember that in the Old Testament, if the Israelites sinned unintentionally, they were still responsible to offer a sacrifice for that offense (Lev. 5:17,18).

You may be tempted to say, "I do not want to blame my parents for my behavior." There is a difference between *excusing*

287

and *explaining* your behavior. If you are excusing your wrong behavior because of what others did to you, that is wrong. But if you explain how others' behavior has affected you, that may give further understanding. Once you acknowledge what they have done to you, you need to forgive them for your own good. If you fail to assign responsibility to people for their sin, you will not forgive, and you will remain wounded and in bondage.

In your prayer, be as detailed as you feel necessary, but avoid details of sexual sin. It is important to name the sin (he raped me) but it does not need to be described in detail for healing to take place. If there is a legitimate need to express the details, they can be written in a private journal or shared with a counselor or mentor friend of the same sex.

CONFESS ALOUD

Why should you confess aloud others' sin before the Lord? Verbal confession seems to be one of the ways of God. At salvation we are told, "If you confess with your mouth Jesus is Lord and believe in your heart that God raised Him from the dead, you will be saved" (Rom. 10:9). For healing, James says, "Confess you sins to one another and pray for one another, so that you may be healed." (Jam. 5:16). We see this same pattern in a prayer for forgiveness (I Jn. 1:9; Lev. 16:21). It is also important to acknowledge out loud that you realize it is the Lord's responsibility to punish the offender for their sin. This acknowledges that revenge is biblical and just, but it clarifies the One responsible to administer it, if He deems it necessary (Rom. 12:19).

Once when I led a woman in this prayer, she stopped abruptly and exclaimed, "I don't want my dad to hurt!" I asked her to let us finish the prayer, and then she would understand. Because after I lead a person to acknowledge that it is the Lord's responsibility to punish them, I quickly add, "Only because of the sacrificial death of Christ on the cross, we ask that He would grant

288

the offender grace, mercy and pardon, just as He has granted to us." This is the basis of the Lord's prayer in Matt. 6:9-13.

In the prayer, I asked Hona to face her mom and tell her what she had done to her, adult-to-adult and to add anything else she wanted her to know, feel or understand. This is like closure at a funeral when you speak to loved ones that have died. It is for your benefit, not theirs. Usually one of the last steps of the grieving process is saying, "Goodbye." At this point I told Hona to tell her mom that she acknowledged it is the Lord's responsibility to punish her, but only because of Christ's death on the cross she has asked Him to grant her grace, mercy and pardon, just like He has granted to her. Then she sent her mother and her sin over to the Lord Jesus and said, "Goodbye."

The New Testament Greek word, forgiveness (apohiemi), literally means *to send away.* You have a place to send offenses, namely to the Lord Jesus, and those sins were nailed to the cross (Col. 2:14). The word, *Goodbye,* indicates you are done; it is over. At the end of this chapter we will provide a sample prayer to consider.

IDENTIFY THE LIES

You would think that the wounds would be the most damaging effect of people's offenses, but traumatic events are like a double-edged sword. They wound the heart emotionally, and then they instill a lie. Typically, the hurt needs to be identified and healed through forgiveness before the power of the lie can be broken.

Most lies were instilled at the time of the offense or soon afterward. If you lived with critics as Hona and Jenny did growing up, lies can be instilled in the core belief system of your black box. You were made to *feel* you cannot do anything right. If you were sexually violated, a lie could be inserted that you are dirty, damaged goods that no one would ever want. And these lies often served as a basis for a pattern of immorality in one's youth and early adulthood. It can be a set-up to tolerate physical and emotional abuse in a marriage.

Surprisingly, it is not always the offenses/hurts that are as damaging as the lies instilled in the child's emotional memory. Continuing to live from a heart that is hurt indicates the lies from those wounds are still embedded and controlling your life. Emotional pain can be Satan's opportunity to instill lies in the mind. He is a liar and the father (reproducer) of lies. He does not stand for truth or reality (Jn. 8:44). He set up spiritual and physical death when he distorted truth in Adam and Eve's mind and manipulated them to eat from the tree of the knowledge of good and evil (Gen. 3:1-7).

Lies are like barnacles on a ship. They attach themselves and slow the ship down, and, in some cases, cause the ship to sink. Usually the ship can still function but not at its intended potential. Instilled lies do just that: you can still function but not as effectively.

Most of us are clueless as to the lies that gained entrance into our hearts as a result of hurts. If a parent abandons his child, this betrayal can convey lies to the child that he is bad, defective, worthless, unwanted, a mistake or unlovable. My father abandoned me. The meaning I put on that was my father did not love me. Then I believed the lie that I was not lovable, even though I knew God created me to give and receive love. My dad had left long ago, the offense was history, but the infused lie had energy of itself and was deeply embedded in my belief system. It became a managing emotion that I was not lovable. Behind that negative emotion was a festering lie of which I was oblivious. Lies often endure long after the effects of the wound diminish.

Your first task in disarming the lie is to discover its existence and realize what effect it has had on your thinking and behavior. Some common lies are:

- I can't do anything right.
- I'm a failure.
- I'm not lovable.
- The sexual abuse was my fault.
- I am damaged goods.
- If people really knew me they would not like me.
- God does not like me.
- I am unforgivable.
- God does not care.
- I caused my parents' problems.
- I must perform to be accepted.
- I deserve to suffer for life for what I have done.
- I can't help myself. That is just the way I am.
- I don't deserve to be happy.
- It is too late to start over.

Lies usually surface when you are confessing or acknowledging to God, out loud, the offender's sin against you. They may also surface as someone is telling his story. For this reason, I keep two lists as people share their stories; first, the offenses they experienced or the sins they committed and second, the lies they believed because of these events.

DENOUNCE THE LIES

What do you do with the lies? It is important to renounce (reject, repudiate, disown) the lies you believed as a result of people's hurts or the events of life (car accident, premature death of a parent, debilitating disease, etc.). Your real battle is between the kingdom of light (God's truth) and the kingdom of darkness (Satan's lies). You cannot get rid of the negative emotions behind Satan's lies by trying not to think of them. This is denial. We must bring God's truth and reality to the wound and the lies that infected the wound. Once the lies have been identified as lies, and not truth, they, then, must be renounced as lies. This breaks the ties and the power the lies have had over you. These lies are mental strongholds the evil one has used to control and deceive you. Remember, you always have the power of choice. When a lie comes to the front door of your mind, you can do nothing and it can creep in, or you can slam the door (renounce the lie), deny it entrance, command it to leave (resist the devil), and stay in control of your thoughts (2 Cor. 10:3-5).

Satan, the father of lies, (Jn. 8:44), will be driven from heaven during the tribulation, after a career of accusing believers to God, pointing out all our sins and failures. The tribulation saints in heaven "...triumphed over him [Satan] by the blood of the Lamb and the word of their testimony..." (Rev. 12:10,11). To remove Satan, they affirmed the presence of the blood of the Lamb and stated their testimony (who they were in Christ).

When guiding people in prayer, either during the confession time or after it, I have them clearly state the specific lies. They must assume full responsibility for their own thoughts. Then I simply lead them to affirm that Jesus is their Lord and Savior (their testimony), then acknowledge the blood of the Lord Jesus and renounce the lies. If there is any demonic influence behind the lies, we command it to leave because we are the temple of the Holy Spirit and it has no place (ground or authority to be) in us (I Cor. 6:19; Eph. 4:27).

This is just one way to resist Satan as we are commanded to do in James 4:7. The Greek word for *resist* is literally *to take a stand against*. But your resistance of Satan in your life must be preceded by your submission to God.

REPLACE THE LIES

To renounce the lies is good but will not last unless you replace them with biblical truth. Jesus warned the Pharisees that when an unclean spirit comes out of a person and their life is clean but empty, that unclean spirit will return bringing seven other spirits more wicked than himself (Matt. 12:43-45). For this reason, renouncing a lie must be replaced immediately by the truth of Scripture. Once the lies are exposed, renounced and replaced, Satan's power over you is broken.

Hona believed she was worthless and had spent her entire life attempting to disprove that lie by getting married, having children and becoming a doctor. It did not work. So in our prayer, I had her state, "Lord, Jesus, I have believed a lie these 38 years that I am worthless. I now acknowledge and renounce that lie in Jesus' name and I affirm the truth that I am very valuable in Your sight, so much so, that You chose to die to pay for my sins. If there is any evil influence behind that lie, I affirm that You are my Lord and Savior (testimony) and I acknowledge the blood of Christ and come against the unclean influence (resist) and command it to leave. This body is the temple of the Holy Spirit and you must leave. I now choose to believe that I am not only valuable, but I am chosen before the foundation of the world, the daughter of God, a saint, an ambassador of Christ and a royal priestess. I, now purpose in my heart to live out the new reality as His Holy Spirit gives me strength to do it" (I Jn. 1:6,7; Rom. 6:13; Eph. 4:20-24).

Will these lies seep back into your thinking from time to time? Possibly. But you do the same thing you do with a forgiven sin when the memory returns. "Lord, I remember the lie. I have renounced it once, and now I commit to continue to live out the truth that I am deeply loved and accepted." It is not the memory that takes us down, it is the failure to recall and affirm what you did with it. You do not need to re-renounce the lie again. It is done. Now, choose to live out the truth and reality. The only way lies can have power over you now is if you listen to them, believe them, and act on them.

CUT THE CONTROL OF HISTORY

Hona had a huge list of things that were done to her and the results still controlled her decades later. After she forgave her mother and renounced the lies, I led her in a prayer to cut the control of history. It is similar to talking back the surrendered ground given to Satan through sustained anger (Eph. 4:26,27).

I had her affirm aloud in prayer that she cannot change history, but she can now, in the name of the Lord Jesus, break the power and control those past events have had on her. "Lord, I acknowledge in my heart that I cannot undo history, but I, now in Your name, break the power and control that my history has had on my life. I am a new person in Christ (2 Cor. 5:17), and You came to destroy the works of the devil" (I Jn. 3:8).

ACCEPT THE CONSEQUENCES

In my opinion the hardest part of forgiveness is the next step. You must affirm that you now accept upon yourself all the consequences (losses) of the offender's sin against you. But, you can then ask God to take all the losses and turn them into a benefit for His glory, for family and friends and a better quality of life for yourself. Failure to do this important step could result in bitterness later toward God for the loss, even though Satan may have been behind it.

The enemy of your soul meant the pain and loss for your permanent hurt or destruction, but God allowed it for His purpose and glory and for your benefit to prepare you to help others (Gen. 50:20). Your task is to praise God for what He will do in your life and in the lives of others as a result of what you experienced (Phil. 2:13; I Thess. 5:18). If the truth be known, you *will* live with the consequences, either in blessing or bitterness; it is your choice. I suggest choosing to live as an example of God's healing grace (Matt. 5:16; I Tim. 1:16). It was by His wounds we were healed (I Pet. 2:24), and by your wounds, others can be healed (2 Cor. 1:6).

NOW YOU ARE READY

Your corrected past is now your primary training to help others work through their problems. You are a living, breathing example of what the Word and grace of God can do. No, you are not perfect; He has only begun His healing, maturing work. It is a life-long process and journey until Jesus returns or you go to be with Him (Phil. 1:6).

By helping others, you have the capacity to fulfill the entire law of Christ by carrying another's burden (Gal. 6:2; Jn. 13:34). Some of the greatest leaders and authors of our time were once deep failures. Both Max Lucado (author) and Franklin Graham (leader) stand as trophies of God's grace and examples for you to follow.

I HAVE A QUESTION

Is it better to take a person through the forgiveness section before you do the emotional freedom steps?

> It is not necessary to take a person through the forgiveness material first. The emotional freedom approach is one use of the forgiveness tool. I rarely cover the forgiveness material before I use the emotional freedom tool.

Once you have taken a person through the emotional freedom steps, if the old lies come back, do you just renounce them and affirm the truth or do you need to go through the forgiveness steps again?

> When an old lie returns, rebuke the evil one behind the lie and affirm the truth. I sometimes ask God to show us where that lie is coming from in case there is an old hurt behind the lie. Remember, a hurt is not the most damaging thing but the *lie* the evil one inserts at the time of the hurt. Forgiveness releases the emotional connection to the offense and offender. Renouncing the

lie releases or disconnects us from the lie. The same lie can come back because the evil one never gives up (1 Peter 5:8).

Does it sometimes take two to four sessions with the steps to emotional freedom? If the Lord brings up other people or issues that were not dealt with in the first session, do you go back and repeat the steps for emotional freedom?

Often you are dealing with layers or multiple hurts from multiple sources. That is why I use the tool of asking what level the anger is (on a scale of 1-10) when we start. When we go through the process the anger may decrease to a level of four. Then we ask God to tell us where the four is coming from. Usually there will be other hurts that will surface.

Personally, I believe the emotional freedom tool should become a regular personal practice. When I feel a negative emotion, I personally ask God where it is coming from. It may be just a need such as a challenge to my faith or trust. It does not always have roots in a hurt or it may be a test or a dart (scheme) from the evil one (2 Cor. 2:11). Satan loves to pick the scabs off old wounds to get you to redo the work of God in your life to make you think it didn't work before.

The hardest part after one goes through the emotional freedom steps is to undo the past habits that were developed by the old lie and start living out the truth in a practical way. Long-held habits are usually the hardest to break because the grooves are so deep in the brain. We will experience a *knee jerk* (quick reaction) from the past but all we have to do is remind our self that it is not necessary to act out the old pattern again because we are living out the truth now. Remember, the past that is not worked out biblically is always present in one form or another.

NOW WHAT?

You are the most important person in someone's life. Your past was your present preparation to be a change agent in someone else's life. But no two people-helpers serve others exactly the same way. Each of us have different gifts and talents. It would be to your benefit to have in mind some practical basic principles that experienced, focused disciplers have found to be helpful. Relax. These principles we will share are not complicated. They are entirely doable. See for yourself!

SAMPLE HEALING PRAYER

"Lord, I come before you personally because you have told me to do so. This is my dad. I realize he can't say or do anything but stand there."

"I have come to realize my dad hurt me by yelling at me and screaming at the top of his voice, telling me, "You'll never amount to anything."

"He instilled the lie that 'I can't do anything right.' I affirm you are my Lord and Savior and I hold up the blood of Christ and I come against that lie and renounce it in the name of the Lord Jesus."

"I acknowledge in my heart that it is your responsibility to punish him, but I pray that you will grant him grace, mercy, and pardon just like you granted to me."

(Turn and face your dad.) "Dad when I was a kid you lost your temper with me and yelled at me and told me I would never amount to anything. I realize it is the Lord's responsibility to punish you, but only because of His death on the cross, I have asked Him to grant you grace, mercy and pardon just like He has granted to me. I now send you and your sin over to the Lord Jesus Christ and I say 'goodbye.'"

(Now address the Heavenly Father)

"Lord, I acknowledge my own anger, bitterness and even hatred for my father. I now take back all the ground I have given to Satan. I now purpose in my heart to use that new energy and freedom for Your honor and glory, for my family and friends, and for a better quality of life for myself."

"I recognize I cannot change history, but now in the name of the Lord Jesus Christ, I break (end, cut) the control the history has had on me. I now accept upon myself all the consequences of Dad's sin against me. I ask you to convert all those losses into a benefit in my life. I thank and praise You for all that You are going to do in me and in those You bring into my life."

"I now picture myself as a trophy of Your healing and an example of what You can do for those who turn to You with their pain. I purpose in my heart to look for opportunities to help others with the tools that I have learned through my own experience."

Chapter 15
GAIN CONTROL OVER
NEGATIVE EMOTIONS - PART II

• Permit yourself to feel your managing emotions.

• Let emotions reveal how you view yourself and how others view themselves.

• Identify the negative events that are feeding the emotions.

• Do not minimize what God reveals.

• Do not excuse offenders' wrong behavior.

• Go directly to Jesus and confess your offenders' sin.

• Trust God to comfort you in the process.

• Denounce lies and replace with truth and reality.

• When the lies return, affirm you have renounced and replaced them with truth.

• Cut the control of history.

Chapter 15
SMALL GROUP QUESTIONS

1. How have negative emotions affected the way you view life?

2. What reality about yourself or someone else was hard for you to acknowledge?

3. What emotion or responsibility were you trying to avoid?

4. Describe the difficulty in assigning responsibility for a hurt to someone you dearly loved. How did you do it?

5. How did you feel when you identified the specific lie(s) that you believed? How did you make this discovery

6. Describe your adjustment in learning to live out the truth that replaced a lie.

7. How did living out the truth affect those around you? What adjustments did they experience?

8. What is your strategy when a lie attempts to re-enter your mind?

9. How have you cut the control of your history?

10. What are the consequences of others' offenses that you have had to accept? How are you dealing with them today?

Chapter 16
INCORPORATE A BASIC
PEOPLE-HELPING PLAN

It sounds so complicated! How do you start? Good question! No two people counsel or disciple exactly the same way every time. Jesus did not heal everyone in the same way as far as it is recorded in Scripture. God will lead you in different ways as you reproduce yourself in others, but a general guideline may be helpful as you get started.

Many people believe that counseling or discipling is only dispensing information but it doesn't always involve information. When someone is deeply grieving the death of a loved one, we are not told to lecture those who weep, instead to weep with those who weep (Rom. 12:15). So, we will survey at least five aspects of discipleship counseling: identification, information, application, motivation and affirmation. Each offers much room for creativity. You may not use all five with everyone. These are simply guidelines, not a formula. As an added bonus, these principles work as relational tools as well.

IDENTIFY EMOTIONS

When Rod first came to see me, he was short of breath, confused and very emotional. He seemed to mumble, jumping from one topic to another. His eyes were red from crying and he was filled with anxiety. I led in a short prayer, asking God to comfort Rod and to enable him to share his heart.

His dad had just died. He loved his dad, but he had never showed any love toward Rod. As a result, Rod was sad, angry, depressed and confused with all the conflicting emotions he was experiencing. What was *my* task? What was the first thing Rod needed? While he poured out his heart, he needed compassionate understanding, the first aspect of identification. Psychiatrist Dr. Theodore Rubin clearly affirms that, "compassion is the strongest human therapeutic agent in existence. Its possibility is almost limitless" (Compassion, p. 4). This is where Rod needed a sincere sign by my tone of voice, body language and facial expressions that I was not only listening but was feeling, at least in a small way, his grief. His ability to unload on me without my censoring, judging, criticizing or shaming was the starting point of his healing.

God will use your identification through understanding to open the mind and heart of the hurting person whether the hurt was done to them or by them. Broken men who begin to realize the damage their affair has caused, still need some compassionate identification, even though their pain was self-inflicted and they are now facing the shame and consequences.

Sympathetic identification is the most effective way of building a healing relationship which will open a person to your counsel later. Dr. Jerome Frank believes that everyone, with a small amount of human warmth, common sense, sensitivity to human problems, and a desire to help, can benefit many candidates for psychotherapy (Tan. P. 53).

Dr. Selwyn Hughes recounted that as a young man, he sat in church with a deep spiritual problem he could not resolve. Leaving the church, sad and dejected, a man tapped him on the shoulder and said, "May I have a word with you for a moment?" Selwyn reported, "Never, as long as I live, will I forget the impact he made on me as he said, '*I could not help from noticing that something is bothering you. I am not a counselor and I do not have great experience helping people with their problems, but I can promise you one thing – I am a good listener and I care.*' Those last two words were just what I needed. Within minutes I shared my problem and although he was unable to fully unravel and solve it, I left that service walking on air, all because someone cared" (Hughes, p. 13).

The gentleman who ministered to Selwyn identified with his emotions appropriately. Multitudes of studies continue to demonstrate that it is empathy or the ability to feel or at least acknowledge the emotions of the one hurting that lays the groundwork for everything else that is done in a discipleship or parenting setting. Most wounded people find some healing through relationships, especially if the discipler can connect with them on an emotional level. Dr. Gary Collins confirms that many research studies show that effective counselors succeed, not so much because of their theoretical orientation or technique, but because of their empathy, warmth, and genuineness (Collins, p.33).

Regardless of how skilled or sophisticated a counselor you may be, it is the ability to connect with the counselee that is first and foremost. You must grasp, on some level, what a counselee feels and communicate this understanding in a way that the counselee recognizes that you do connect with them. Genuine compassion is a prerequisite for the ministry of biblical discipleship. The Apostle Paul reflected this as he discipled his converts, "Who is weak without my feeling that weakness? Who is led astray and I do not burn with anger?" (2 Cor. 11:29). He mirrored these same thoughts to the Galatians, "Oh my dear children, I feel as if I am going through labor pains for you again, until Christ is fully developed in your lives" (Gal. 4:19).

As Rod poured out his heart, I validated his emotions by saying, "That had to hurt," "I'm so sad you went through that," "Rejection really hurts," "That was quite a loss." I kept asking, "How did that feel?" Then, I would acknowledge those emotions because his emotions needed a voice and validation. I would slowly shake my head and even wince when I heard horrific things his dad said or did to him while Rod was trying to get his dad to display love towards him in even the smallest way. Now his dad was gone, and Rod had lost the last chance for his dad to express love at any level.

Some hurting people do not work through their grief (losses) because they may have been told to be strong or not to cry. They may have had their emotions minimized, "You shouldn't feel that way." What Rod needed most now was to know his emotions were normal.

One way to work on identifying with hurting friends is to give them permission to express their emotions appropriately. I will say, "It is okay to cry, to grieve. It is normal to hurt or feel anger at this time." It is okay to say, "Ouch!" In my office I will offer a tissue box, which is one more way to indicate it is normal to cry. With Rod, I told him to take his time because I know that grieving is a very important part of healing.

You can identify with people in their weaknesses, "I've had to go through that with my dad. It was not fun." And if appropriate, you may share a past failure, hurt, or loss you experienced to further identify with them. But summarize without much detail because this is the other person's turn to unload *his* heart.

One advantage recovering alcoholics have in helping other alcoholics is they know first-hand the struggle to get and to stay sober. When you can share an illustration from your life, it may help to free the other person to identify and process his own issues. Secular psychological training now encourages therapists to share personal past or present struggles with clients when appropriate. This honesty with discretion can be a source of strength as the counselee continues his journey toward healing. The Apostle Paul role-modeled this with the Corinthian Church when he admitted, "I was with you in weakness, in fear and in much trembling" (1 Cor. 2:3).

Paul continued to identify with his sinful, abusive past in order to help others deal with their sin in the present. He referred to himself as a former blasphemer, persecutor and verbal abuser and Paul still pictured himself as a major sinner, "Christ Jesus came to the world to save sinners, among whom I am foremost of all" (I Tim. 1:13). Note the verb he used, not I *was* but I *am* foremost of all. He felt that what he did in the past earned him the title of the worst sinner that ever lived, at least in his mind. But he held himself up as an illustration that God will save anyone who comes to Him, confesses his sin and repents. If He would save Paul, He would save anyone. Paul identified with our needs. Yes, he knew he was forgiven, but the memories remained fresh in his mind for the purpose of helping others to process their memories.

Your past is the picture frame around your life. It may be the key that helps you identify with a hurting person. Women who have been sexually abused have instant identification with other victims. Their past does not define their present. It *discipled* them to be who they are today, illustrators of how to forgive their abusers. My past with an alcoholic father prepared me to help others in the present.

One of the purposes of the body of Christ is to demonstrate compassion to those who are hurting, "And if one member suffers, all members suffer with it" (1 Cor. 12:26). Your focus is to listen and understand, not to judge, criticize, condemn, evaluate or plan your response. There will be time for your evaluation and response later.

This was a good time for me to mirror Rod's words and feelings. "Am I hearing you say your dad never hugged you or told you he loved you?" This pattern helped me understand and confirm what Rod was saying. I was also making a list of the hurts inflicted by his father because I knew Rod would need to process those hurts later through forgiveness. I also kept track of the lies his dad instilled in Rod, "You're no good." "You'll never amount to anything." "You never did a thing for me." This was said to Rod just after he had remodeled his dad's bathroom, cleaned out his garage, fixed the kitchen plumbing and cleaned his house from top to bottom.

Next, you can admit you have needs, too. Spiritual leaders sometimes give the impression they have no needs and therefore something must be wrong with you when you have needs the leader never had. This prideful perspective makes God sick, "Because you say, 'I am rich, have become wealthy, and have need of nothing,'" (Rev. 3:16,17). It is hard to identify with a perfect person.

Finally, you can affirm that the other person's feelings, including anger, are valid. This affirmation is a deep desire of one in emotional pain or in a troubling conflict. If however, his pain triggers unprocessed pain in you, you may want to seek further healing for yourself. We are all wounded warriors, and you may need to refer him to someone else.

IDENTIFY THE NEED

Rod was in no condition to identify his need. He would say, "I need relief. This is killing me. My dad left a financial mess. Relatives are swooping in to claim his things. People have lied about me." Rod's issues were legion regarding his father. To work through the pain and loss was a process. It was only after we saw an honest x-ray of his needs and identified the conflicts and who was responsible for what, that we could move forward, one step at a time. He had to grieve his father's death, forgive him for the abuse, accept the losses, renounce the lies he was led to believe, replace them with truth, identify what was in his circle of responsibility, stop taking responsibility for others' actions and accept the fact people are sometimes irreconcilable.

Before you deal with a need, I would be sure there is agreement on what the real issues and needs are. If the counselee does not agree on the need or issue, he will tend to resist your counsel. If he does not believe his arm is broken, he will not let you put a cast on it. Your goal is to avoid arguing with him. So, I said to Rod, "When you think through all that your father has done, do you think you might need to consider forgiving him so you can be free from that abusive history?" "Yes, I know I need to do it; I just don't know how." What a set-up! I shared the Jesus Jail concept and led him through a forgiveness prayer naming each offense. Then we concluded by renouncing the lies that were instilled in him by his father.

Sometimes a client will just tell you a story or describe a situation, hoping you will guess the need. I have lost track of the number of times I guessed the need, addressed it, then had him tell me near the end of the session, "I had a question I wanted to ask you." Because of this repeated mistake, I now pointedly ask if he has a specific question before we continue. Sometimes I will suggest the question and get an affirmative response, "Yeah, that's it!" But by asking the question, it forces him to think through what his needs are. If he expects you to guess it and do his thinking for him, that is not discipleship. That is enabling him to be passive when he needs to be active.

INFORMATION

Identifying with a person in various ways and agreeing with his needs are a good start. But appropriate information (insights, clarification) may need to precede change. Failure of the counselee to change his core belief system (heart) will result in only temporary change of behavior. God led Paul to write eleven chapters in Romans to cover all the important theological issues before he issued his *therefore* to us to present our bodies as a living sacrifice to God (Rom. 12:1). Paul knew we would not be willing to change our behavior until our thinking had been changed first. Paul subsequently laid out a list of behavioral changes He wanted us to make, but the heart needed a complete overhaul first. He as much as said so in verse two by explaining the process leading to changed behavior. Do not let the world system squeeze you into its mold, but go through a process from the inside out by changing your thinking (Rom. 12:2).

307

Many of the issues your friends may be facing are results of attempting to deal with life out of their old perspective and understanding. Your task may be to give them new information or perspective before they are ready to make a significant change in their thinking and behavior. At this point, the decision is theirs. The number one criteria for *success* in counseling or discipleship is still obedience. God does not bless the *knowers* of His Word, only the *doers* (Jam. 1:25).

I have learned to ask permission before I share specific information. This opens the door of the mind and a willingness to listen. People tend to resist and even get angry when we share unsolicited information. You will observe this when parents give unsolicited advice to adult children; it can be rejected and resented. Asking permission shows respect. They may respond, "Sure, that's why I came to see you." But some of the information may not be what they wanted to hear. It is a myth that everyone who seeks help really wants it. But you do not know this until you try.

With Rod, I asked, "May I offer a suggestion?" or "Would you be open to a suggestion?" Most of the time he was very open, so I would say, "May I share something with you?" I did not ask permission every time I offered an insight or Scripture. A few times were enough unless I knew that the information may be a new perspective and hard for him to accept.

CLARIFY MISINFORMATION

It is one thing to give new information but quite another to clarify or correct wrong information shared by sincere people. Paul assigned Timothy to remain in Ephesus to do just that, to stop teachers from teaching doctrine that was contrary to Scripture (I Tim. 1:3,4). People were accepting fables as truth and started arguments that did not lead to godly edification. People's opinions were shared as valid, biblical doctrine. Sadly, today there are preachers and teachers sharing things they were told without checking to see if it is the truth.

We mentioned earlier that people are told to forgive and forget. That is impossible! Those who tell them this may not know what to do with the memories. I also hear, "You need to forgive yourself." There is not one verse in the Bible that supports that. I Jn. 1:9 makes it clear that "when we confess our sin, we are [forgiven and] cleansed from all unrighteousness." *All* means *all*. But if you do not *feel* forgiven or cleansed, then your core belief has been infused with a lie that you are not forgiven. That results in false feelings of guilt. False guilt and true guilt feel the same. So, false guilt must be tested with truth (I Jn. 4:1), the lie discovered, renounced and the truth affirmed.

It is your task to study and understand the Scripture so you will not be misled by false doctrines, beliefs and opinions of men. Many of these false doctrines are found in cultural traditions handed down from generation to generation. When a person is saved but has not sought to be transformed in his thinking, he may mix faulty cultural traditions with Scripture.

While teaching in China, I opened a session with question and answer. A young lady preceded her question by saying, "In our culture..." Before addressing her question, I drew an open Bible on the white board with a line down the center indicating God's plumb line of truth. The two lines off to each side represent culture and every culture deviates from God's standard (Rom. 3:23).

I explained that anything in her culture that that does not violate Scripture, keep and enjoy but anything that violates Scripture must be reevaluated and changed. Scripture is the plumb line of truth.

For example, in the Filipino culture, the oldest son has as much authority over his siblings as the parents. God never gave a child a parent's responsibility. It robs him of his childhood and gives him a responsibility that he is not emotionally mature enough to handle.

The Word of God is cross-cultural. Having taught in over 20 countries, I have found that basic biblical truth can be appropriately applied in every culture. Guilt is guilt. Shame is shame. Fear is fear. I work hard to avoid imposing western culture on anyone and claiming it is biblical. When this principle was not adhered to in early missionary endeavors, we exported western-cultural Christianity. There are on-going efforts today in modern missions to address this issue.

Jesus alerted His hearers that some religious men and women teach their opinions as if they were doctrines of God (such as self-forgiveness). "But in vain, they worship Me, teaching as doctrine the precepts [ideas] of men" (Matt. 15:9). This is serious! The Apostle Paul referred to false doctrines as the doctrines of demons which many will follow. "Now the Spirit expressly says that in latter times some will depart from the faith, giving heed to deceiving spirits and doctrines of demons" (I Tim. 4:1). For example, Mormons believe they will actually become a god. Their thinking is reversed. They believe Jesus was a man who became God instead of God who became man (Phil. 2:5-11). They believe they, too, will become a god as Jesus did.

Wrong thinking (theology) in a person's core belief can be at the root of personal problems and conflicts. As a people helper, you must first identify what a person is thinking or believing and whether or not it is biblical. You may need to start from what he *feels* to determine what he *believes*. If, for instance, he says, "I feel God does not love me," ask him to substitute the word, *think,* for *feel.* When he states he thinks God does not love him, then you have something concrete to work with. Emotions are not subject to truth (reality) but thoughts can be tested with truth.

When he gets in touch with his negative emotions, then, in prayer, ask God to reveal to him, the thoughts, events, hurts or lies behind his emotions which can be dealt with from Scripture. Often emotions are based on lies that feel truer than the truth. Your task is to look for any lies that were embedded in his thinking as a result of past pain: "I'm no good; I'm damaged goods; God cannot forgive me; I'm not loveable."

Years ago, a dentist asked to see me. His family called him a controller. Since controlling tends to come from fear, I asked him where he thought the fear was coming from. He did not know, so we went to prayer as he was feeling his fear. He abruptly stopped and said, "I know." God revealed a memory of an incident when he fell out the back door of the car his dad was driving. As he was falling, a thought entered his mind, "You are alone." From that day forward, he vowed he would never be alone, so he manipulated everyone to be dependent on him so they would not abandon him. We went back to prayer and I had him verbally state it was a lie that he was alone. He renounced the lie, then affirmed out loud the truth that God said He would never abandon him and from that day forward he would live out the truth. He realized that the lie was a scheme of the evil one to attack him (Eph. 6:11).

Another simple illustration in dealing with feeling and truth is to take a piece of paper, fold it lengthwise and write on the top left side, *Feelings*, and on the right side, *Facts* (or reality). Ask the person to name the feelings he or she is struggling with as you write them in the left column. On the right side, write the truth from Scripture or reality.

Yes, he can do this in his head, but it will have much more impact if it is written down. I have had people say after doing this exercise, "This negative list is worse than I thought." In reality it is not worse, it is just that they see it for what it is now. This process is just one way to test negative feelings with the truth of Scripture, just as we are to test false prophets with truth (I Jn. 4:1).

APPLICATION

Many people I am privileged to counsel are Christians and have a working knowledge of Scripture. They may have been in church for years, but for the most part, they have not learned how to practically apply the Word of God. It is not from a lack of desire but a lack of know-how. In our training sessions or personal counseling, we make a special effort to explain how to apply Scripture and principles from Scripture using analogies and word pictures that people can relate to.

The concept of circles of responsibility is the practical application of Rom. 12:18. "If possible, as much as it depends on you, be at peace with everyone." I take the phrase, "As much as it depends on you," and draw a circle and put the person in that circle. Because conflicts involve other people, I add a second or third person in the same circle. Then I take each person out of the big circle and give each one his own circle of responsibility. I have written an entire book on the application of this one verse, *You Can Work it Out.* This practical concept has spread around the world in books, sermons, small group studies and counseling materials because it is a practical application of Scripture. Much teaching and preaching emphasize you *should, ought* and *must.* That sounds great, but most people want to know *how.*

In people-helping, with every verse or insight you reference, be sure to also teach how to put it into practice. Failure to do so will only create more guilt and a sense of failure. If I tell a man he needs to love his wife more, I might as well tell him to fly to the moon. Instead, I give him Dr. Gary Smalley's list of *One Hundred Ways to Love Your Wife.* I do not tell him to do all one hundred. I encourage him to give this list to his wife and ask her to select two or three items that are meaningful to her. One or two things done on a regular basis are better than a hundred things not done (Smalley, *If Only He Knew*, pp. 36-39).

This is where small *t* truth comes in. Those *One Hundred Ways to Love Your Wife* are not in the Bible, but they come from thousands of hours of counseling and research. None of them violate Scripture. They are practical ways to apply Scripture. And there are many specific actions defined in Scripture that are practical. The Apostle Paul wrote a whole chapter on ways to be a living sacrifice (Rom. 12). He knew telling people to love each other sounded nice, but they needed some practical instruction of what to do. So, he penned I Corinthians 13 which defines what love is not and what it is. It is a very *How-To* chapter.

People need at least two things from you: they need to be told what they should do and clearly mentored how to do it. Equally important, they need to adopt biblical core beliefs behind these actions. This will mean a change in their thinking (Rom. 12:2). Instruction plus a heart change will result in gradual behavior change. The key behind all of this is an unconditional commitment to obedience (Jam. 1:25).

MOTIVATION

You could wish everyone was motivated to do the right thing. God has many ways to motivate us to obey Him from the heart. One obvious way is through His Word. We have 39 books in the Old Testament of history, poetry and prophets written for at least one reason described by Paul, "Now all these things happened to them [in the Old Testament] as examples [warnings] and were written for our admonition, upon whom the end of the ages has come" (I Cor. 10:11).

The verbs, *happened* and *written*, are imperfect verbs which means they took place in the past from time to time and were written down from time to time. Why? As examples, though not *just* examples, but for our admonition. Admonition is made up of two concepts, *to put*, plus, *the mind*. Put these two together and you have, *to put into the mind* or we would say, "They were written to drive a point home."

The Old Testament is full of men and women of faith and failure. God tells it like it is so we can learn from them and be motivated to obey Him. "All Scripture is given by inspiration of God and is profitable for doctrine, for reproof, for correction [and training] in righteousness" (2 Tim. 3:16). Reading Scripture can provide a lot of motivation.

When we fail to listen to His Word, God sends His works. Most people are not motivated to obey until there is a high level of physical or emotional pain. Dr. Larry Crabb says, "During literally thousands of hours spent in trying to help couples, he found that the major obstacle getting in the way was stubbornness, not a lack of understanding" (Understanding, p. 18). Nehemiah described how God sent His Word to His people first through the prophets, but they would not listen until God allowed them to experience a great deal of pain. "For many years You were patient with them. By Your Spirit You warned them through Your prophets. But they paid no attention so You gave them [Israel] into the hands of the neighboring peoples" (Neh. 9:30). Pain is often what motivates people to get help. Life and relationships are not working for them. One reason God allows problems or consequences is because of their choices. God's works can be the basis of His discipline for correction, not punishment (Heb. 12:5-11).

God also motivates us through His Spirit (Jn. 16:8-11). He convicts us of sin, especially unbelief, of which we need to confess and repent. We can ask His Spirit to search our hearts to reveal the source of our anxious thoughts and any offensive ways that need to be corrected (Ps. 139:23,24).

Another way God can motivate us is through other people. Paul confronted Peter for his hypocrisy in abandoning the Gentile Christians to be with the Jewish Christians. He feared rejection by the Jews if they saw him eating with the Gentiles (Gal. 2:11-14). When we see a brother who has been overtaken by sin, we are to go to him and seek to restore him to spiritual usefulness (Gal. 6:1). Remember, God has chosen to limit

Himself to work through you. You are the most important person in someone's life whether you know it or not.

LEVELS OF MOTIVATION

Every person has an invisible scale in the back of his mind. On one side is a desire (motivation) to experience gain and on the other side is a fear of loss. God illustrated these two scales with two mountains in Israel. Mt. Gerizim represented blessings and Mt. Ebal represented curses. If Israel obeyed God, they would be blessed; if they failed to obey, they would be cursed (Deut. 27:11-13). So, God gave them a physical reminder of potential personal gain or of personal loss.

There are two questions that must be answered in the counselee's mind before they make an attempt to change behavior. First: "Is it worth it to me?" (If it isn't, why waste the effort?). He must see the personal benefit. The second: "Can I do this?" (If not, why try?). Any suggestions you make to a counselee or disciple will go through this gain/loss filter.

The gain/loss perspective has at least three levels of motivation. First is a desire for God's gain or a fear of God's loss. When the prophet, Nathan, confronted King David for his adultery and murder, he told David that he had caused the enemies of God to blaspheme Him. The greatest loss was not David's; it was God's (2 Sam. 12:14).

Joseph resisted the sexual advances of Potiphar's wife's because he could not betray his master but, even more than that, he told her, "How can I do this great wickedness and sin against God?" (Gen. 39:9). Uppermost in Joseph's mind was a concern for God's reputation.

The second level is a desire for others' gain and fear of others' loss. This level caused Paul a lot of personal, internal conflict. He said, "For I am hard-pressed between the two, having a desire to depart and be with Christ, which is far better [personal gain]. Nevertheless, to remain in the flesh is more needful for you" [desire for others' gain] (Phil. 1:23-24). The basis for husbands to lay down their lives for their wives is the example of Christ who laid down His life for us. "Jesus did not come to be served [personal gain] but to serve [others' gain] and to give His life as a ransom for sin" (Matt. 20:28).

The third level is a desire for my gain or a fear of my loss. Sometimes according to our spiritual level, we will change for God's sake or for another's sake, but mostly our motivation is for our own gain or loss. God even appeals to us on a personal level reminding us that all believers will stand before the judgment seat of Christ to receive what we deserve according to what we have done (2 Cor. 5:10). This explains why Paul said, "I discipline my body and bring it into subjection lest when I have preached to others, I, myself, should become disqualified" [personal loss] (I Cor. 9:27). For this reason, throughout a counseling session, I stress the personal benefit of applying God's Word in principle or precept. If they do not want to forgive after I've explained how and why, I will ask, "Do you really want to destroy yourself with anger and bitterness? Is it really worth it?"

AFFIRMATION

It may come as a surprise that not everyone who comes for counseling is doing things wrong. Many times, I have affirmed a person for what they are doing right and will hear, "Thank you, I so needed to hear that." Confirmation that a person is going in the right direction encourages a hurting person. I have commented, "I could not have said that any better," "That was a great idea; I never thought of that" and may follow up on that by saying, "I'm going to use that." Often, I will say, "That's a positive," even if it is a small one because I know they are struggling to believe they can do something or that their difficult marriage even has a chance. Just the fact that they ask for help is a positive step.

For most people, encouragement is a powerful motivator, especially if they highly value you and your opinion. The word *encouragement* means *to keep going in a positive direction.* "Let another man praise you and not your own lips" (Prov. 27:2). Encouragement is so important that God commands us to do it for others daily (Heb. 3:13).

IN SUMMARY

You may not use all the aspects of discipleship counseling in one session. Your friend may just need a compassionate listener or guidance in following through with practical application. You may have to appeal to him on the various levels of motivation. He may be struggling to know if he did something right as he seeks to follow through with what you have shared. He may want or need to hear you say, "Well done, my good and faithful servant."

Finally, you may find yourself going from one aspect to another. This will more likely be your experience. Be reassured that God has promised to lead you as you trust Him for direction (Prov. 3:5,6).

CONGRATULATIONS!

You did it! Yes, it is a little overwhelming at first so take baby steps. Share these tools as often as God gives you opportunity. Realize not everyone will be open to learn, but those who are will someday say to you what I have heard for 55 years, "Thank you, you changed my life." "My kids are talking to me now." "Our marriage has never been better." I'm so glad I'm no longer controlled by guilt and shame." The list goes on and on. As I now think of you, I picture the hundreds of those who will let their light (life) shine in such a way that others will see their change, glorify God for it ...and thank *you* for making it possible (Mt. 5:16).

Chapter 16
INCORPORATE A BASIC
PEOPLE-HELPING PLAN

- Identify and acknowledge the emotions.

- Determine the need.

- Share information when appropriate.

- Identify and clarify misinformation.

- Practically apply Scripture to specific issues.

- Understand the levels of motivation.

- Help motivate obedience to Scripture.

- Affirm right words and/or actions.

- Realize you may not use all five aspects all the time.

- Be sensitive to the Holy Spirit to direct you.

Chapter 16
SMALL GROUP QUESTIONS

1. What struggle would you have in identifying with someone else's emotions? Why might that be the case?

2. Where in Scripture have you observed someone responding to another's emotions?

3. In what areas do you feel you could connect with a person on an emotional level?

4. How do you feel when you listen to a speaker who sounds like he/she is *perfect* or always has it all together?

5. What difficulties do you have determining someone's need? What is helping you determine those needs?

6. What faulty ideas did you have to change to match truth or reality?

7. What religious concepts have you changed as you grew more knowledgeable in Scripture?

8. What specific practical applications of Scripture have you made? What difference have they made in your life?

9. What motivated you to make changes in your life? How did others attempt to get you to change with guilt, shame and fear? How did you resist it?

10. In what ways has your life changed or been influenced by someone affirming you? Who affirmed you and how did they do it?

BIBLIOGRAPHY

Adams, Jay. *The Unchangeable Christ;* The Christian Counselor's Manuel.

Augsburger, David. *Caring Enough to Confront.* Glendale: Regal, 1993.

Bobgan, Martin. *How to Counsel from Scripture.* Chicago: Moody Press, 1983.

Carter, Les. *Good 'N' Angry.* Grand Rapids: Baker Book House, 1983.

Chapman, Gary. *The Five Love Languages.* Chicago: Northfield Publishing, 1995.

Cloud, Henry, John Townsend. *Boundaries.* Grand Rapids: Zondervan Publishing, 1992

Collins, Gary. *How to Be a People Helper.* Wheaton: Tyndale House, 1995.

Crabb, Larry. *Correction.* Nashville: Word Publishing, 1997.

Crabb, Larry. Understanding People. Grand Rapids: Zondervan, 1981.

Detzler, Wayne. *New Testament Words in Today's Language.* Wheaton: Victor, 1986.

Egan, Gerard. *The Skilled Helper.* Monterey California: Brooks/Cole, 1975.

Ferguson, David, Don McMinn. *Emotional Fitness.* Irvine: Intimacy Press, 2003.

Friel, John, Linda Friel. *Adult Children: The Secrets of Dysfunctional Families.*

Deerfield Beach: *Health Communications,* Inc., 1988.

Friel, John, Linda Friel. *An Adult Childs Guide to What's Normal.* Deerfield Beach: Health Communication, 1990.

Friesen, James G. *Living from the Heart Jesus Gave You.* Van Nuys: Shephard's House, 2000.

Hughes, Selwyn. *Helping People Through Their Problems.* Minneapolis: Bethany House Publishers, 1991

Lynch, Chuck. *I Should Forgive, But...* Nashville: Word Publishing, 1998.

Lynch, Chuck. *You Can Work It Out.* Nashville: Word Publishing, 1999.

Lynch, Chuck. *Mending Fences, Healing Hearts.* North

Charleston, Create Space, 2011.

Lynch, Chuck. *God's Peace in Your Home*. North Charleston, Create Space, 2016.

Mason, Paul. *Stop Walking on Egg Shells*. New Harbinger Publications. Oakland: New Harbinger, 1998.

Meier, Paul. *Don't Let Jerks Get the Best of You*. Nashville: Thomas Nelson, 1993.

Meier, Paul, Frank Minirth. *Happiness is a Choice*. Grand Rapids: Baker Book House, 1978.

Newsweek. January 1998

Nicoll, Robertson. *The Expositor's Greek Testament*. Grand Rapids: Eerdman's, 1983.

Oliver, Gary, H. Norman Wright. *Raising Kids to Love Jesus*. Ventura: Regal, 1999.

Robertson, Archibald T. *Word Pictures in the New Testament, Vol III*. Nashville: Broadman Press, 1930.

Rubin, Theodore. *Compassion and Self-Hate*. New York: Ballentino, 1975.

Smalley, Gary. *If Only He Knew*. Grand Rapids: Zondervan, 1982

Smalley, Gary. *The DNA of Relationships*. Wheaton: Tyndale, 2004.

Stoeher, Fred. *Every Man's Battle*. Colorado Springs: Waterbrook Press, 2000.

Tan, Siang-Yang. Lay *Counseling*. Grand Rapids: Zondervan, 1991.

Thomas, Gary. *Sacred Marriage*. Grand Rapids: Zondervan, 2000.

Vine, W.E. *Vine's Complete Expository Dictionary*. Nashville: Thomas Nelson, 1989.

Walvoord, John, Roy Zuch (Editors). *The Bible Knowledge Commentary, New Testament*. Colorado Springs: Victor Publish., 1983

Wright, Norman H. *Crises Counseling*. San Bernardino: Here's Life Publishers, 1985.

Yancey, Phillip. *Disappointment with God*. Grand Rapids: Zondervan, 1988.

Zilbergeld, B. *The Shrinking of America: Myths of Psychological Change*. Boston: Zondervan, 1981.

For additional learning opportunities
please visit:

http//www.help4living.org

Made in the USA
Columbia, SC
27 March 2022

58111168R00178